READ,
WRITE, REVISE

A GUIDE TO ACADEMIC WRITING

READ,
WRITE, REVISE

A GUIDE TO
ACADEMIC WRITING

MARY JANE SCHENCK
UNIVERSITY OF TAMPA

ST. MARTIN'S PRESS
NEW YORK

Executive Editor: Susan Anker
Project Editor: Julie Nord
Production Supervisor: Julie Toth
Text Design: Levavi & Levavi
Cover Design: Darby Downey
Cover Photo: Michael Zide
Graphics: G&H/Soho

Library of Congress Catalog Card Number: 87-060515

For information, write
St. Martin's Press, Inc.
175 Fifth Avenue
New York, NY 10010

ISBN: 0-312-00293-9
Instructor's Edition ISBN: 0-312-01285-3

Acknowledgments

"A Way of Writing," by William Stafford. First appeared in *Field*, #2, Spring, 1970. Reprinted by permission.

"Freewriting Exercises," by Peter Elbow. From *Writing Without Teachers*. Copyright © 1973 by Oxford University Press and reprinted with their permission.

Acknowledgments and copyrights are continued at the back of the book on page 298, which constitutes an extension of the copyright page.

Preface

Read, Write, Revise: A Guide to Academic Writing is a composition text that combines reading and writing to develop the skills students need in their academic courses. Each chapter has a dual title and focus, reflecting the thematic content of the readings, which are paired with instruction in writing for different purposes. The book is directed primarily at multilingual students in first-year college writing courses, advanced intensive English progams, special writing classes for graduate multilingual students, or advanced adult learners.

The thematically grouped readings have been chosen for their topical interest and their potential for provoking critical thinking preparatory to writing assignments. The readings include three types of writing: selections describing the writing process, narrative and descriptive passages from autobiographical works, and essays. The readings in this text are meant to be used primarily as a stimulus for discussion and writing topics. The selections are appropriately challenging for an academic setting, and they represent the level of reading students will encounter in classes in other disciplines. The supporting materials, such as the introductions, discussion questions, vocabulary, and idioms lists, are there to aid the students in comprehending advanced material. The readings assume a vocabulary of approximately five thousand words. Therefore, any word or its derivatives that could be found in the *New Horizons Ladder Dictionary* is not glossed; unusual terms, names, events, or places are included in footnotes; other difficult vocabulary words that merit additional study for college-level students are included in the vocabulary lists and exercises.

This book emphasizes academic writing. Each chapter presents, through its reading and writing instruction, assignments for various purposes: writing from experience, writing to inform, to analyze, to form a judgment, and to persuade. The process of writing is presented from prewriting activities through multiple drafting, revision, editing, and final proofreading, all of which are included in the context of the purpose emphasized in each chapter. The difference between revision and editing is explained and stressed through the inclusion and analysis of multiple student drafts so students will learn that revising an essay involves more than recopying to correct spelling errors.

The discussion of each part of the writing process is designed to be just long enough to be instructive and short enough to keep the emphasis in the course on the students' writing, rather than on reading about writing. As someone once said, "On a scale of human interest, reading about writing ranks right along with watching bowling on TV." In completing the many exercises, activities, and writing assignments included here, students have ample opportunity to write.

The first chapter offers instruction in writing relatively short personal pieces. From Chapter 2 on, each chapter includes instruction in writing a complete, longer narrative or essay, so that by the end, each student will have finished six assignments for evaluation. Each finished product will have gone through at least two drafts and usually three before its final submission. The work that the students put into drafts and the instructor's corresponding work in commenting on them is far more important for the development of writing abilities than a large number of graded or evaluated final pieces.

This text attempts to demystify the process of creating a polished final draft by including short explanations of writing strategies, examples of students' multiple drafts, and assignments to guide the students' own writing. All the explanations and models of student writing are meant to suggest ways of helping multilingual students understand the type of writing required in American colleges and universities. Nothing in this text, however, should or can substitute for extensive writing done by students in the class and careful responses from instructors and peers. It is my hope that *Read, Write, Revise: A Guide to Academic Writing* will help students and instructors enjoy the process of developing themselves through writing.

ACKNOWLEDGMENTS

The students I've taught during the past ten years in both ESL and freshman composition classes have inspired this text. Having always had difficulty finding materials appropriate for an advanced bilingual student, I decided to write a text that would reflect how I teach my own students to develop their writing for college-level work. I have also been greatly inspired by the exciting research in the field of composition over the past ten years and by friends I made through my involvement in the Council of Writing Program Administrators (WPA), CCCC, Gulf TESOL, and national TESOL.

Special thanks go to the following students from recent classes whose writing I have used in this text: Abdullah Almaimanee, Luis Alonso, Hoang Bui Van, Jose Corcione, Bichnga Do, Alberto Grajales, Thomas Hogstedt, Jose Jimenez, Niclas Karlsson, Jean-François Laverdure, Minh Mai, Phuong Mai, Thuong Nguyen, Tim Paschalidis, Carlos C. Perez, Regina Prestefelippe, Marcelo G. Riemer, Ivelisse Silva, Annika Svensson, Sachiko Taketani, John Voravarn. Their bright minds and their willingness to try out the drafting process and many readings have made teaching them and writing this text a pleasure.

Thanks also go to my secretary Ruth Cash, who has helped out with some of the typing, duplicating, and formatting; to my editor Susan Anker, not only for encouraging me to do the text but also for many a good conversation about female juggling acts; and to my project editor, Julie Nord, and to my reviewers (listed below) for making the text much stronger as a result of their perceptive critiques.

Alexandra Krapels, University of South Carolina

Elizabeth Rorschach, City College, CUNY

Lynn M. Goldstein, Monterey Institute of International Rules

Gay Brookes, Borough of Manhattan Community College

Vivian Zamel, University of Massachusetts, Boston

JoAnne Liebman, University of Arkansas at Little Rock

Susan Jenkins, Director, Intensive English Communication Program, Pennsylvania State University

Most of whatever strength the text has is due to the students, editors, and reviewers; the flaws are entirely my own.

Mary Jane Schenck
University of Tampa

Contents

Note to Students

The most accurate definition of writing, I believe, is that it is the process of using language to discover meaning in experience and to communicate it.

—*Donald Murray*

In school or on the job, many people feel apprehensive about being asked to write because they think they have nothing to say, or because they worry about making mistakes. If you too think that writing is not one of your strongest talents, keep in mind what Donald Murray says— writing is a means of discovering and communicating *your* ideas and your feelings. To help you feel more confident about expressing yourself in writing, this book will teach you techniques that will make starting an assignment easier and finishing it more satisfying.

First, some myths about good writers:

They know exactly what they want to say.

They are organized.

They don't make many mistakes.

They just begin and it all comes out quickly.

If you are a new or inexperienced writer, you may think that students who get good grades in writing just have a "gift for writing." Perhaps we all think that, because we don't see other writers working—we only see the results. The process many experienced writers use, whether they are students or professionals, is actually no great mystery, however, and the following ideas describe more accurately what they do:

They write often and a lot.

They are willing to begin without having a plan.

They don't worry too much about mistakes at first.

They use writing to discover their ideas.

They write and rewrite frequently.

Much of the material in this book is designed to help you see the process that good writers use.

Why should we try to write well? Henry Miller says: "Writing, like life itself, is a voyage of discovery." If writing is a process of discovering meaning in our experiences, as Donald Murray and Henry Miller suggest, then you will find out that it is more than just a part of your education—it is an education itself. It is the best way to discover yourself and learn new ideas in academic work or in your personal activities.

This book will introduce you to some interesting readings and to the process of writing responses to these and other experiences. We begin with personal writing because that is often the easiest and most natural place to start, but most of the book will help you with typical academic writing assignments. Throughout the book you will be introduced to things you can do before writing, to the process of revising from one draft to another one, and finally to polishing or editing a final version. The reading selections are written by professional writers, but the sample papers have been written by students very much like you. Note that student work is typeset to look like it was done on a typewriter or word processor, but, of course, most of it was originally handwritten.

If writing is, in fact, a voyage of discovery and not just a difficult academic chore, then imagine yourself now getting ready to take off on an interesting adventure. What you find during the voyage will be directly related to how much of yourself you put into the process, that is, the process of reading, reacting, and writing about your feelings and ideas.

Chapter One

ON WRITING

Language is the mother, not the hand-maiden, of thought; words will tell you things you never thought or felt before.

—*W. H. Auden*

Donald Murray *(1924–)*

Donald Murray received his B.A. degree from the University of New Hampshire in 1948 and then went to work on the Boston Herald *as a reporter. He rose to editorial writer there before joining* Time *magazine as a contributing editor. He won a Pulitzer Prize for editorial writing in 1954. He has published extensively in a variety of forms— journalism, magazine articles, fiction, and academic writing. He is currently an Associate Professor of English at the University of New Hampshire and has written several texts on writing for instructors and students.*

Why Write?

Sometimes we write just for ourselves, to record what we have seen or felt or thought. Sometimes we write to celebrate experience. Many times we write just to find out what it all means, for by writing we can stand back from ourselves and see significance in what is close to us. 1

Most of the time, however, writing is a private act with a public result. We write alone to discover meaning. But once that meaning is discovered, once we understand what we have to say, then we want or need to share it with other people. 2

Sometimes that need precedes the impulse to write. We receive an assignment and have to write a paper, an examination, a memo for the boss, a news story. We may have to report an experiment, turn in a poem, write a skit, send out fund-raising publicity, create a job résumé, complain about being badgered[1] for a bill we've already paid. There are hundreds of writing tasks we may have to perform. We may have to write speeches, books, brochures, letters of sympathy, case histories on patients. But whatever writing we do, if it is to be done well we have to go back to gather information and make sense of it. 3

We can't write writing. Some readers think professionals who turn out political speeches or company reports can use language to weave a meaning without information. I've been hired as a ghostwriter[2] and know we can't. First we have to understand what the candidate is trying to do, or why the company has made a profit or a loss. We have to do 4

---

[1]Bothered, from the badger, an animal known for its persistant aggressiveness.

[2]Someone hired to write for someone else; the actual writer is a ''ghost'' in the sense that his or her name will not be credited for the work.

research and attempt to build a meaning from the product of our research that a reader can understand.

The writer may write to inform, to explain, to entertain, to persuade, but whatever the purpose there should be, first of all, the satisfaction of the writer's own learning, the joy and surprise of finding out what you have to say.

There are many side benefits to writing. Writing allows you to discover that you have a voice, a way of speaking that is individual and effective. It allows you to share with others and even to influence others.

Writing can bring attention to you or to your ideas. It can add to your job skills, and it can improve your grades. Writing can give you power, for we live in a complicated technological society, and those people who can collect information, order it into significant meaning and then communicate it to others will influence the course of events within the town or nation, school or university, company or corporation. Information is power.

If you have the ability to find specific, accurate information and fit it together in a meaningful pattern through language you will have the pleasure of making something that was not there before, of finding significance where others find confusion, of bringing order to chaos. If you can do this clearly and gracefully you will have readers, for people are hungry for specific information ordered into meaning.

And if you write, when you look out your window you will see what you had forgotten and, by writing, you may discover what it means. My attention turns from my uncle carrying me to my grandmother standing by the door of the living room. She approves more by not frowning than by smiling. I study the set of that stern mouth and begin to wonder how much her glance still governs me. If I write about her I may find out.

♦ COMPREHENSION/DISCUSSION QUESTIONS

1. What was interesting to you about this selection?

2. What kinds of writing is Donald Murray referring to in the first paragraph?

3. What does he mean when he says, "writing is a private act with a public result?" [2]*

4. What does "We can't write writing" [4] mean?

*Numbers in brackets refer to paragraph numbers in readings.

5. What are the various purposes for writing, according to Murray? Are there other purposes?

6. Why do you think the last paragraph is so different from the preceding ones?

7. What does the last sentence mean?

8. Do you agree with Murray that information is power? Cite some specific examples from your own experience.

9. Do you ever write for fun? What do you write other than class assignments?

10. When you write in English, how does it differ from writing in your native language?

Prewriting: Getting Started

Prewriting is an oral or written activity used to help the writer come up with ideas for longer written assignments. Although we may think of prewriting as a step to be taken only before a longer composition is started, it actually can be used at any time during the process of writing if the writer needs help in generating new ideas, more details, or connections between ideas.

Prewriting exercises not only help you find something to say but also improve your writing skills by providing more opportunities to write. Practice in writing, no matter how short the exercise, is certain to make you feel more self-confident about your writing and to improve your skills.

Various types of prewriting exercises will be explained in detail throughout this chapter, but one of the simplest ways to begin is to write an answer to a question.

◆ PREWRITING EXERCISE: QUESTION/ANSWER

1. Write a few sentences in response to the following questions:

What is your name?

Where are you from?

What do you want others in the class to know about you?

Share what you have written with someone sitting near you. Then introduce your partner to the whole class by reading aloud what he or she has written. Repeat this exercise or variations on it during the first few classes until everyone gets to know each other. Variations on the questions might be: what are you planning to study? how long have you lived here? have you been a student at another college or university? or do you live with your family? The class should suggest questions they would like to ask each other in order to get to know each other better.

2. Now write a few sentences in response to the question: how do you feel when you are asked to write for a class?

Share your writing with another student.

Sample Student Writing

Here are some uncorrected examples of what other students have written in response to the second question.

I like to write because is a scape from reality. I usually write about what I am thinking, and when I do it is like telling all my problems to a person. Sometimes get solutions to those problems and sometimes, I just forget them. I like free writing, is like a relaxation, specially in those cases when you can not said what you are thinking. I like to write about personal feelings, problems and satisfaction. Most of the time I write for myself, or for a very special friend.

Joe Corcione

I personally think that writing is a good thing for many reasons. When you write you practice and exercise your mind to work faster and get the words onto the paper rapidly.

I like to write because it is a great way to express my feelings. No one can know what I am thinking if I don't tell them. If I want I can let them read about of what I think.

It is good to write because when you have a good idea you can write it so that it is difficult to forget. If you don't loose the paper.

My favorite writings are poems. In which I write everything that comes in my mind of a specific theme. Some of them are from experiences that I had with my friends others are of what I think about life or about the problems that many people has with life and how the people are working with them.

Carlos Perez

To tell the truth writing has not been nor is it now my strongest subject. I remember that since I learned how to write in primary school I didn't like it, but there was always someone behind us to tell us that we had to keep writing for the rest of our lives. On the other side I like to read a lot. It is always easier to read someone else's writing than to write our own lines.

I never had the talent of writing because I don't feel I can express myself that way, I prefer to speak, it is more direct way of communicating and it takes less time to do it.

The only way I can write freely and without any problem is free writing because I don't need to apply any grammatical rule or plan and it comes out the same way I am thinking. It is the nearest approximation to spoken word.

Perhaps it is just a matter of laziness or impatience.

I am sometimes lazy with the things that do not interest me too much or perhaps I do not have the required patience of doing one thing that could be done in a faster and more expressive way like spoken word.

Who knows, perhaps written english at the university will make of me a write loving person or on the contrary it will increase my aversion to writing.

Marcelo Riemer

♦ DISCUSSION QUESTIONS

1. Which of the students' ideas about writing are similar to Donald Murray's?

2. Why do you suppose Marcelo feels that writing is more difficult than reading? Do you think this is true?

3. Do you share any of the other ideas expressed by these student writers about their writing?

Peter Elbow *(1935–)*

Peter Elbow teaches at the University of Massachusetts (Amherst). He has held a Danforth Fellowship and published extensively on teaching writing as well as on Chaucer. The following selection is from his book Writing Without Teachers, *published by Oxford in 1973.*

Freewriting

The most effective way I know to improve your writing is to do   1
freewriting exercises regularly. At least three times a week. They are
sometimes called "automatic writing,"[1] "babbling," or "jabbering"
exercises. The idea is simply to write for ten minutes (later on, perhaps
fifteen or twenty). Don't stop for anything. Go quickly without rushing.
Never stop to look back, to cross something out, to wonder how to spell
something, to wonder what word or thought to use, or to think about
what you are doing. If you can't think of a word or a spelling, just use a
squiggle or else write, "I can't think of it." Just put down something.
The easiest thing is just to put down whatever is in your mind. If you get
stuck it's fine to write "I can't think what to say, I can't think what to
say" as many times as you want; or repeat the last word you wrote over
and over again; or anything else. The only requirement is that you *never*
stop.

What happens to a freewriting exercise is important. It must be a   2
piece of writing which, even if someone reads it, doesn't send any
ripples back to you. It is like writing something and putting it in a bottle
in the sea. The teacherless[2] class helps your writing by providing max-
imum feedback. Freewritings help you by providing no feedback at all.
When I assign one, I invite the writer to let me read it. But also tell him
to keep it if he prefers. I read it quickly and make no comments at all
and I do not speak with him about it. The main thing is that a freewriting must never be evaluated in any way; in fact there must be no discussion or comment at all.

Here is an example of a fairly coherent exercise (sometimes they are   3
very incoherent, which is fine):

> I think I'll write what's on my mind, but the only thing on my
> mind right now is what to write for ten minutes. I've never done

---

[1] Writing without plan or revision; writing from the subconscious.

[2] A word Elbow made up to describe a class where teacher are not the sole influence; students teach themselves and each other.

this before and I'm not prepared in any way—the sky is cloudy today, how's that? now I'm afraid I won't be able to think of what to write when I get to the end of the sentence—well, here I am at the end of the sentence—here I am again, again, again, again, at least I'm still writing—Now I ask is there some reason to be happy that I'm still writing—ah yes! Here comes the question again—What am I getting out of this? What point is there in it? It's almost obscene to always ask it but I seem to question everything that way and I was gonna say something else pertaining to that but I got so busy writing down the first part that I forgot what I was leading into. This is kind of fun oh don't stop writing—cars and trucks speeding by somewhere out the window, pens clittering across peoples' papers. The sky is still cloudy—is it symbolic that I should be mentioning it? Huh? I dunno. Maybe I should try colors, blue, red, dirty words—wait a minute—no, can't do that, orange, yellow, arm tired, green pink violet magenta lavender red brown black green—now that I can't think of any more colors—just about done—relief? maybe.

HOW FREEWRITING EXERCISES HELP

Freewriting may seem crazy but actually it makes simple sense. Think of the difference between speaking and writing. Writing has the advantage of permitting more editing. But that's its downfall too. Almost everybody interposes a massive and complicated series of editings between the time words start to be born into consciousness and when they finally come off the end of the pencil or typewriter onto the page. This is partly because schooling makes us obsessed with the "mistakes" we make in writing. Many people are constantly thinking about spelling and grammar as they try to write. I am always thinking about the awkwardness, wordiness, and general mushiness of my natural verbal product as I try to write down words.

But it's not just "mistakes" or "bad writing" we edit as we write. We also edit unacceptable thoughts and feelings, as we do in speaking. In writing there is more time to do it so the editing is heavier: when speaking, there's someone right there waiting for a reply and he'll get bored or think we're crazy if we don't come out with *something*. Most of the time in speaking, we settle for the catch-as-catch-can[3] way in which the words tumble out. In writing, however, there's a chance to try to get them right. But the opportunity to get them right is a terrible burden: you can work for two hours trying to get a paragraph "right" and discover it's not right at all. And then give up.

[3]Do it any way you can.

Editing, *in itself*, is not the problem. Editing is usually necessary if we   6
want to end up with something satisfactory. The problem is that editing
goes on *at the same time* as producing. The editor is, as it were,
constantly looking over the shoulder of the producer and constantly
fiddling with what he's doing while he's in the middle of trying to do it.
No wonder the producer gets nervous, jumpy, inhibited, and finally
can't be coherent. It's an unnecessary burden to try to think of words
and also worry at the same time whether they're the right words.

The main thing about freewriting is that it is *nonediting*. It is an   7
exercise in bringing together the process of producing words and putting them down on the page. Practiced regularly, it undoes the ingrained
habit of editing at the same time you are trying to produce. It will make
writing less blocked because words will come more easily. You will use
up more paper, but chew up fewer pencils.

Next time you write, notice how often you stop yourself from writing   8
down something you were going to write down. Or else cross it out after
it's written. "Naturally," you say, "it wasn't any good." But think for a
moment about the occasions when you spoke well. Seldom was it
because you first got the beginning just right. Usually it was a matter of a
halting or even garbled beginning, but you kept going and your speech
finally became coherent and even powerful. There is a lesson here for
writing: trying to get the beginning just right is a formula for failure—
and probably a secret tactic to make yourself give up writing. Make
some words, whatever they are, and then grab hold of that line and reel
in as hard as you can. Afterwards you can throw away lousy beginnings
and make new ones. This is the quickest way to get into good writing.

The habit of compulsive, premature editing doesn't just make writing   9
hard. It also makes writing dead. Your voice is damped out by all the
interruptions, changes, and hesitations between the consciousness and
the page. In your natural way of producing words there is a sound, a
texture, a rhythm—a voice—which is the main source of power in your
writing. I don't know how it works, but this voice is the force that will
make a reader listen to you, the energy that drives the meanings through
his thick skull. Maybe you don't *like* your voice; maybe people have
made fun of it. But it's the only voice you've got. It's your only source of
power. You better get back into it, no matter what you think of it. If you
keep writing in it, it may change into something you like better. But if
you abandon it, you'll likely never have a voice and never be heard.

Freewritings are vacuums. Gradually you will begin to carry over   10
into your regular writing some of the voice, force, and connectedness
that creep into those vacuums.

◆ COMPREHENSION/DISCUSSION QUESTIONS

1. Restate what you remember about Elbow's main points.

2. According to Elbow, how are you supposed to do freewriting?

3. Why do you suppose he says that it's fine if freewriting is incoherent?

4. Why do we edit our writing more than our speech?

5. When should editing be done?

6. What are the advantages of doing freewriting exercises?

7. Throughout paragraph 9, Elbow refers to finding your "voice" in writing. What does he mean?

8. What do you suppose he means when he says that freewritings are "vacuums"?

9. Have you ever done any freewriting? If so, did you enjoy it?

10. What are the similarities between Murray's ideas about writing and Elbow's?

◆ VOCABULARY

Write a definition of the following words, indicating their specific meaning in context. Are you familiar with other forms of the same word (such as "babble")?

babbling [1]	inhibited [6]
feedback [2]	interpose [4]
garbled [8]	jabbering [1]
halting [8]	mushiness [4]
ingrained [7]	squiggle [1]

Fill in the blanks with the appropriate vocabulary word. As you look at each sentence, consider not only the meanings of the words but also what part of speech must be used in the blank in order for the sentence to be correct.

1. This is not writing; this is a _____ on the page.

2. English teachers have an _____ habit of correcting grammar.

3. The message was so _____ I couldn't understand it.

4. Please don't be _____ about speaking English; you do quite well.

5. _____ is a quality of bad apples.

6. The small stream made a _____ sound.

7. When babies start to walk they take _____ steps.

8. The parrot was _____ to everyone that walked by.

9. If you give the tutor your rough draft, she will give you some _____.

10. Seeing that a fight was about to start, the man _____ himself between the arguing boys.

♦ FIGURES OF SPEECH: EXPANDING YOUR MEANING

Figures of speech are single words or phrases that mean something more, or something different, from what they literally say. The purpose of a figure of speech is to create an association of one idea with another, to make meanings clearer or more interesting, and to express ideas or feelings in new ways, i.e.,* to enhance and extend language. Figures of speech are used in speaking as well as in writing. They can be very simple, such as "she inched her way through the door" or "the baby is the light of my life." Or they can be quite complex, as they are in poetry. "An aged man is but a paltry thing, / a tattered coat upon a stick" (W. B. Yeats, "Sailing to Byzantium") or "Come, night; come, Romeo; come thou day in night; / For thou wilt lie upon the wings of night / Whiter than new snow upon a raven's back." (Shakespeare, *Romeo and Juliet* III, ii). For the purposes of this book, however, you will not be studying figures of speech as literary ornaments. The purpose of pointing them out here is to show you how often figures of speech are used in all forms of writing. As you go through this book, they will be pointed out so that your reading comprehension will improve.

In the preceding selection, Elbow uses some figures of speech to make his points. For example, in "[Freewriting] *doesn't send any ripples back to you*"·[2], Elbow has used the word "ripples" which properly describes the ring-shaped movements that radiate back toward the shore if an object is dropped in the water. He means that since freewriting is not read or graded by an instructor, it sends nothing back to the

---

* I.e. = *id est*, Latin for "that is," meaning "for example." It is always punctuated as it is here, surrounded by commas.

writer. Here's another example: "Almost everybody interposes a massive and complicated series of editings between the time words start to be born into consciousness and when they finally *come off the end* of the pencil or typewriter onto the page" [4]. The words are not literally "coming off" the end of the typewriter. But with this figure, he creates the contrast between the slow thinking process when we are too worried about editing and the sudden appearance of some words as if they were dropping out of the pencil or typewriter.

How would you explain the following figure of speech from Elbow's writing? "Make some words, whatever they are, and then *grab hold of that line and reel in as hard as you can*" [8].

Prewriting

Freewriting: Writing Without Stopping As Peter Elbow explains, freewriting (another form of prewriting) means writing without stopping for any reason, especially not to correct or to rewrite. You should attempt to fill up the time given for freewriting (perhaps 5–10 minutes) without letting the pen or pencil stop. The purpose is to loosen up your thinking, to get ideas flowing; so even if you think you have no ideas, write over and over again the last words you wrote, "this is dumb" or whatever, until new words and ideas come into your mind. Do not criticize yourself or worry about grammar, punctuation, or spelling. This is not graded writing, and it probably won't even be seen by the instructor.

Your instructor may ask you to freewrite without any hint of a topic, but sometimes it is good to begin with a word, statement, or question that will prompt your ideas. For example, your instructor might ask you to write what you think about a particular key word from a reading assignment or an idea from a class discussion.

Whatever the assignment and time limit, remember that words will come if you let them. If you open your mind and keep the pen or pencil moving, the words you write during freewriting may surprise you. Don't forget to turn off your "editor." Write what you want to, not what you think someone else wants you to write.

Note in the following examples that the students sometimes repeat a word or write a word in their native language rather than stopping when they couldn't think of the next word or idea. Since freewriting is unrevised, there are naturally many errors, but that does not mean they are not interesting writing and useful starting points for the writer. As you read them, ask yourself what is most interesting, what emotions do the writers reveal, and what else would you like to know about these writers?

Sample Student Writing

The two students' responses below are to the assignment, "Write for 10 minutes on a childhood memory, or about your first day on campus." These examples are uncorrected.

When I was young, in the age of 5 to 7 years old. I was afraid of the Santa Claus. At every Christmas, I went to bed from 5:00 pm until 11:00 pm to be able to stay up all night long. My cousins woke me up each time in my room, because Christmas was always at my house. Then, I waited for the Santa Claus, to see him I look thru the freezy windows and walked by the cheminée. My parents said to me to go into the kitchen and take the beer's Santa Claus. There was always noise from the cheminée, my old cousins were doing this noise and, I always thought that it was the Santa Clause. Once arrived in the house, he always sits on the same chair, the big red one. I couldn't sit on his laps, because I was too afraid of him. I just give him his beer and walked away, he scared me. Today it's fun to remember this and that it was my uncle who made the big Santa Claus.

Jean-François Laverdure

I came here in middle of the night, didn't know where I where or what do. I just followed my friend to a room where we were supposed to live. It was a rather small room and there were two beds and nothing else. I didn't like it. They said that we were supposed to live with some american boys and I worried about it. We tried to change so that my Swedish friend and I could live togheter but because of the insurance—it was impossible. I was scared about living with someone else because of the language but I realized now I would be able to learn English much faster but it's nice to have a friend to talke Swedish with and study toghether with. With With With With With With. The next morning we meet all guys in the soccer team they were all very nice. They played all very good soccer which surprised me. I thought they didn't know soccer at all but they did. Know I don't know what write down but I hope I will remember something to write down. I haven't what shall I do-oh gosh. Yes about the food. I have never seen such a fat people as the american. They can't know anything about right diet. But if you look in cafeteria you realize that they must be fat if they are supposed to eat that kind of food. I hope I won't be fat. But I dont think so.

Thomas Hogstedt

◆ FREEWRITING EXERCISE

Write for 10 minutes nonstop on one of the following ideas:

> a specific scene you observed today
>
> your first impression of school
>
> a childhood memory
>
> what you thought about after reading the selection by Peter Elbow

Follow-up Writing   (may be done in class or outside class): Look back over your prewriting and choose the sentences you like best. Take those sentences and rewrite them to make them the best you can. Since the whole point of this book is to teach you to revise and edit your own work, you cannot be expected to know everything about the process at this point. You can, however, begin by trying to look over your writing to make it as clear as possible and as error-free as possible. Then show this piece of writing to your instructor and/or share it with a partner in the class. After they have seen it, keep this writing for yourself.

William Stafford *(1914–)*

William Stafford received his Ph.D. from the University of Iowa in 1954 and taught at Lewis and Clark College from 1948 until he retired. He won the National Book Award for Traveling Through the Dark, *a collection of his poetry. He has published five other volumes of poetry, one nonfiction work, and a collection of essays entitled* Writing the Australian Crawl *(1978), which describes his process of writing poetry. The following selection is taken from those essays.*

Writing

A writer is not so much someone who has something to say as he is   1
someone who has found a process that will bring about new things he
would not have thought of if he had not started to say them. That is, he
does not draw on a reservoir; instead, he engages in an activity that
brings to him a whole succession of unforseen stories, poems, essays,
plays, laws, philosophies, religions, or—but wait!

Back in school, from the first when I began to try to write things, I   2
felt this richness. One thing would lead to another; the world would give
and give. Now, after twenty years or so of trying, I live by that certain
richness, an idea hard to pin, difficult to say, and perhaps offensive to
some. For there are strange implications in it.

One implication is the importance of just plain receptivity. When I   3
write, I like to have an interval before me when I am not likely to be
interrupted. For me, this means usually the early morning, before others
are awake. I get pen and paper, take a glance out the window (often it is
dark out there), and wait. It is like fishing. But I do not wait very long,
for there is always a nibble—and this is where receptivity comes in. To
get started I will accept anything that occurs to me. Something always
occurs, of course, to any of us. We can't keep from thinking. Maybe I
have to settle for an immediate impression: it's cold, or hot, or dark, or
bright, or in between! Or—well, the possibilities are endless. If I put
down something, that thing will help the next thing come, and I'm off.
If I let the process go on, things will occur to me that were not at all in
my mind when I started. These things, odd or trivial as they may be, are
somehow connected. And if I let them string out, surprising things will
happen.

If I let them string out. . . . Along with initial receptivity, then, there   4
is another readiness: I must be willing to fail. If I am to keep on writing,
I cannot bother to insist on high standards. I must get into action and
not let anything stop me, or even slow me much. By "standards" I do

not mean "correctness"—spelling, punctuation, and so on. These details become mechanical for anyone who writes for a while. I am thinking about what many people would consider "important" standards, such matters as social significance, positive values, consistency, etc. I resolutely disregard these. Something better, greater, is happening! I am following a process that leads so wildly and originally into new territory that no judgment can at the moment be made about values, significance, and so on. I am making something new, something that has not been judged before. Later others—and maybe I myself—will make judgments. Now, I am headlong to discover.[1] Any distraction may harm the creating.

So, receptive, careless of failure, I spin out things on the page. And a wonderful freedom comes. If something occurs to me, it is all right to accept it. It has one justification: it occurs to me. No one else can guide me. I must follow my own weak, wandering, diffident impulses.   5

A strange bonus happens. At times, without my insisting on it, my writings become coherent; the successive elements that occur to me are clearly related. They lead by themselves to new connections. Sometimes the language, even the syllables that happen along, may start a trend. Sometimes the materials alert me to something waiting in my mind, ready for sustained attention. At such times, I allow myself to be eloquent, or intentional, or for great swoops[2] (treacherous! not to be trusted!) reasonable. But I do not insist on any of that; for I know that back of my activity there will be the coherence of my self, and that indulgence of my impulses will bring recurrent patterns and meanings again.   6

This attitude toward the process of writing creatively suggests a problem for me, in terms of what others say. They talk about "skills" in writing. Without denying that I do have experience, wide reading, automatic orthodoxies[3] and maneuvers of various kinds, I still must insist that I am often baffled about what "skill" has to do with the precious little area of confusion when I do not know what I am going to say and then I find out what I am going to say. That precious interval I am unable to bridge by skill. What can I witness about it? It remains mysterious, just as all of us must feel puzzled about how we are so inventive as to be able to talk along through complexities with our friends, not needing to plan what we are going to say, but never stalled for long in our confident forward progress. Skill? If so, it is the skill we all have, something we must have learned before the age of three or four.   7

---

[1]Totally immersed, involved.

[2]Sudden descents or sweeping motions.

[3]Sets of beliefs, usually traditional in nature.

A writer is one who has become accustomed to trusting that grace, or   8
luck, or—skill.

Yet another attitude I find necessary: most of what I write, like most   9
of what I say in casual conversation, will not amount to much. Even I
will realize, and even at the time, that it is not negotiable. It will be like
practice. In conversation I allow myself random remarks—in fact, as I
recall, that is the way I learned to talk—, so in writing I launch many
expendable efforts. A result of this free way of writing is that I am not
writing for others, mostly; they will not see the product at all unless the
activity eventuates[4] in something that later appears to be worthy. My
guide is the self, and its adventuring in the language brings about communication.

This process-rather-than-substance view of writing invites a final,   10
dual reflection:

1. Writers may not be special—sensitive or talented in any usual   11
sense. They are simply engaged in sustained use of a language skill we all
have. Their "creations" come about through confident reliance on stray
impulses that will, with trust, find occasional patterns that are satisfying.

2. But writing itself is one of the great, free human activities. There   12
is scope for individuality, and elation, and discovery, in writing. For the
person who follows with trust and forgiveness what occurs to him, the
world remains always ready and deep, and inexhaustible environment,
with the combined vividness of an actuality and flexibility of a dream.
Working back and forth between experience and thought, writers have
more than space and time can offer. They have the whole unexplored
realm of human vision.

♦ COMPREHENSION/ DISCUSSION QUESTIONS

1. What does Stafford mean when he says that a writer "has found a
    process that will bring about new things he would not have
    thought of if he had not started to say them" [1]?

2. What is "receptivity" [3] as Stafford describes it?

3. When should a writer not insist on high standards?

4. What does Stafford think about the value of writing skills?

5. How is the word "witness" used in paragraph 7?

6. Who is he writing for? Why?

7. What did you think about after you read this selection?

----

[4]Comes to some conclusion, results in.

8. Have you ever tried to write any poetry or fiction (stories)? Did you enjoy it? Do you think you are good at it?

9. Do you think the process Stafford describes for writing would help you to begin an academic assignment? Why or why not?

10. What points do Murray, Elbow, and Stafford have in common?

♦ VOCABULARY

Write out a definition of the following words, indicating their specific meaning in the context of the essay. Are you familiar with other forms of these words, such as "diffidently?"

diffident [5]	negotiable [9]
disregard [4]	nibble [3]
elation [12]	receptivity [3]
implication [2]	resolutely [4]
maneuver [7]	stalled [7]

Fill in the blanks with the appropriate vocabulary word. As you are searching for the right word, remember to consider not only meaning but also the part of speech that belongs in the sentence.

1. When she won the prize, her face showed her _____ _____.

2. All the terms of this agreement are _____.

3. Stafford says that _____ is important in order to start writing.

4. The army marched _____ toward the enemy.

5. The rains have continued for three days because a tropical storm is _____ off the coast.

6. Does the driveway leave you any room to _____ your car?

7. At first, the students were _____ around their teachers.

8. The only _____ to be seen in this paragraph is that the writer is opposed to required courses.

9. If you aren't hungry, you just _____ at your food.

10. She doesn't care; she has complete _____ for others' feelings.

♦ IDIOMS

An idiom is an expression that has an accepted meaning different from the literal meaning of the words. Study the meanings of the idioms below, referring back to the sentence in which they were used. Does the context help you to understand them?

1. "Hard to pin" [2]—normally "hard to pin down" meaning difficult to describe, define, or explain.

2. "I'm off [3]—I have started.

3. "string out" [3]—lead from one thing to another.

4. "Spin out" [5]—similar to "string out"; often refers to telling a story; from the action of pulling thread off a spinning wheel.

Prewriting

Freewriting   Practice what Stafford calls "receptivity." Get up early or find some quiet time during the day when you can go off by yourself and freewrite for 15 minutes or longer on:

anything you observe or think about.

your definition of "creativity"

how important you think it is to write well

Brainstorming: Making Quick Lists   When you use a process of quickly listing words or phrases associated with a subject, it is another form of prewriting called "brainstorming." You force your brain to discharge its ideas quickly, as an electrical storm discharges its energy in thunder and lightning. (One of my students used to call this form of prewriting "brain-thundering.") Brainstorming can be done individually or in small groups, but most of the time in this text it will be an individual exercise. It is a very effective way for you to generate ideas for writing assignments or to prepare for class discussion of a reading assignment. The best results will occur if you do not stop to worry about the order or logic of the words or phrases that come into your mind. For instance, if your instructor asked you to brainstorm for 5 minutes on the idea of college life, you might make a list like the one we've called Brainstorming List A (page 20).

Your responses to the same suggestion will vary at different times depending upon your feelings at the particular moment you do the list. Brainstorming is an exercise in "free association" during which you write down whatever words occur to you without trying to organize your thoughts. It is called a prewriting exercise precisely because it is a

BRAINSTORMING LIST A

classroom	hungry
books	cafeteria
studying	bad food
tired	homesick

method of getting started on written work and is not supposed to be corrected. This type of prewriting, just like freewriting, might be the first step to a longer piece of writing or might be used to get going again if you run out of ideas in the middle, or at some point in the process of writing a longer piece.

List B was generated by a student in response to the suggestion that she think about her first day on the campus. It is shown here (below) just as she wrote it, including the errors.

BRAINSTORMING LIST B

big hot building
many student
don't know way to go
feel nervous
friendly people
much paper
lines to wait

◆ BRAINSTORMING EXERCISE

Try brainstorming on your own. Remember that you do not write sentences as you do in freewriting. For this exercise write only words or phrases, as in the above examples. Write for 5 minutes on one of the following:

the room you are sitting in

American television

something funny

Once you have brainstormed, you can take your list as a starting point for a writing assignment. For instance, you could take the most interest-

ing or most surprising words on your list, mark them with an asterisk
(*), and then write about them.

Look at the following examples from a brainstorming on "the room
you are sitting in":

blackboard*	books everywhere
words*	people writting
different coulours	too quiet
nice carpet	studying
many chairs	
many students*	

My brainstorm is about my classroom. The blackboard in
the class I'm sitting in is full of words, because many students were studying before I came here.

Tim Paschalidis

classroom	participation
teacher	blackboard
companionship*	English compositions
homework	desk
books	students
study	writing
awake	dictionaries

I think that companionship is the actitude that should
match with all of the other separates ideas that come to my
mind. We need companionship to feel better and get some
productivity.

Luis Alonso

teachers	books	wastbasket
students	pens	quiet*
girls	papers	nervous
boys	eraser	ceiling
clothes	thinking	bookbag
blackboard	floor	noise*
chair	glass	words
shoes	light*	eraser

The room is quiet because everybody is working on their
assignment. The air conditioner break off the noise. The
room is bright.

Phuong Mai

Now try a brainstorming exercise as a whole class. Take your instructor's or a student's suggestion for a starting point. It might be something
like, "How would you describe this room?" or "How could we learn
about each other's backgrounds?" The instructor should write the question or a key word on the board and then jot down the ideas as quickly
as they are called out by the students. After the brainstorming is completed, students could write down several sentences describing the best
ideas mentioned during the brainstorming.

Journals: Writing for Yourself   An excellent way to learn
more about writing and yourself is to keep a journal. A journal is more
than a diary, which is just a record of the day's events. A journal is a
place to write down bits and pieces of your experience, a conversation
overheard, a description of an especially interesting person, or some
feelings about an event. You may also want to look back over your
journal entries for ideas to be used when your instructor assigns longer
pieces of writing that will be drafted and finally turned in for evaluation. Some instructors will want you to keep the journal on your own
time, outside class, but others may want you to bring it to class each
day.

Your instructor will give you some specific directions about how to
keep a journal, but here are some general suggestions:

◇ Purchase a bound notebook with blank lined or unlined pages to
be kept separate from any other notebook.

◇ Write only on the right-hand pages, so you will have blank pages
for later additions and revisions. This will also allow you to fold
over the page to keep a classmate from reading it during group
exercises, if the material you wrote is too private. These journals
are "public" ones because they will be used in class, but occasionally you will find yourself writing something that is "for your eyes
only."

◇ Experiment with different colors of ink and types of pen (don't use
pencil). Part of the fun of writing is the physical act of holding the
pen and seeing the way the writing looks.

◊ Date all entries, and note the location where you are writing.

◊ Give yourself time limits, or follow your instructor's guidelines about how often and for how long you are to write. Don't leave it for when you are tired from other studying. Devote some of the best part of your day to this activity.

Like freewriting, journal keeping can be done by generating your own topics or in response to a suggestion. Write in your journal for 20 minutes on one of the following topics:

> reactions to the idea of doing a lot of writing in this course
>
> a success or failure in past writing assignments
>
> one of your former teachers of writing/English
>
> reactions to what has happened to you today (not just descriptions)

Sample Student Writing

As you will see in the following examples from student journals, writing about an interesting memory, a recent event, or feelings is a good way to find self-expression. These journal entries may provide excellent sources of material for later writing assignments, as will be demonstrated in later chapters. Journal entries are *not* graded, but your instructor will probably give you credit for keeping the journal in a consistent and serious way.

These examples have not been corrected.

The first day in campus was a mess. Lines for this and lines for that. Class conflicts everywhere, lots of meeting overlaping each other. Heat, sweat and tears. Its difficult to start putting my eyes on a text book, not used to it since I graduated in Buenos Aires. The classes were all overcrowded and some air conditioners were not working properly. I hope in winter the weather will be better. The drop add process is really a pain in the neck, they should be using a computer terminal after all that is one reason to have a data processing center. Two hours of waiting in line to add one miserable class. I was lucky I only had one. I hope that in the future things will be better organized. The instructor were ok but there is a lot of work to do at home. Less time to play with baby. The administrative staff were very gentle and explained everything I wanted to know perhaps they are paid to be kind and helpful but anyway it's better to have a paid smile rather than a sour face in front of you stop if that doesnt want or doesnt care about the job they are assigned—

Marcelo G. Riemer

I've been here for two weeks and I'm missing home already. I would like to be with my friends from Montreal, have fun with them, party with them, just for one night but I have to see them. The life here is fun, really different but still fun. I miss my girlfriend, I've been with her for 2 1/2 years so it was very hard to leave her at Montreal. I can't forget her, she's so nice and smart. We talk each other twice a week and we write letters, that makes it harder. I would like to be Christmas in two weeks but it's in four months. It's a chance, guys are so nice here, they help me with my english and everything I have difficulty with. Anyway I'm doing the best I can and wait to see my friends soon. Hope that it's going to pass pretty fast.

Jean-François Laverdure

Today my journal is about the ticket given by the Police Department. Recently, I received a ticket because I was park in a wrong space. That day, I parked my car in the visitor lot, because I couldn't find any parking available in the blue section. I parked there after been around the parking for twenty minutes. I think was unfair that the policeman give it to me that ticket. I know, I parked wrong but I had to park in any space available, because I had a class at ten o'clock in the morning. Also, I think that I'm in the university to study and not to spent my time trying to find a parking. I think that everyone in the university should have freedom to park in any lot available that is designed to park cars.

That day I went to the police department to ask about the ticket and the lady there told me that I could appeal, and I did. In the appeal letter, I asked the Police Board to answer me a question. I asked them this: If they were in my position, what would they do. Also, I asked them, what can I do if I can't find any parking in my design section. I appeal not to don't pay the ticket, I did because I want to know what I should do the next time that I doesn't find a parking. I think that if I pay for a decal parking, I have the right to park in any space available.

Ivelisse Silva

Small Group Exercises

Many exercises in this book are based on small group work. Working together—collaborative learning—is an excellent way to build up your ability to express ideas both orally and in writing. It is a model of learning that will require you to be an active learner rather than a passive receiver of information. You will be expected to work with and help other students in the class in order to develop your speaking and writing in situations that are close to real life.

Just think about how you learned your language at home, or how you learn a new skill on the job. In those situations, growth occurs because the members of a family or the people in an office or factory perform as a team, helping and interacting with each other. Of course, one person (an instructor, a parent, a chief engineer) teaches or gives directions when new information must be learned, but he or she does not always dominate the learning experience. It is the collaboration of the whole group which develops and sustains the growth of individual learners. So too with small group exercises in a class: they are not often used to learn new material. Instead, they are used when analysis, synthesis, or evaluation of material is required.

Small group exercises are especially useful for discussions of reading material and for developing ideas during the process of writing a composition. One of the most basic types of small group exercise is group brainstorming and consensus building.

Brainstorming

1. Divide into groups of 3–4 students, and pull chairs or desks together in a circle.

2. Choose one student as a recorder who will take notes or be a spokesperson for the group, as required.

3. Have a student or the instructor suggest an idea from a reading or writing assignment (some models are presented below).

4. Brainstorm silently in writing for 3 minutes.

5. Read aloud your lists in turn while others listen and the recorder jots down notes (this can be done on large sheets of paper on a flip chart if you desire).

6. Brainstorm aloud again for 5 minutes and have the recorder add new ideas to the list.

The exercise could stop here, with directions from the instructor to do some follow-up writing or go on to another stage of the small group learning process. Suggestions for some follow-up writing include:

explain what you think the best ideas were

explain whether you learned anything from this process

Consensus Building

The exercise described above may also be continued to reach a consensus. A consensus is a statement of an opinion, position, or point that everyone in the group agrees upon. It is arrived at through discussion that takes into account everyone's opinions, and cannot be done by voting. In other words, discussion and some compromising on wording or positions should be pursued with respect for all points of view. Voting must be avoided because it is just a method for determining the majority. A consensus means that *everyone* in the group can support the position, although not everyone has to agree with the same degree of enthusiasm.

After completing the brainstorming exercise above, the small groups should discuss the ideas they have listed and determine the best of all (or the most practical, most realistic, etc., depending on the subject being discussed). The groups should come to an agreement (consensus) by listening and talking to each other long enough to hear each person's opinion. A time limit, however, should be set by the instructor, so that the group will be motivated to move quickly toward a compromise and not just argue back and forth. The recorder should report the result to the whole class. Then the class can work on a final consensus on the best solution to the issue.

Here are some suggested topics for this exercise:

What would help you to write more often?

Why do people think they write poorly?

How could the native English-speaking students be more helpful to you?

How can foreign students meet American students?

Approaching Composition Through Prewriting Exercises

Any of the prewriting exercises presented in this chapter—question/ answer, brainstorming, freewriting, journal keeping, or small group exercises—can be used to help you in the process of composing a longer piece of writing. Not every strategy works for everyone equally well, so now that you know how to do several different types, you can choose which one you think will give you the best results. Your instructor may also suggest that you try other strategies that will be presented later in this text. Remember also that you can stop at any point in the writing process and do a prewriting just to get ideas flowing on a specific point.

After you have done some prewriting, you will probably be eager to do something more with what you've put down on paper. You are used to being asked to write for an instructor and having to turn it in, but you may not be as used to paying attention to the process of how you get from an assignment to the final product. The following chapters are designed to show you how to prepare your writing for your ''public''— another student, the whole class, or your instructor—through the process of writing drafts, doing revisions, and learning to edit the final draft. It can't all be explained in these first few pages, but one important point to keep in mind as you start is that the process of preparing a written assignment for someone else to read includes several phases, which you will move through, repeat, and even occasionally do all at the same time. If that sounds confusing, just keep in mind that writing, like thinking, does not move in straight lines, even though we try to make it do so. We go back over what we have thought or said, revising our approach and our opinions, correcting grammar, and sometimes doing all of those things at once. The writing process is similar.

Without further explanations, you can begin the process of moving from one of the initial phases in writing, prewriting, to composing itself by doing one of the following assignments.

♦ WRITING ASSIGNMENTS

1. Take one or more of the prewritings you have done that ask for information about yourself. Select what you like the best, and write several paragraphs describing yourself, your background, your goals, and something about why you have come to this particular school. Rewrite these paragraphs to make them as clear and as well organized as you can. Then share your writing with a partner in class, and ask if he or she can help you see any places that are not clear. Revise to the best of your ability, and then correct any errors you see. Do not, however, be too worried at this point about making mistakes. Your instructor may want to collect this piece of writing to comment on, or you should keep it for yourself.

2. Take one or more of the prewritings you wrote on your feelings and experiences with writing. Select what you think are the most important points and write several paragraphs telling the class about your attitudes toward writing. Follow the directions for completing the assignment as in assignment 1.

3. Do a new prewriting on any topic that you choose. After you finish, look at it and decide which ideas are particularly interesting. Then write a paragraph explaining these ideas or telling your class about your topic. Follow the directions for completing the assignment as in (1).

4. If you have ever done any creative writing (poetry or stories) or would like to try that sort of writing, do a prewriting activity to get you started on a poem or story. Then complete the assignment as in the first exercise.

Writing Folder   Whenever you do writing for class, especially when you have worked on drafts of your assignments, keep them in a folder. It is important for your instructor to be able to look at drafts in evaluating the final product, and you will have an interesting file of your work to consult and use to demonstrate your progress at certain checkpoints throughout the class.

Chapter Two

IMPORTANT PLACES/ IMPORTANT PEOPLE

Writing from Experience

I write to find out what I'm thinking about.
—Edward Albee

Charles LeBaron (1943–)

Charles LeBaron was born in New York City and received a B.A. from Princeton and an M.A. in teaching from Harvard before working as a social worker in California and New York City. He decided to return to school to attend Harvard Medical College at the age of thirty-four. In his book Gentle Vengeance, *he describes his medical education at one of the best universities in the world. It begins with his reaction, upon arriving late at night, to the fancy lobby of the dorm and the bare room he will have. In his "first day" experience, he worries about how he will fit in and how he will handle his finances.*

Before reading the first selection, write for 10 minutes in your journal on your impressions of a "first day" at school.

Beginnings

I arrived at Harvard in the middle of the night with all my worldly   1
possessions, from an apartment in the Lower East Side, jammed into a
rented station wagon. Vanderbilt Hall, the medical school's sole dormitory, was an ivy-covered effort at an Italian palazzo[1] with odd touches
of Spanish hacienda and Ruskin Gothic decorations.[1] A small, stone
rotunda[2] served as lobby, its curved ceiling painted in elaborate designs
of gold and green and red. Sculpted into that dome was a coat of arms[3]
whose charges incorporated twined serpents and retorts and apothecary's vials.[4] Around the lintel[5] was an inscription in French: "In the
field of observation, chance favors only the prepared mind."

Off the lobby were side chambers with Persian rugs, dark wood   2
paneling, leather armchairs, a grand piano, and paintings of nineteenth-
century physicians with pork chop whiskers[6] and impressive scowls. I
picked up the keys to my room from a security guard behind a desk and

---

[1]Palazzo = palace; hacienda = ranch house; Ruskin Gothic = an imitation of the style of the great medieval cathedrals. Ruskin was a nineteenth–century British writer, and art critic who helped to make a Gothic revival popular.

[2]Round room.

[3]Emblem or heraldic sign of a family.

[4]A retort is a closed laboratory vessel with an outlet tube; apothecary's vials are small glass bottles used by pharmacists.

[5]Horizontal beam above a window or door.

[6]Large bushy whiskers.

went upstairs. After the Versailles[7] of the lobby, the living quarters seemed like barracks—cement staircases, low ceilings, plain white paint, long sets of identical doors. Inside my room there was a desk, dresser, and a narrow, hard bed. A pamphlet of rules on the desk informed me that animals, birds, and reptiles were forbidden, along with waterbeds and stolen goods. I had to carry an official identification at all times, I might be relocated without notice to another room, and a false alarm might result in my "imprisonment in a jail or house of correction for not more than one year." Nevertheless, after the mice and cockroaches and lack of heat in the tenement where I'd stayed in New York, this was quite livable.

After moving my cardboard boxes upstairs, I took a midnight stroll   3
around the campus in the warm September night. The medical school was on the other side of the city from Cambridge and the rest of Harvard, sequestered among museums and parks, surrounded by private hospitals. But a block away, across Huntington Avenue, was the all-black ghetto of Roxbury: squat projects,[8] broken glass, gutted cars. Harvard maintained a private police force to patrol its possessions and protect its students.

In contrast to the undergraduate campus, whose tree-lined squares of   4
colonial buildings created an air of genteel, courteous traditions, even intimacy, the medical school was designed around the turn of the century as one great quadrangle of Roman temples facing a massive, empty lawn. The temples, with their five-story marble columns and giant capitals,[9] seemed to shine of their own in the night, without need of nature's superfluous moonlight.

At thirty-four, I was the oldest student in the first-year class, perhaps   5
in the whole school. And one of the least prepared as well. While nine-tenths of my classmates had been science majors, some even having completed advanced degrees and doctorates, I'd never been exposed to anything but literature and history years ago as an undergraduate at Princeton.[10] Over the decade since then, I'd worked in semimenial capacities in various hospitals and institutions, and it was only by going to night school for the past two years that I'd gained the bare minimum of credits in chemistry and physics and biology. With that kind of scanty and eccentric background, could I survive?

And what I'd be studying, the human body, was, from that tiny bit I   6
knew about it, such a dazzlingly complex biological organization—our

[7]palace of Louis XIV, located outside Paris.

[8]Federally or locally funded housing for poor people.

[9]Decorative top of a column.

[10]Ivy League university; one of the most prestigious American universities, located in New Jersey.

tissues will respond to concentrations of hormones more dilute than a teaspoon of sugar in an Olympic swimming pool; each ounce of skeletal muscle is latticed[11] with forty miles of blood vessels; we can detect sounds so faint that the vibrations they set up in our eardrums have amplitudes no greater than the diameter of a hydrogen atom. Unfortunately, it was anomalous facts such as these, rather than the required information, that I tended to retain. The most painful experience known to man was said to be the passage of kidney stones.[12] But did I remember that last tidbit from introductory biology or from Montaigne,[13] who'd devoted some essays to the philosophical import of that experience? And the kidney itself—now what was that? I tended to get it mixed up with the liver. One had to do with urine, and the other . . . ? It was two in the morning; I'd ask someone at registration tomorrow. . . .

Everybody looked almost excessively wholesome and normal— bright, eager, twenty-three-year-old faces, only a few beards, almost no long hair. About a third of us came from Harvard, Princeton, or Yale, only five or six like me were older than thirty, a quarter of the class was female, about a sixth black or Hispanic. The women and minorities were relative newcomers; thirty years or so before, neither would have been seen in that amphitheater.

Since I'd half expected a bunch of gnomes[14] with inch-thick glasses, sunken chests, and calculators already in hand, the general appearance of the class was a distinct relief. There seemed none of those flippant, harsh, cynical expressions I'd gotten to know so well on the faces of doctors from my days in the hospitals. In fact, the principal spirit seemed to be freshness and enthusiasm.

That evening I was in my room, unpacking and going over how I was going to spend my money for the year. The class had been invited, en masse,[15] to a reception at Dean Nathaniel Hasting's house, a palatial affair down the street from the Longwood Cricket Club.[16] But with the rush of picnics, cocktail parties, and general festivities in our honor, I hadn't even had time to find my toothbrush or towels in the cartons that were stacked like an obstacle course around my bed. So I skipped the reception, and after arranging my belongings I was trying to draw up a budget for myself for the year.

[11]Criss-crossed.

[12]Mineral salt deposits that form in the kidneys.

[13]Sixteenth-century French philosopher who invented the essay form.

[14]A fabled, dwarflike creature who supposedly lives underground.

[15]French for "all together."

[16]A social club for playing "cricket," an English game similar to American baseball.

In contrast to most of the class, my financial situation was simple.   10
Both my parents were dead; I had no brothers or sisters, no rich relatives, and no money of my own. Whatever Harvard decided I needed,
that's what I had to live on. And this nine-by-thirteen dorm room was
home.

In the afternoon I'd visited the financial aid office, signed some   11
papers, and gotten a voucher. Harvard fixed the yearly cost of atten-
dance at twelve thousand dollars. It had awarded me a scholarship of
thirty-five hundred and was lending me the rest. Which meant I'd leave
medical school with a debt of about thirty thousand dollars. That
amount was too large to be real for me. The most I'd ever made in my
life was around a thousand a month; for long periods in the past, it'd
been more like three or four hundred. Well, I'd worry about the thirty
thousand later. Meanwhile, what did I have to live on now?

Financial aid had paid my dorm rent, then allowed me seventeen   12
hundred to live on for the year. OK, let's say five hundred a year for
books, clothes, telephone, soap, transportation and so forth. That left
me with twelve hundred for food. Or a hundred dollars a month, or
about three dollars a day, or—just a second . . .

A dollar a meal? How was I going to manage that? A salad down in the   13
dining hall cost two dollars!

Well, I was going to have to figure out some way. Maybe cook for   14
myself in my room. And movies were certainly out, so were bookstores,
trips out of town, and restaurants. Running and walking were cheap, so I
could do a lot of that. It'd just take a while getting used to. A dollar a
meal.

♦ COMPREHENSION/DISCUSSION QUESTIONS

In addition to writing something before you read, it is a good idea to
write something immediately after you read. Your instructor may want
you to prepare some or all of these questions in writing before class
discussion or may ask you to do some of the other exercises before class.
Even if you only prepare these questions for oral review, try to get into
the habit of writing briefly in your journal something about how you
reacted to the reading, questions you have, and points you think should
be discussed. These directions will not be repeated with each selection;
just follow your instructor's directions for each specific assignment.

1. What kind of person do you think the author is? What is his
   background? Which details tell you this?

2. What sort of reputation does Harvard have? Is the outside of the
   building and the downstairs what you would expect there? Why?

3. What does the quotation, "In the field of observation, chance favors only the prepared mind" [1] have to do with the rest of the selection?

4. Do you have any idea, from what he wrote, what has motivated him to go to medical school?

5. In what ways does LeBaron feel different from his fellow students? In what ways do their faces reassure him? Which details tell you this?

6. What does he mean that the amount of his future debt is not real to him?

7. Do you think he will succeed in medical school? Why or why not?

8. Did this narrative remind you of any "first day" experiences you have had? Which parts are similar to your experiences?

♦ VOCABULARY

Write a definition of the following words and one or two other forms of the same word.

amphitheater [7]	hormone [6]
amplitude [6]	newcomer [7]
anomalous [6]	palatial [9]
cynical [8]	semimenial [5]
eccentric [5]	sequestered [3]
flippant [8]	squat [3]
genteel [4]	superfluous [4]
ghetto [3]	tidbit [6]
gutted [3]	voucher [11]

Fill in the blanks with the appropriate vocabulary word. Appropriate verb or noun endings have been put in parentheses.

1. The jury will be _____ until the trial ends so that they won't be influenced by the media.

2. They gave him a _____ that indicated he had paid all his fees.

3. Universities often have a large _____ in which lectures are given.

4. Professors are sometimes considered _____ because of their absentminded ways or odd clothing.

5. The dog loves to eat little _____(s) from the table.

6. After many disappointments, a person may become _____ about the world.

7. The president of the university lives in a _____ house on the golf course.

8. The construction crew _____ the building before starting to rebuild it.

9. A long, low building could be described as _____.

10. For a straight-A student to make a F on this quiz is an _____ situation.

♦ IDIOMS

Study the meaning of these idioms. Refer back to the sentence in which they were used. Does it help you to understand them? Try writing a sentence of your own using each one.

1. "going over" [9]—reviewing, thinking about.

2. "have to live on" [10]—resources, amount of money available to spend.

♦ JOURNAL ENTRIES

Write for 20 minutes in your journal on one of the following or on anything that you thought about after reading this selection:

the students at this school

an ideal place to live

your favorite or best subject of study

♦ SMALL GROUP WORK: CIRCLE WRITING

Sit in groups of 3–4 students. One student should begin a story by writing a sentence and then pass the paper to another student, who also writes a sentence and then passes it along. Each student takes three turns. The last person should read the "story" aloud to the small group. If time permits, a spokesperson should read it aloud to the entire class.

Story topic: what might happen to a new student during the first few days here?

Maxine Hong Kingston (1940–)

Maxine Hong Kingston was born of Chinese parents in San Francisco and graduated from the University of California at Berkeley in 1962. She did graduate work before moving to Hawaii, where she has taught English in high school and at the university level. She won the National Book Critics Circle Award in 1976 for her autobiographical novel, Woman Warrior: Memoirs of a Girlhood Among Ghosts, *from which this selection is taken. Here she begins with a detailed description of a metal tube which held her mother's diplomas and a photo of her mother with her graduating class from a Chinese medical school. Kingston recounts how her mother went off to school as a grown woman and her initial experiences when she met her new classmates.*

Before reading the selection, write in your journal for 10 minutes about your own mother's education or early adulthood.

Mother

Once in a long while, four times so far for me, my mother brings out   1
the metal tube that holds her medical diploma. On the tube are gold circles crossed with seven red lines each—"joy" ideographs[1] in abstract. There are also little flowers that look like gears for a gold machine. According to the scraps of labels with Chinese and American addresses, stamps, and postmarks, the family airmailed the can from Hong Kong in 1950. It got crushed in the middle, and whoever tried to peel the labels off stopped because the red and gold paint came off too, leaving silver scratches that rust. Somebody tried to pry the end off before discovering that the tube pulls apart. When I open it, the smell of China flies out, a thousand-year-old bat flying heavy-headed out of the Chinese caverns where bats are as white as dust, a smell that comes from long ago, far back in the brain. Crates from Canton, Hong Kong, Singapore, and Taiwan have that smell too, only stronger because they are more recently come from the Chinese.

Inside the can are three scrolls, one inside another. The largest says   2
that in the twenty-third year of the National Republic, the To Keung School of Midwifery,[2] where she has had two years of instruction and Hospital Practice, awards its Diploma to my mother, who has shown

---

[1]Chinese characters; symbols, representing ideas.

[2]School training women to deliver babies.

through oral and written examination her Proficiency in Midwifery, Pediatrics, Gynecology, "Medecine," "Surgary,"[3] Therapeutics, Ophthalmology, Bacteriology, Dermatology, Nursing, and Bandage.. . .

The school seal has been pressed over a photograph of my mother at the age of thirty-seven. The diploma gives her age as twenty-seven. She looks younger than I do, her eyebrows are thicker, her lips fuller. Her naturally curly hair is parted on the left, one wavy wisp tendrilling off to the right. She wears a scholar's white gown, and she is not thinking about her appearance. She stares straight ahead as if she could see me and past me to her grandchildren and grandchildren's grandchildren. She has spacy eyes, as all people recently from Asia have. Her eyes do not focus on the camera. My mother is not smiling; Chinese do not smile for photographs. Their faces command relatives in foreign lands— "Send money"—and posterity forever—"Put food in front of this picture."[4] My mother does not understand Chinese-American snapshots. "What are you laughing at?" she asks.

The second scroll is a long narrow photograph of the graduating class with the school officials seated in front. I picked out my mother immediately. Her face is exactly her own, though forty years younger. She is so familiar, I can only tell whether or not she is pretty or happy or smart by comparing her to the other women. For this formal group picture she straightened her hair with oil to make a chin-length bob[5] like the others'. On the other women, strangers, I can recognize a curled lip, a sidelong glance, pinched shoulders. My mother is not soft; the girl with the small nose and dimpled underlip[6] is soft. My mother is not humorous, not like the girl at the end who lifts her mocking chin to pose like Girl Graduate. My mother does not have smiling eyes; the old woman teacher (Dean Woo?) in front crinkles happily, and the one faculty member in the western suit smiles westernly. Most of the graduates are girls whose faces have not yet formed; my mother's face will not change anymore, except to age. She is intelligent, alert, pretty. I can't tell if she's happy.

The graduates seem to have been looking elsewhere when they pinned the rose, zinnia, or chrysanthemum on their precise black dresses. One thin girl wears hers in the middle of her chest. A few have a flower over a left or a right nipple. My mother put hers, a chrysanthemum, below her left breast. Chinese dresses at that time were dartless, cut as if women did not have breasts; these young doctors,

3

4

5

[3]Misspellings of "medicine" and "surgery."

[4]They command their descendants: Keep our memory alive forever.

[5]A short, straight haircut for women.

[6]A natural indentation on the area below the mouth.

unaccustomed to decorations, may have seen their chests as black expanses with no reference points for flowers. Perhaps they couldn't shorten that far gaze that lasts only a few years after a Chinese emigrates. In this picture too my mother's eyes are big with what they held—reaches[7] of oceans beyond China, land beyond oceans. Most emigrants learn the barbarians' directness—how to gather themselves and stare rudely into talking faces as if trying to catch lies. In America my mother has eyes as strong as boulders, never once skittering off a face, but she has not learned to place decorations and phonograph needles, nor has she stopped seeing land on the other side of the oceans. Now her eyes include the relatives in China, as they once included my father smiling and smiling in his many western outfits, a different one for each photograph that he sent from America. . . .

The last scroll has columns of Chinese words. The only English is "Department of Health, Canton," imprinted on my mother's face, the same photograph as on the diploma. I keep looking to see whether she was afraid. Year after year my father did not come home or send for her. Their two children had been dead for ten years. If he did not return soon, there would be no more children. ("They were three and two years old, a boy and a girl. They could talk already.") My father did send money regularly, though, and she had nobody to spend it on but herself. She bought good clothes and shoes. Then she decided to use the money for becoming a doctor. She did not leave for Canton immediately after the children died. In China there was time to complete feelings. As my father had done, my mother left the village by ship. There was a sea bird painted on the ship to protect it against shipwreck and winds. She was in luck. The following ship was boarded by river pirates, who kidnapped every passenger, even old ladies. "Sixty dollars for an old lady" was what the bandits used to say. "I sailed alone," she says, "to the capital of the entire province." She took a brown leather suitcase and a seabag stuffed with two quilts.

At the dormitory the school official assigned her to a room with five other women, who were unpacking when she came in. They greeted her and she greeted them. But no one wanted to start friendships until the unpacking was done, each item placed precisely to section off the room. My mother spotted the name she had written on her application pinned to a headboard,[8] and the annoyance she felt at not arriving early enough for first choice disappeared. The locks on her suitcase opened with two satisfying clicks; she enjoyed again how neatly her belongings fitted together, clean against the green lining. She refolded the clothes before putting them in the one drawer that was hers. Then she took out her

6

7

[7]Areas that stretch out over long distances.

[8]The decorative frame at the head of the bed.

pens and inkbox, an atlas of the world, a tea set and tea cannister, sewing box, her ruler with the real gold markings, writing paper, envelopes with the thick red stripe to signify no bad news,[9] her bowl and silver chopsticks. These things she arranged one by one on her shelf. She spread the two quilts on top of the bed and put her slippers side by side underneath. She owned more—furniture, wedding jewelry, cloth, photographs—but she had left such troublesome valuables behind in the family's care. She never did get all of it back.

The women who had arrived early did not offer to help unpack, not wanting to interfere with the pleasure and the privacy of it. Not many women got to live out the daydream of women—to have a room, even a section of a room, that only gets messed up when she messes it up herself. The book would stay open at the very page she had pressed flat with her hand, and no one would complain about the field not being plowed or the leak in the roof. She would clean her own bowl and a small, limited area; she would have one drawer to sort, one bed to make.   8

To shut the door at the end of the workday, which does not spill over into evening. To throw away books after reading them so they don't have to be dusted. To go through boxes on New Year's Eve and throw out half of what is inside. Sometimes for extravagance to pick a bunch of flowers for the one table. Other women besides me must have this daydream about a carefree life. I've seen Communist pictures showing a contented woman sitting on her bunk sewing. Above her head is her one box on a shelf. The words stenciled on the box mean "Fragile," but literally say, "Use a little heart." The woman looks very pleased. The Revolution[10] put an end to prostitution by giving women what they wanted: a job and a room of their own.   9

Free from families, my mother would live for two years without servitude. She would not have to run errands for my father's tyrant mother with the bound feet[11] or thread needles for the old ladies, but neither would there be slaves and nieces to wait on her. Now she would get hot water only if she bribed the concierge.[12] When I went away to school my mother said, "Give the concierge oranges."   10

Two of my mother's roommates, who had organized their corners to their satisfaction, made tea and set a small table with their leftover travel   11

---

[9]Envelopes would have a red mark to warn whomever received the letter that it contained no bad news, as opposed to envelopes with a black mark that would warn of death.

[10]The Communist Revolution of 1949.

[11]Refers to the old Chinese custom of tightly wrapping the feet of girls so that as women they would have very small feet.

[12]French for the person in charge of security in a building. In this case also someone in charge of furnishing hot water to the residents.

food. "Have you eaten, Lady Scholar?" they invited my mother. "Lady Scholar, come drink tea," they said to each of the others. "Bring your own cup." This largess moved my mother—tea, an act of humility. She brought out meats and figs she had preserved on the farm. Everyone complimented her on their tastiness. The women told which villages they came from and the names they would go by. My mother did not let it be known that she had already had two children and that some of these girls were young enough to be her daughters.

♦ COMPREHENSION/DISCUSSION QUESTIONS

1. How do you think the author feels toward her mother?

2. Why is the mother not smiling in the photograph?

3. How is the mother different from other graduates in the photograph?

4. Who are the barbarians? [5]

5. What do we learn from this selection about the impact of immigration? If you are an immigrant, does this match your experience?

6. What does it mean that the mother "has not learned to place decorations and phonograph needles, nor has she stopped seeing land on the other side of the oceans"? [5]

7. What does the author mean when she says, "In China there was time to complete feelings." [6]

8. What do we learn about the mother's nature from paragraph 6?

9. Why do you suppose that privacy is so important to the women?

10. Can you explain what the "daydream of women" [8] is?

11. What is the point of giving the concierge oranges [10]?

12. How do the women at the school treat each other?

13. What was interesting to you about this selection?

14. Do you admire the mother? Why or why not?

15. What did you learn about China from this selection?

♦ VOCABULARY

Match the following vocabulary words with the definitions given below them.

atlas [7] pry [1]

canister [7] scroll [2]

crinkle [4] servitude [10]

humility [11] sidelong [4]

imprinted [6] skittering [5]

largess [11] spacy [3]

pinched [4] stenciled [9]

1. skipping or moving about quickly _____

2. a book of maps _____

3. absence of pride or self-assertion _____

4. toward the side, laterally _____

5. the condition of being a servant or slave _____

6. generous giving _____

7. lettered or designed using a pattern with cut-out shapes through which the ink passes to make the letters or designs _____

8. dreamy, lost in thought _____

9. squeezed between the fingers, cramped _____

10. a roll of parchment or paper with writing on it _____

11. marked by pressing or stamping _____

12. to remove or open by force _____

13. a metal container _____

14. to wrinkle or put ripples in something _____

◆ FIGURES OF SPEECH

Study the following sentences and try to explain the figures of speech.

1. "When I open it, *the smell of China flies out, a thousand-year-old bat flying heavy-headed out of the Chinese caverns where bats are as white as dust*, a smell that comes from long ago, far back in the brain." [1]

2. "Her naturally curly hair is parted on the left, one wavy wisp *tendrilling* off to the right." [3]

3. "Chinese dresses at that time were dartless, cut as if women did not have breasts; these young doctors, unaccustomed to decorations, may have seen their chest as *black expanses with no reference points for flowers.*" [5]

4. "To shut the door at the end of the workday, which *does not spill over into evening.* [9]

5. "The words stenciled on the box mean 'Fragile,' but literally say, 'Use a little heart.'" [9]

♦ JOURNAL ENTRIES

Write in your journal for 20 minutes on one of the following, or write on anything you thought about after reading the Kingston selection.

feelings about my family

a memory from childhood

leaving home

♦ SMALL GROUP WORK: SIMPLE CONSENSUS

Divide into groups of 3–4 students and choose a recorder. List aloud small cultural differences (such as the attitude toward smiling for photographs mentioned in the Kingston selection or the way people greet each other) that exist between your home culture and the one where you are now. The group is to listen while each member lists his or her ideas; no one should criticize or debate the points (5 minutes). The group should then discuss and come to an agreement on the most unusual idea (or least known, most serious, most interesting) to be presented to the whole class (10 minutes). After the class has listened to each recorder, it should discuss and agree upon one of the cultural differences to use for further brainstorming. In the final stage, the class should brainstorm aloud, with one of the recorders writing on the board or on large sheets of paper ways to make other people aware of and tolerant of this difference (10 minutes).

Follow-up Writing Write a brief description of the cultural difference discussed and the results of the class brainstorming. As with all short writing assignments, keep this as part of an "idea" file for future writing assignments.

Maya Angelou *(1928–)*

Maya Angelou is a poet, playwright, professional stage and screen performer, musical composer, and author of two autobiographical works, I Know Why the Caged Bird Sings *(1970), from which the following selection is taken, and* Gather Together in My Name *(1974). In the passage below, Angelou describes an important figure in her development as a lover of literature. Mrs. Flowers was the first person to get Marguerite to talk after she went into a self-imposed silence after being raped by her mother's boyfriend.*

Before reading, write for 10 minutes in your journal about a visit you took as a child to the house of an adult you didn't know well.

Mrs. Flowers

Mrs. Bertha Flowers was the aristocrat of Black Stamps.[1] She had the grace of control to appear warm in the coldest weather, and on the Arkansas summer days it seemed she had a private breeze which swirled around, cooling her. She was thin without the taut look of wiry people, and her printed voile[2] dresses and flowered hats were as right for her as denim overalls for a farmer. She was our side's answer to the richest white woman in town.   1

Her skin was a rich black that would have peeled like a plum if snagged, but then no one would have thought of getting close enough to Mrs. Flowers to ruffle her dress, let alone snag her skin. She didn't encourage familiarity. She wore gloves too.   2

I don't think I ever saw Mrs. Flowers laugh, but she smiled often. A slow widening of her thin black lips to show even, small white teeth, then the slow effortless closing. When she chose to smile on me, I always wanted to thank her. The action was so graceful and inclusively benign.   3

She was one of the few gentlewomen I have ever known, and has remained throughout my life the measure of what a human being can be. . . .   4

One summer afternoon, sweet-milk fresh in my memory, she stopped   5

---

[1]Stamps is a small town in Arkansas, in the South. At the time of this story (the 1930s and early 1940s), residential areas were still strictly segregated between black and white people.

[2]A very light fabric.

at the Store to buy provisions. Another Negro woman of her health and age would have been expected to carry the paper sacks home in one hand, but Momma said, "Sister Flowers,[3] I'll send Bailey[4] up to your house with these things."

She smiled that slow dragging smile, "Thank you, Mrs. Henderson. I'd   6 prefer Marguerite, though." My name was beautiful when she said it. "I've been meaning to talk to her, anyway." They gave each other age-group looks."[5] . . .

There was a little path beside the rocky road, and Mrs. Flowers   7 walked in front swinging her arms and picking her way over the stones.

She said, without turning her head, to me, "I hear you're doing very   8 good school work, Marguerite, but that it's all written. The teachers report that they have trouble getting you to talk in class." We passed the triangular farm on our left and the path widened to allow us to walk together. I hung back in the separate unasked and unanswerable questions.

"Come and walk along with me, Marguerite." I couldn't have refused   9 even if I wanted to. She pronounced my name so nicely. Or more correctly, she spoke each word with such clarity that I was certain a foreigner who didn't understand English could have understood her.

"Now no one is going to make you talk—possibly no one can. But   10 bear in mind, language is man's way of communicating with his fellow man and it is language alone which separates him from the lower animals." That was a totally new idea to me, and I would need time to think about it.

"Your grandmother says you read a lot. Every chance you get. That's   11 good, but not good enough. Words mean more than what is set down on paper. It takes the human voice to infuse them with the shades of deeper meaning."

I memorized the part about the human voice infusing words. It   12 seemed so valid and poetic.

She said she was going to give me some books and that I not only   13 must read them, I must read them aloud. She suggested that I try to make a sentence sound in as many different ways as possible.

"I'll accept no excuse if you return a book to me that has been badly   14 handled." My imagination boggled at the punishment I would deserve if in fact I did abuse a book of Mrs. Flowers'. Death would be too kind and brief.

---

[3]"Sister" is a term of respect which does not indicate a blood relationship.

[4]Her grandson.

[5]As women of similar age, they exchange a look that communicates what they are thinking about Marguerite.

The odors in the house surprised me. Somehow I had never con-   15
nected Mrs. Flowers with food or eating or any other common experience of common people. There must have been an outhouse,[6] too, but
my mind never recorded it.

The sweet scent of vanilla had met us as she opened the door.   16

"I made tea cookies this morning. You see, I had planned to invite   17
you for cookies and lemonade so we could have this little chat. The
lemonade is in the icebox."

It followed that Mrs. Flowers would have ice on an ordinary day,   18
when most families in our town bought ice late on Saturdays only a few
times during the summer to be used in the wooden ice-cream freezers.

She took the bags from me and disappeared through the kitchen door.   19
I looked around the room that I had never in my wildest fantasies
imagined I would see. Browned photographs leered or threatened from
the walls and the white, freshly done curtains pushed against themselves
and against the wind. I wanted to gobble up the room entire and take it
to Bailey, who would help me analyze and enjoy it.

"Have a seat, Marguerite. Over there by the table." She carried a   20
platter covered with a tea towel.[7] Although she warned that she hadn't
tried her hand at baking sweets for some time, I was certain that like
everything else about her the cookies would be perfect.

They were flat round wafers, slightly browned on the edges and   21
butter-yellow in the center. With the cold lemonade they were sufficient
for childhood's lifelong diet. Remembering my manners, I took nice
little lady-like bites off the edges. She said she had made them expressly
for me and that she had a few in the kitchen that I could take home to
my brother. So I jammed one whole cake in my mouth and the rough
crumbs scratched the insides of my jaws, and if I hadn't had to swallow,
it would have been a dream come true.

As I ate she began the first of what we later called "my lessons in   22
living." She said that I must always be intolerant of ignorance but
understanding of illiteracy. That some people, unable to go to school,
were more educated and even more intelligent than college professors.
She encouraged me to listen, carefully to what country people called
mother wit.[8] That in those homely sayings was couched the collective
wisdom of generations.

When I finished the cookies she brushed off the table and brought a   23
thick, small book from the bookcase. I had read *A Tale of Two Cities*[9]

---

[6]Outdoor toilet.

[7]Cloth used to dry dishes.

[8]Native intelligence, common sense.

[9]A novel written by Charles Dickens.

and found it up to my standards as a romantic novel. She opened the first page and I heard poetry for the first time in my life.

"It was the best of times and the worst of times . . ." Her voice slid in and curved down through and over the words. She was nearly singing. I wanted to look at the pages. Were they the same that I had read? Or were there notes, music, lined on the pages, as in a hymn book? Her sounds began cascading gently. I knew from listening to a thousand preachers that she was nearing the end of her reading, and I hadn't really heard, heard to understand, a single word. 24

"How do you like that?" 25

It occurred to me that she expected a response. The sweet vanilla flavor was still on my tongue and her reading was a wonder in my ears. I had to speak. 26

I said, "Yes, ma'am." It was the least I could do, but it was the most also. 27

"There's one more thing. Take this book of poems and memorize one for me. Next time you pay me a visit, I want you to recite." 28

I have tried often to search behind the sophistication of years for the enchantment I so easily found in those gifts. The essence escapes but its aura remains. To be allowed, no, invited, into the private lives of strangers, and to share their joys and fears, was a chance to exchange the Southern bitter wormwood[10] for a cup of mead with Beowulf or a hot cup of tea and milk with Oliver Twist[11] When I said aloud, "It is a far, far better thing that I do, than I have ever done . . ."[12] tears of love filled my eyes at my selflessness. 29

On that first day, I ran down the hill and into the road (few cars ever came along it) and had the good sense to stop running before I reached the Store. 30

I was liked, and what a difference it made. I was respected not as Mrs. Henderson's grandchild or Bailey's sister but for just being Marguerite Johnson. 31

◆ COMPREHENSION/DISCUSSION QUESTIONS

1. How would you describe Marguerite's attitude toward Mrs. Flowers?

---

[10]A plant used to make a bitter medicine.

[11]She exchanges her bitterness (see above) for an escape into literature. She figuratively drinks a cup of mead, a type of beer, with the hero of an early English heroic epic and tea with the young hero of Dickens' novel, *Oliver Twist*.

[12]Spoken by Sydney Carton, in *Tale of Two Cities*, at the end as he offers his own life to save another man.

2. What does her wearing gloves tell us about Mrs. Flowers' personality?

3. What does paragraph 5 tell the reader about Momma's attitude toward Mrs. Flowers?

4. What method does Mrs. Flowers use to get Marguerite to talk?

5. Do you think Mrs. Flowers is right about the value of reading aloud? What is reading aloud compared to?

6. Explain Mrs. Flowers' statement that Marguerite should "be intolerant of ignorance but understanding of illiteracy" [22].

7. What is the meaning of paragraph 27?

8. What did you think of Mrs. Flowers?

9. Is there any special adult outside your family who was like a Mrs. Flowers to you when you were young?

10. Did this reading teach you anything about black culture in the United States during the early 1940s?

◆ VOCABULARY

Match the following words with their definitions listed below.

aura [29]	leer [19]
benign [3]	sophistication [29]
boggle [14]	snag [2]
couched [22]	swirl [1]
denim [1]	taut [1]
gobble [19]	vanilla [16]
inclusively [3]	wafer [21]
infuse [11]	

1. to move in a spiral, or a circular manner _____

2. to include everything _____

3. tight, smoothly stretched _____

4. a flat, round cookie or cracker _____

5. an invisible atmosphere surrounding something _____

6. coarse cotton cloth _____

7. flavoring used in desserts _____

8. eat quickly, swallow food almost whole _____

9. overwhelm, confuse _____

10. being worldly or other than natural _____

11. not harmful _____

12. to pour into, to impart _____

13. expressed, put into words _____

14. to hook or tear _____

15. to look at with scorn or with sexual implications _____

♦ IDIOMS

Study the following idioms. Does their context help you to understand their meaning? Write a sentence using each one.

1. "Bear in mind" [10]—remember.

2. "Freshly done" [19]—recently washed.

3. "Mother wit" [22]—natural intelligence, cleverness.

4. "Pay a visit" [28]—visit, call on someone.

♦ FIGURES OF SPEECH

Try to explain the meaning of the following comparisons and figures of speech.

1. ". . . It seemed she had *a private breeze which swirled around, cooling her.*" [1]

2. ". . . *Her printed voile dresses and flowered hats were as right for her as denim overalls for a farmer.*" [1]

3. "Her skin was a rich black that would have *peeled like a plum* if snagged. . . ." [2]

4. "One summer afternoon, *sweet-milk fresh* in my memory. . . ." [5].

5. "She smiled that *slow dragging smile* . . ." [6]

6. "*I hung back in the separate unasked and unanswerable questions.*" [8]

7. "Browned photographs *leered or threatened* from the walls. . . ." [19]

8. "Her voice *slid in and curved down through and over the words.* . . . Her sounds began *cascading gently.*" [24]

♦ JOURNAL ENTRIES

Write for 20 minutes on one of the following topics:

an important learning experience from your childhood

the kindest person you have met

a special book you read as a child

an experience that made you feel important

♦ SMALL GROUP WORK

Divide into groups of 3-4 students. The instructor may give each group a different question about the reading to discuss, or you as small groups can decide on your own questions. Two examples might be: what is the secret of Mrs. Flowers' success with Marguerite? Why do you think she is more successful than Marguerite's Momma could be with her?

Discuss answers to the question and have the recorder write down some answers that everyone in the group can agree on (10 minutes). Choose another student to be the spokesperson for the group. Each spokesperson will present the question and answers to the entire class. Allow a few minutes for discussion by the whole class of each question. 15 minutes).

Follow-up Writing Write for 5 minutes on whichever question and answers seemed the most interesting to you, no matter which group it came from originally. Keep this for your idea file.

WRITING FROM EXPERIENCE

As each of the writers in Chapter 1 mentioned, writing is a process that requires you to open your mind and to be willing to explore feelings and ideas. Once you open up and let the words start flowing by doing a prewriting activity of some kind, you are ready for the rest of the process that includes composing and reworking a longer piece until it is ready for your public to see. This process, from the point of generating ideas to the polishing of the final draft, includes several steps that are done both sequentially and recursively. In other words, there is a sequence, as in any process, but the writer also repeats cycles of revisions and often works on several procedures simultaneously. It is not a mechanical process of following steps 1, 2, 3, with perfection guaranteed at step 3. But it is also not a great mystery accomplished only by the ''gifted.'' We, as readers, just don't see how a writer has achieved a polished text. We don't see all the early drafts, the scratched-out paragraphs, the paper thrown away when something wasn't going well. The purpose of this book is to help you see the process by looking at examples from other student writers and by practicing it yourself.

Most of the writing you did for Chapter 1 was for yourself, to reflect on what you were experiencing and to describe yourself and your attitudes toward writing. The last assignment asked you to take one of the prewritings, write a few paragraphs, and then rewrite until you felt that your writing was as good as you could make it. In this chapter, the goal is to begin explaining what it means to *rewrite* a composition. Later chapters will add more instruction on the revision process. Before we go further, here are some important definitions of terms used throughout this text:

draft—a written version

discovery draft—a draft written to think through what the writer wants to say

multiple drafting—the process of writing many drafts to achieve a good final draft

peer review—students reading each others' papers to assist each other in revision

revision—rewriting to improve major points: development, organization, and clarity

editing—rewriting to correct grammar, usage, word choice, spelling, punctuation, etc.

proofreading—a final reading of a draft to check for mistakes

Drafting: From Prewriting to Composing

At times writing assignments are made and finished work is required so quickly that you don't have time to revise. An in-class essay exam or a quick letter to meet a deadline are examples. Most writing situations, however, allow you time to think and revise before the piece is due to be turned in. Most of the work in this text is designed to show you how to use the process of multiple drafting, revising, and editing to achieve a very good finished piece.

To move from prewriting to composing a draft is not difficult. You may even find that for some assignments, when you have ideas, it is just as easy to start by writing several paragraphs or pages. This type of prewriting is called a discovery draft—a lengthy piece of writing that allows you to explore what you want to say without worrying about anything other than expressing what is on your mind. Whether you want to base your draft on a prewriting exercise or begin directly with a discovery draft, here are some suggestions for getting started with composing:

◊ Find out from the instructor what length assignment you should have in mind—is it a paragraph, several paragraphs, or several pages?

◊ Assemble the paper and pens (or pencils) you want to use. It's more fun to use materials you like, special pens and your favorite type of paper. Most instructors will let you be creative in a draft, although they probably will have guidelines for the final draft.

◊ If you are writing outside class, set aside time and find a location that will be good for concentration. Some writers work well in silence; others can concentrate in the midst of total chaos. Experiment with different locations to find out what suits you best.

◊ Look at your prewriting or discovery draft and think about what you want to communicate to your reader.

◊ Start writing quickly. Do not allow yourself to waste time worrying about the first sentence or first paragraph. Since there will be many occasions to rewrite that first part, don't let it become a stumbling block. Try to write the full target length at one sitting.

◊ As you write the draft, concentrate on what you want to say or describe, not on how well you are saying it.

◊ If either a typewriter or a word processor is available to you, try getting used to composing at the keyboard. If you write a rough draft on the machine, it will be much easier to "see" what the text looks like, and you will also find it easier to make revisions. Even if you don't type, you should get someone to type early drafts for you as often as possible because you will get a much better sense of what your paragraphs look like.

Sample Student Writing

Here is an example of a short composition that began as a journal entry (all examples of student writing are uncorrected).

Journal Entry

Well, this time I want to write about a Malibu surf trip. It was 4:30 in the morning when I woke up, everybody was sleeping in my home, so I took my surfboard and went out of my home. All the place was so quiet. I went downstairs and opened the main door. It was cold outside, it was a full moon, and a lot of stars.

I put my surfboard on the racks on the top of the car and started it. I saw no cars in the streets, it was so early.

I picked up a friend of mine and we started the trip. By 5:15 we were at the bridge, the America's Bridge, that connects South America and North America. It was sunrise when we stop to eat something in a little town on the side of the road.

At 6:30 we were about to Malibu beach, it was a muddy road in the middle of the jungle. We were listening some music, when suddenly we were there, Malibu beach. There were four to five foot waves a perfect ride, with incredible tubes. It was like a Mag trip.

Alberto Grajales

Draft 1

It was 4:30 in the morning, when I woke up, my room was so dark. The tic-tac of my alarm clock was the only sound that I could hear in the still night. Everybody was asleep in my home.

I opened the door of my room carefully, because my brother was moving in his bed and I didn't want to wake him up, it was too early.

Then I went to the bathroom, I brushed my teeth and washed my face, the water was very cold.

At approximately 4:45, I took my stuffs and left my house. The garden was so quiet, it was cold and very silent outside. I could see the full moon and a lot of stars in the cloudless sky.

I put the surfboard over the racks on the top of the car and started it. There were no cars in the streets, it was early.

I picked up a friend of mine and we began the trip to the beach. By 5:15 we were at the "America's Bridge," that connects South America and North America. It was sunrise, when we stoped to eat something in a little restaurant on the side of the road.

At 6:30 we were driving to Malibu beach again. It was a muddy road in the middle of a jungle. On both sides of the road there were flocks of cows grazing. The curves in the road made an uncomfortable trip, but we were listening to some good music wich comforted us and in no time at all we were at Malibu beach. There were four to five foot waves, a perfect ride. It was like a magazine trip.

♦ DISCUSSION QUESTIONS

1. What is the difference between the journal entry and the "composition?"

2. Would you like to know more about this trip?

3. What would you tell the writer to add as he continues to work on this piece?

Here is another example that started with a brainstorming.

pretty, looks young, work, perfume,* little, study, purse, shoes, skirts. Warm, white, lipstick, makeup, beautiful,* dark black hair. Stuff. paperworks, headache,* medicine, vitamin pills.

MY MOTHER

I was so sad to leave home. Because I might not see my mother for a long time. My mother is very pretty. She is very little. She works part time. When I was in 4th grade she made me study so hard. She wanted me to enter the private good junior high school. After 2 years I made it. Then she stop saying study hard or anything. Actually I got bad grades while I was in junior high. Because I didn't study hard. But I tried to study hard and hard while I was in high school. I got very good grades. I found out that studying is for me not for anybody else. You have to study for yourself. I study for my-self and for my mother. I want to make her feel happy and let her know that her child is not stupid.

I like my mother. I miss her a lot. She puts perfumes. They smell so good. I like her putting her makeup on.

Well, she has some problems. She often has bad headaches. That's very bad. She has head-ache once or twice a month. Sometimes, she can't get up. She feels sick. She can't do anything because of the bad headache. I hope she gets well.

Sachiko Taketani

Prewriting

Look back at one of your journal entries or the notes from the small group work to get some ideas. It may also be good to do a fresh prewriting on a topic from the readings. Choose either a brainstorming or freewriting exercise.

Brainstorming Choose one from among the following or develop your own starting point:

> where you live compared to LeBaron's room
>
> the first person you met on campus
>
> a favorite family member
>
> the most influential person in your childhood
>
> a great teacher

Freewriting Write for 10 minutes nonstop on:

> your first day at a new school
>
> what you think it would be like to live with as few possessions as Kingston's mother
>
> going off on your own for the first time

After you have completed the prewriting, look over it for a few minutes and then write a draft of 2–3 pages based on the ideas you got during the prewriting. Put it away for a while (even an hour or two will help), and then reread it. Make a few notes in the margins to yourself about what you would like to change, or go ahead and make the changes. Then retype, reprint, or recopy it, to make it clear enough for someone else to read.

Hold this piece of writing until you read the next section. To prepare for peer review, make a list of questions you would like your partner to answer about your draft.

Peer Reviewing: Questions from Your Readers

How do you know what to revise? How can you go further than you did on your own? If you are an especially good reader of your own work, you might be able to see many places where revision is necessary. But, generally, how do you find out whether something you make is good? You ask someone else what he or she thinks. A cook does well to ask a "taster" to test the sauce before it is brought to the table for the guests. Likewise, a writer needs to test ideas and expression with a reader before the writing is considered finished. Thus, throughout this text, you will find references to having other students, your peers, as well as your instructor read your work *during* the process of writing it, not just after you think it is completed.

Peer reviewing is the process of reading and commenting on another student's composition during the drafting process. The reviewer plays the role of an intelligent reader who reacts and comments upon the writing as a friend might do, not as an instructor does who "corrects" a student's work. Peer reviewing is a process that can be done orally or in writing, depending upon the preferences of your instructor.

The use of peer reviewing does not mean you must be constantly dependent on someone else's opinion of your work before you do revisions. You can and should train yourself to be analytical about your own work. But sometimes it is easier to help other people and to receive their advice than it is to "re-see" your own writing. Using the feedback of your peers and your instructor is not meant to replace you as a reader of your own work. There will still be many times when you must become your own reader, so you need to learn what sorts of questions you should be asking about your own work.

Each time you do a peer review in this text, you will be asked to respond to specific questions that vary with the kind of paper you are writing. You will find them on the peer review sheets in Appendix A at the end of this book. These questions are just a guideline; your instructor may want to suggest other questions, and you may have your own. For an assignment to write a description, the peer reviewer might be asked to comment on the use of detail, which is of major importance in this type of writing.

When choosing someone to exchange papers with, choose someone other than your best friend (who might not be objective), and choose someone who does not share your native language, if at all possible. A basic rule is: Always start your response with a positive comment, such as "I really liked your first paragraph because . . ." or "I thought the description of your house was terrific because. . . ." Everyone is sensitive, and nothing is accomplished by offending the writer. As a peer reviewer, you are supposed to offer helpful reactions, not harsh criticism. Therefore it is important to respond only to the questions the instructor or the writer poses—don't give the writer a list of what's wrong.

Here is how a brief oral peer review should work.

1. Choose a partner and exchange papers.

2. Read them silently.

3. Then discuss the answers to whatever questions your instructor or the writer may suggest. Two good ones at this point would be:

   What is most interesting?

   Where would you like more detail?

4. Remember to begin with a positive comment.

5. Do not correct anything for the writer.

If the peer review is to be done in writing, use peer review sheet 1 (see appendix A).

Now exchange the piece of writing you did above, and do either an oral or a written peer review.

Revision: Rewriting for Your Reader

The words revision, editing, and proofreading describe different parts of the writing process. Look back at the definitions of these terms given earlier in this chapter, and note that *Revision* refers to major rewriting. On your own or with the help of a peer reader, you must be able to look at your writing and see what major changes need to be made. Perhaps you will need to rethink and reword your main points or to take a completely different approach to your topic, depending upon what your reader has said about your rough draft. You must decide whether you need more supporting detail or less in some places and whether the overall organization is effective. You will practice revision with every assignment in this text, but as you begin, keep in mind that when you are asked to revise, it does not mean just correcting some of the grammar and spelling.

Here are three important elements to consider as you move from the earliest draft to the next one. As you become more skilled, you will think about these elements even before you write a rough draft. If your primary goal was to concentrate on writing "about" something at first, then you should now turn your attention to *purpose*, *audience*, and *development* and keep them in mind as you revise.

Purpose   As Donald Murray said, people write for many reasons—to inform, to entertain, or to persuade, among others. The selections in this chapter were all autobiographical, real experiences of the authors which were probably fictionalized* to some degree. One purpose of personal writing, which comes either from experience or from the writer's imagination, is to help the writer reach self-expression. But writers write for an audience too, and another purpose of personal writing done for an audience is to entertain and inform. To inform does not mean giving the reader a report as much as it means sharing an experience or feeling that might become as meaningful to the reader as it was to the writer. To entertain means to keep the readers' attention and appeal to their imagination.

When you choose a topic or when your instructor suggests one, the assignment may imply the purpose. If, for instance, you are asked to write about your first experiences at school or an important person in your life, the assignment implies autobiographical writing, like the readings in this chapter. Other topics or writing situations may lead to different purposes.

Many times, when you start your revisions, you will realize that your writing wanders from one point to another without much focus. You may not have identified clearly, for yourself or for your reader, what the purpose is. Therefore, as you begin revision, ask yourself:

> Why am I writing this?
>
> What do I expect my audience to get from this?
>
> Is each paragraph consistent with that purpose?

Be willing to delete something, even a whole paragraph, if, on the second reading, you realize it doesn't fit your purpose. It may be something interesting by itself, but if it doesn't fit the purpose, then it will distract or confuse your reader.

---

*Written through the imagination, fiction being that which is not factual.

Audience   We all know from experience that sometimes we can't read something because it is just too difficult, too boring, too outrageous, or too silly. In each case the writers have missed us as an audience. Maybe they didn't want us to be their audience, but if they did, something went wrong. If a computer expert, for instance, intends to write a textbook for undergraduates, the expert must use a vocabulary and examples that are appropriate for the student who will be a beginner, not a vocabulary appropriate for other experts. Writers can make many choices to adjust their words, examples, and even subject matter to reach different audiences. As a student writer, you need to think about who your audience is. If you think about it, you know this is true; it is unlikely that you would want to share your personal letters to a friend with your instructor or with students you don't know. Either the vocabulary, the subject, or the grammar might not be for the "public." Likewise, in doing writing for a class, you need to think about different aspects of your audience (your peers and your instructor). Among the characteristics you should consider are their ages and their educational background.

◆ EXERCISE: WRITING FOR AN AUDIENCE

Get together with two other students in the class and list characteristics of the people in the class that should be considered in writing something for them. Keep in mind cultural and religious differences. Each small group should report aloud to the whole class what characteristics they have identified. Then the whole can discuss how being aware of those characteristics will modify or change certain aspects of each student's writing.

Development   Development means building a simple statement or idea into a more complete and understandable text for your audience. You may often find yourself writing very little and then thinking there is nothing left to say. Working on development, however, should help you find much more to say and to communicate to your audience. The primary strategies for developing personal writing are description and narration, or storytelling. As is true of most good writing, description and narration depend upon the use of detail, examples, and illustrations. The differences between these words are not great. Perhaps details are smaller units of meaning than examples, and illustrations slightly larger or longer than examples. Illustrations can be short narratives, or stories within stories. Descriptions and narrations both contain mixtures of details, examples, and illustrations, but one paragraph may depend more on one kind of development than on another.

Good development means having enough of these elements to make your writing interesting and clear while avoiding too many details where they are not necessary. In other words, you should avoid being either too general and too brief, on the one hand, or being too repetitous and too long-winded, on the other. Naturally, there are no easy rules to guide you here, just your own critical abilities and the critical abilities of the readers who will help during the drafting process.

◆ DEVELOPMENT EXERCISE

To understand better the use of details, examples, and illustrations, look at the following paragraphs from the readings in this chapter and see if they give you a sense of some of the different patterns of development.

Detail	LeBaron, paragraphs 1, 2, 7
	Kingston, paragraphs 1, 2, 3, 4
	Angelou, paragraphs 1, 2, 21
Example	LeBaron, paragraphs 5, 6
	Kingston, paragraphs 5, 10
	Angelou, paragraphs 10, 29
Illustration	LeBaron, paragraphs 10–11
	Kingston, paragraph 11
	Angelou, paragraphs 5–6, 23–24

Sample Student Writing

Now compare Alberto Grajales' first draft (p. 52) to his second one, which he revised after a peer reviewer told him what he thought was interesting and where more detail was needed (Peer Review 1, p. 60).

Would you have given the same advice as the peer reviewer did (check your own response to the earlier question 3)?

Draft 2

It was 4:30 on a Saturday morning when I woke up. My room was very dark. The tic-tock of my alarm clock was the only sound that I could hear in the still night. Everybody was asleep in my home.

My brother was moving in his bed and I didn't want to wake him up. It was too early and he needed resting because he works hard in my father's store every day including Saturdays and Sundays. So I carefully opened the door of my

Peer Review 1
Personal Writing

Writer: *alberto grajales*
Peer Reviewer: *Ivan Fernandez*

1. What is most interesting?

> I like the first lines — good scene with detail. I liked trying to imagine where they were since I not been there Makes me want to go surfing.

2. Where would you like to have more detail?

> More details about his family or house Maybe he could explain more about the trip and what he did. He didn't say much about his friend.

room, and went to the bathroom where I brushed my teeth and washed my face. By the way, I remember that the water was very cold because the water heater wouldn't work until 6 o'clock, one hour after my mother wakes up to make breakfast.

At approximately 4:45 I left my house and took the back that has all the things that I need for the trip. It was cold and very silent outside. The garden was very quiet and there was no wind. I could see the full moon and alot of stars in the cloudless sky. I put the surfboard over the racks on the top of the car and started it. There were no cars on the streets for which reason I could go fastest and got to my friend's house earlier. I had to honk only two times before he came out. As fast as we could we put his surfboard over the racks and we started the trip to the beach. By 5:15 we were at the "America's Bridge" wich connects South America and North America at Panama. It was a typical tropical sunrise, full of colors, those that reflected on the water created a beautiful picture to the human eye. Then we stopped to eat something in a little restaurant on the side of the road.

At 6:30 we were driving to Malibu Beach again. It was a muddy road, the smell of the wet grass made a sensation of freshness in that humid jungle. On both sides of the road there were herds of cows grazing freely on the fields.

The curves in the road made an uncomfortable trip, but we were listening to some good music which comforted us and in no time at all we were at Mailbu Beach; a beautiful beach with white sands and crystal waters. The sun's heat was strong and the waves were four to five feet. That made for an unforgettable trip.

♦ REVISION EXERCISE

Now take the piece your peer reviewer read and try some revisions that respond to what the reviewer said. Pay particular attention to the following:

> Delete anything that doesn't fit your purpose or that seems repetitious.

> Expand with more details or examples according to what the reviewer said and your own judgment about whether you have enough detail.

> Consider who your audience is. Is their general knowledge sufficient for them to understand what you have written? Consider the other questions the class discussed about audience.

This is a good point at which to do another peer review session (use peer review sheet 2) and/or to turn this piece in to the instructor for his or her comments. Once you have seen the peer reviewer's comments or have had a conference with the instructor, you are ready to do more revision and then begin your editing.

Editing: Correcting Your Draft

When you complete your revisions, you can concentrate on editing. This includes checking for and correcting:

> grammar—sentence structure, verb forms and tenses, agreement of subjects, verbs, pronoun reference, etc.

usage—word choice, apostrophe use, capitalization

punctuation

spelling

At first, it may be difficult to edit your own writing, but with practice and the help of your instructor, peers, and tutors in the writing center (if you have a tutor available to you), you will become a good editor. You can help yourself edit by reading your draft aloud. Often that will help you to catch errors, especially in agreement, if you make an effort to pronounce the endings of words. When you are editing, you need to read your work slowly and concentrate on each word and each sentence. If your instructor or the tutors in the writing center can help you to identify patterns in the errors you make,* you can then concentrate on watching for those errors in particular. Naturally, you cannot correct everything, and you should not let yourself become frustrated by that fact. Editing your writing takes time and dedication to overcoming your particular patterns of error.

Sample Student Writing

One way to learn editing is to practice on someone else's work. Here is a short draft that has some errors in it. Go over it as a class and try to find places that need to be corrected. What particular ''patterns of error'' does this student have?

Hawaii is one of the most alive and fascinating place I have been. I arrived there by accident in an early morning when the sun begins to take over the night. I came to Hawaii for a change of flight from Malaysia to North America. The plane which I was suppose to take was broke down before I got there. The pilot told us that they have an electrical problem in the left turbine of the plane. And he also told us that it won't be ready for a week or two. I thought to myself that this is a chance of a life time to see the dream city.

The pilot had an assistant took us to a huge hotel located about six miles away from the airport. They said they were very please to help us if we have any problems. I got to my room and worried so much about the bill for room and food. I

---

*Write a list of your errors by categories, i.e., verb forms, agreement, apostrophe use, etc.

didn't have that much money with me and also didn't have American Express. I asked the assistant how do I go about paying for the bill and he told me that the flight company will take care of all that. "This is great!" I thought to myself.

I woke up very early in the morning after the longest sleep of my life. I'm now ready to enjoy the wonderful city that I've been waiting for. My hunger about seeing the city made me wake all my friends up to get ready. We took a walk down the street away from the hotel. It was too early in the morning so we hardly saw anybody, but it was beautiful to us. The street runs along the bay. There are quite a few coconut trees on the beach and modern buildings along the other side. After a while, the city began to wake up with all the noise of cars, people, ships, and horns. All the noise jammed into one little space. The atmosphere was totally different from a few hours ago.

In the afternoon, went to the beach to catch a little sun and waves. There were many people on the beach and quite a few activities. I saw people surfing, swimming, playing volley-ball, and lying in the sun. The lifestyle is totally different around there compare to other places. People seemed to enjoy life very much and don't worried about other things. It was very hot in the sunshine, but there were few spots were very cool which were the mountain's shadows. Most of the tourist were hide under those spots, because they could not stand the hot weather.

At night, the city stand out against the dark of night. It was very cool; I could feel the breeze in the air and into my face. While walking down the street, I could hear the trees rustling from the cool wind. The wind was so cool that make my body chilled through to my soul.

We had such a good time which made the time rolled quickly. We were then on the fourth day on that island and the bad news came. The assistant came back and told us that our plane had fixed. We were leaving on the fifth day instead of one or two weeks. We left the city before we wanted to, but it is still there for another time.

Thuong Nguyen

When you are ready to edit the piece you have been working on, concentrate on the types of errors you know you are likely to make from your instructor's or tutor's comments. In the early stages of learning to edit, it will help to pay particular attention to a few potential problems at a time, rather than worrying about everything at once. For now, read the draft that you revised and look especially for the following:

> subject/verb agreement

> verb forms (correct past participles, etc.)

> verb tenses

Make whatever corrections you think are necessary. This is the time to consult a tutor, consult your instructor, or use a reference tool such as an English handbook to make certain you are making appropriate corrections.

Proofreading: Catching the Mistakes

Before you turn in a final draft for grading, you must reread for mistakes you have made in copying or retyping. You may also catch errors that have been left in from one draft to another, but certainly you want to avoid leaving in mistakes that are the result of simple carelessness.

You might try one of the following strategies to help in your proofreading;

◇ Read your writing aloud.

◇ Read it word for word very slowly.

◇ Read it backwards.

◇ Have a peer read it.

Check especially for spelling and punctuation errors. Once you have done a careful proofreading, you should be ready to turn in your writing for evaluation.

◆ WRITING ASSIGNMENTS

1. Complete the draft you have been working on throughout this chapter and turn it in for evaluation, or

2. Start a new draft, based on a prewriting related to one of the readings. Whatever the topic, try to make your writing describe something or someone, or narrate some event that you have experienced yourself. Take the prewriting and write a first draft

that will be read by a peer reviewer. At this point you could take it to the writing center, if one is available and if it is a center where tutors are allowed to assist with work in progress. Revise on the basis of the peer reviewer's comments and/or tutor's comments. Turn it in or take it to a conference with your instructor. After hearing or reading the instructor's comments, revise again and edit. You may want to make a second appointment in the writing center, do another peer review in class, or ask for another reading by the instructor. Before you turn in the final draft for evaluation, do a final proofreading with the help of a partner in class.

Guidelines for Submitting Final Papers

Some instructors will have very specific guidelines about what the final draft should look like when it is submitted. Requirements such as writing in ink, typewriting, keeping certain margins, using lined or unlined paper, and using a specific heading are not meant to make life difficult or expensive for students. They are good practice for other classes or for jobs, where the appearance of the final product is important. So find out what your instructor would like and enjoy performing like a professional.

Be certain to keep all drafts and peer review sheets for each assignment. Then you can hand them all in with the final draft for an evaluation of the whole process. Even if your instructor looks only at the final draft at this stage, you can take pride in the progress you made from prewriting to the final draft.

Sample Student Essay for Writing from Experience

The following is an example of the whole process described in this chapter. It is a student paper that you can follow from prewriting through the third draft. Read the drafts and answer the questions.

Brainstorming

Assignment: brainstorm for 5 minutes on where you live.

different colors	no lobby at all in my dorm
same small room*	some furniture
hard bed too	more light*
different architecture*	

Demosthenes ''Tim'' Paschalidis

From Prewriting to Composing

The assignment was: Put an asterisk next to three words from the brainstorming that are interesting or surprising to you. Write several paragraphs about those words, the connections between them, or why they are important.

One of the thinks that I like is architecture. Once I saw a   1
building and I was really surprised of his different style of
structure. And when I see another building one of the best
thinks I see is how it is structured. That happened with my
university. I believe that one of the reasons that I came to this
university was his style, somethink unique.

Of course when I came here for the first time I was like I   2
was lost. But when I went to my room I saw that it was really
small, as small as that room in the passage we read. Unfortunately the light of the day couldn't come in because of the
curtins but also because of the dark paint of the walls. But
anyway I like it because it was cozy. Of course I would prefer
another room but now I had to make this room a part of my
life, to get used to it because it would be my home for a long
time. The room itself wasn't anythink special. Just a plain
room with two beds, one for me and one for my roomate, two
closets, two chairs, almost everything in that room was a
couple.

After writing for a while on the ideas he had circled, Tim wrote a first
draft. The peer reviewer's comments can be read on peer review 2 (p.68).

Draft 1

THE PLACE I LIVE

It is well known that any person takes a style and a kind of   1
thinking from the country he, or she, is from. Because I was
borned and raised in Greece, I believe that I am more interested in historical facts than someone who his country has
not history at all. And one part of my countrys history is architecture.

This is one of the reasons I believe architecture that I chose 2
to enroll in the University of Tampa. On the Bulletin they sent
me, when I was still in Greece, I was really fascinated of the
style of Plant Hall, a style that it was more used to our eastern country, like the east part of Europe or Asia.

And when I came here, I still had the same impresion 3
about the building. It was somethink really different, somethink like an oasis in the middle of the desert. After a small
walk I had around Plant Hall, I went to my room at the Hilton
Hotel, where I stay til they would found me a room on
campus.

After a few days, I finally moved into a dorm. It was really 4
different from the rooms I knew in the main building. Its a
small room, painted in a tone of brown color, with two beds,
two closets, two chairs, and not so much day light, because of
the curtins. My roommate had already moved in and the
room was in a mess. Clothes, luggages and many other
thinks were everywhere.

I really didn't wanted in the beginning to criticiased it, be- 5
cause it would be my home for a long time. And day by day
I'm more used to it. Anyway thats the only way for me to stop
thinking. Thinking about other thinks like my lessons.

I hope that pretty soon I'll feel more comfortable, not only 6
with my room, but also with the new way of living. I know
that it needs a little more time, but I can wait for as long as it
is necessary.

♦ DISCUSSION QUESTIONS

1. What comments would you make to Tim about his draft?
2. What do you think of the peer reviewer's comments (Peer Review
2, on p. 68)?

Draft 2

It is well known that any person takes a style and a kind of 1
thinking from the country he, or she, is from. Because I was
born and raised in Greece, I believe that I am more interested
in historical facts than someone else, whose country hasn't

Peer Review 2　　　　　　　　Writer: _Jim Paschalidis_
Narrative/Descriptive　　　　　Peer Reviewer: _Minh Mai_

1. What did you like the most about this composition?

I like the introduction and the part about photos in the Bulletin. It's interesting he came here because of a building.

2. What is the purpose? Is each paragraph related to that purpose?

to describe this building, this university
yes

3. Is the writing appropriate for the audience?

yes — for students

4. Is there any place that is unclear?

about history in first paragraph — what country has no history? I not understand "Style of Plant Hall"

5. Are there any places where the writer should add more detail or eliminate any repetitions?

describe better Plant Hall — why it is interesting? tell more about room and roommate

got such a background in history. And one chapter of
Greece's past is architecture.

Architecture is one of the reasons I believe, that I've   2
chosen to enroll in the University of Tampa. On a Bulletin
they sent me, when I was still in Greece, when it contained
informations about the history of the college, the cources,
the campus life and generally almost everything I wanted to
know about the University. But especially one part of it really
fascinated me. It was the photos. The main building of the
school, Plant Hall, was something different, something that I
would never believe I could see in a Western country.

The style of Plant Hall was like a dream, like a picture that   3
all of us have from the fairytales concerning the Far East.
And when I finally came at Tampa I was anxius to see it.

When I did so, it was like the photo coming alive. The   4
minarets going up to the sky, with the halfmoons on top of
them, the woodwork around the window-frames sculpture,
the halls, the rooms everything was something unique. The
building was, and still is, like an oasis in the middle of the cement desert.

Finally, after I look over almost every part of the Plant   5
Hall, I went for a small walk around it and then I went to my
room at the Hilton hotel, where I would stay until they could
find me a room on campus.

After a few days, I moved into a dorm. It was really dif-   6
ferent from the rooms I knew in the main building. It was a
small room painted in a grey color, with two beds, two
closets, two chairs and almost everything else was in double.
It seemed like the people who had organized the room, had
think about everything exept personality. The day light was
too difficult to pass throught the curtains, although the windows were big enough. The bathroom was common with another room, which was the Residence Advisors, who gladly
introduced himself to me. My roommate, an Amerikan boy
from the North part of the States, had already moved in and
the room was in a mess. Clothes, luggages, boxes and many
other things were everywhere. It was as if someone was fighting there, before I went.

One of my thoughts, was not to criticize the room because   7
it would be my home for a long time. And day by day I'm
more used to it. Anyway, trying to get used to, not only of my
room, but of everything else too, it would be a way for me to
stop thinking. Thinking about other things, exept my studies and my life here at school and in the States generally.

I hope that soon I'll feel more comfortable, I know that it   8
needs a little more time, but I can wait for as long as it is
necessary.

♦ DISCUSSION QUESTIONS

1. Do you think this draft is more interesting? Why or why not?

2. Has Tim responded well to his peer reviewer's comments?

Now read draft 3 and respond to the questions at the end.

Draft 3

It is well known that any person takes a style and a kind of   1
thinking from the country he, or she, is from. Because I was
born and raised in Greece, I believe that I am more interested in historical facts than someone else, whose country
hasn't got such a background in history. And one chapter of
Greece's past is architecture.

Architecture is one of the reasons I believe, that I've   2
chosen to enroll in the University of Tampa. The bulletin
they sent me when I was still in Greece, contained informations about generally almost everything I wanted to know
about the University. The main building of the school, Plant
Hall, was something different, something that I would never
believe I could see in a Western country. The style of Plant
Hall was like a dream, like a picture that all of us have from
the fairytales concerning the Far East. And when I finally
came at Tampa I was anxious to see it.

When I did so, it was like the photograph coming alive. The   3
minarets going up to the sky, with the half moons on top of
them, the wood-work around the window-frames, the halls,
the rooms, everything was something unique. The building

was, and still is, like an oasis in the middle of the cement desert.

Finally, after I had <u>tooken</u> a tour of almost every part of the   4
Plant Hall, I went for a small walk around <u>it </u>and then I went
to my room at the Hilton Hotel, where I would stay until they
could find me a room on campus.

After a few days, I moved into a dorm. It was a small room,   5
really different from the ones I knew in the main building,
painted in a grey color, with two beds, two closets, two chairs
and almost everything was double. It seemed like the people
who had organized the room, had thought about everything,
<u>exept</u> personality. It was too difficult for the light to pass
through the curtains, although the windows were big
enough. The bathroom was in common with another room,
which was the Residence Advi<u>sors</u>, who gladly introduced
himself to me. My roommate had already moved in and the
room was in a mess. He told me that he was from the northern part of the States. When I saw the room, it was like someone was fighting there, before I arrived. Clothes, luggage,
boxes, and many other things were everywhere. Almost
nothing was in order.

One of my thoughts, was not to criti<u>ciase</u> the room, be-   6
cause it would be my home for a long time. And day by day
I'm more used to it. <u>Anyway, trying to get used to, not only of</u>
<u>my room but of everything else too, for example the different</u>
<u>way that the Americans think, the different style of life, in-</u>
<u>cluding the entertainment, and generally the culture of the</u>
<u>people, but also the climate.</u> So it would be a way for me to
stop thinking. <u>Thinking about other things, exept my stud-</u>
<u>ies here at the school and in the States generally.</u>

I hope that soon I'll feel more comfortable. I know that it   7
needs a little more time, but I can wait for as long as it is necessary.

♦ DISCUSSION QUESTIONS

  1. Note the revision. He has combined paragraphs 2 and 3 of the
     earlier draft. Do you think that this is an improvement? Why or

why not? One sentence was left out. Do you think it should have been? Has he improved the end of paragraph 5 (paragraph 6 in draft 2)? Why or why not?

2. Do you think he should have done more revision in general?

3. Notice the editing:

[2] the second sentence

[3] photo > photograph

halfmoons > half moons

[5] combination of two sentences at beginning

in double > double

had think > had thought

the day light was too difficult > it was too difficult for the light

common > in common

the North part > the northern part

before I went > before I arrived

4. Much more work needed to be done on editing this draft, but Tim probably felt he had already worked on it for a long time. Go through draft 3 and make corrections at each underlined place. Paragraph 6 has two major sentence fragments. As you make corrections be certain you know why they need to be made. These corrections do not relate to anything other than grammatical points, punctuation, or spelling. There also may be errors that have not been underlined.

Chapter Three

AMERICA / AMERICA
Writing to Inform

*Writing and rewriting are a constant
search for what one is saying.*
                              —*John Updike*

Gary Moore *(1951–)*

Gary Moore is a freelance writer and hiker. His hiking trips have included a cross-country trek (on which this article is based) and a walk to Panama from California. The following article appeared in the "My Turn" column of Newsweek. *In this selection, Moore describes how his trip across the United States taught him about the nature of Americans. Contrary to the predictions, he did not encounter violence at every turn.*

Before you read, write for 10 minutes in your journal about what it would be like to take a trip hitchhiking across America.

What America Is Really Like

A 3,600-mile walk has proved to me that America is not as dangerous as many people think. 1

Last May, I set out on foot from Boston. Eight months later, I walked into San Diego, having accepted no rides en route.[1] But it was not the hike's length that astonished many of the backporch and lunch-counter acquaintances that I made along the way; it was the fact that I had not been mugged.[2] 2

Said a waitress in North Texas: "You mean you don't carry no *gun?*" 3

In town after town I was warned that the citizens of the next county or the next state or the next region were likely to fall upon me and do me harm. Yet, invariably when I arrived at these alleged no man's lands, I would feel that I must have taken a wrong turn and wound up somewhere else, for my wary glance was never met with violence. Often it was met with open hospitality. In fact, the whole nation turned out to be amazingly, gratifyingly friendly. 4

Many times, in crowded suburbs as well as on isolated farms, I was invited into people's homes for meals or lodging. At no time did anyone attempt to run me over with a car, or to steal my backpack, or to stab, stomp, or strangle me. I repeat, they did not even try. 5

[1] French for "on the way."

[2] Robbed, usually with some physical violence.

BANJOS AND HOME COOKING

Though it had been predicted that my long hair and beard would   6
bring me to a sad end in Texas, the Lone Star State[3] besieged me only
with repeated helpings of home cooking. The mere fact that I was a
stranger was supposed to spell my doom in the Missouri Ozarks,[4] yet I
was greeted there with backwoods banjo concerts and invitations to go
water-skiing.

In the all-white rural parts of Illinois that surround East St. Louis, it   7
was begrudgingly admitted that I might get through the predominantly
black inner city alive—but certainly not without four or five huge
junkies[5] ordering me to hand over my backpack. Yet, when I persisted in
my suicide mission and entered East St. Louis, I got only a few stares and
an offer from a black businessman to buy me lunch.

Could there possibly be two Americas existing simultaneously in the   8
same space—one, the rather amiable country that is accessible to those
who will see it, the other, the menacing landscape that imprisons those
who see only their fears?

Those who live in the second America—the menacing one—seem to   9
feel that it is jam-packed with one or the other of two groups: murderous "red-necks" or murderous "crazies."[6]

Sufferers of red-neck phobia are usually city dwellers or longer-   10
haired young people who do not realize that in the last five or ten years
the countryside has undergone an important change. Vanished are the
days in the '60s and early '70s when hirsute travelers were thrown into
sheep-dip vats[7] in Wyoming and shot at in Georgia. Perhaps Watergate
and Vietnam[8] have humbled us, for an extraordinary atmosphere of
restraint has settled upon the land. I saw repeated evidence that America's mayhem-minded[9] bigots have turned to dissipating their energies in
grumbling.

---

[3] Texas; the flag of the state has one star.

[4] A mountain range in the Midwest.

[5] Drug addicts.

[6] Red-necks: negative term used by city-dwellers to describe rural people they fear are
prejudiced. Crazies: a negative term for those individuals who seem strange in appearance
or action.

[7] Hirsute means hairy or bearded. During the 1960s farmers might have thrown a
young, bearded man into a tub of chemicals used to treat sheep as a joke or a protest
against his appearance.

[8] Watergate was the scandal that led to President Nixon's resignation. After the Vietnam War, Americans were less sure of themselves in many ways.

[9] Someone intent upon violence or disruption of society.

MURDEROUS LUNATICS

"If you'd a come through here five years ago," I was told by a   11
friendly Oklahoma housewife who invited me in for lunch, "they'd a
got you down and cut your hair. But now, all them that was doin' it, they
have long hair themselves."

This same restraint seems also to have affected other prejudices. In   12
most parts of the country that I crossed, racist attitudes were flour-
ishing—but without the consistent violence of decades past. As I discussed the sudden decrease in violent racism with a Texas newspaper
editor, I mentioned that I had grown up in Mississippi. He looked at me
thoughtfully, then replied, "You're from the South. You know how it
used to be. Don't you think it says a lot about this country—that we can
go through a change like that without a revolution?"

But fears of "Easy Rider"[10] type bigots account for only half of   13
American paranoia. For every anxious suburban longhair there is an
equally distraught smalltown beautician or auto mechanic. The
bugaboo[11] of these people is murderous lunatics. Sometimes the fears
are only of "drug-crazed" lunatics, but often they are more general—
embracing all manner of ax-murderers and stranglers who are seen as
the natural product of a society gone crazy. Like the political assassins of
the '60s and '70s, for instance, or that former Eagle Scout who killed all
those people with a high-powered rifle from atop an observation
tower.[12]

Newspapers and television may be partly to blame for the spread of   14
this kind of anxiety. The same media overkill that made the violent
racists shudder from exposure and reconsider their impulsive deeds has
made violent psychotics seem as abundant and as inescapable as tabloid
headlines about them.

The fallacies of the murderous-lunatic syndrome can be summed up   15
by an incident that happened to me in St. Louis, on a bus-stop bench. I
had stopped there to rest my pack, and was soon joined by a small man
of middle age. He was wearing a football-referee's cap.

He seemed to think that because I carried a backpack, I was hitchhik-   16
ing, and he told me that he just did not see where I got the courage to get
into other people's cars. Why, every day he saw bus seats that had been

[10] A movie of the early 1970s that depicted cruelty and violence against young people
who were part of the "counterculture."

[11] Imaginary monsters, or something that bothers someone intensely.

[12] Reference to the young man who went crazy and shot people from an observatory
tower at the University of Texas. during the 1960s. He had achieved the highest rank in
scouting (Eagle), which indicates he had strong moral training and at one time knew right
from wrong.

carved on with *knives*. I should watch my step, he said, for the world was definitely full of dangerous weirdos.[13]

SHOCK

This rankled[14] me, and I gruffly told my new companion that he was 17 wrong—especially about the abundance of weirdos. The rebuff seemed to stun him like a physical blow—sending him into shock. For a moment, he stared into space, then suddenly he whipped off his referee's cap, snatched a silver whistle from underneath it, blew the whistle, replaced the whistle on his head, replaced the cap on the whistle, and after another pause he began, as if nothing had happened, to talk cooperatively about how safe the country was.

Slowly I realized that when he had first sat down, he had been afraid 18 of me. His unusual behavior was just his way of coping with the hostility he expected to find. But in fact, I was really rather harmless, and so was he.

You see, some rather extraordinary people do exist out there, but 19 they are as benign as the bus-stop referee—if only we would see them as they are, rather than as we fear they will be.

♦ COMPREHENSION/DISCUSSION QUESTIONS

1. What surprised you the most about this reading?

2. Why do you suppose Moore included the ungrammatical quotations [3 and 11]?

3. When he asks "Could there possibly be two Americas existing simultaneously . . ." [8] what does he mean?

4. In paragraph 10, Moore refers to a fear of "red-necks." Who fears these people and why?

5. What changes in American racial attitudes did he notice during his travels?

6. Explain the last sentence in paragraph 12.

7. What is the main idea of paragraph 13?

8. What does Moore say about the role of the media in forming people's attitudes? Do you agree with him?

---

[13] Odd people.

[14] Bothered; irritated.

9. What is the point of his last illustration?

10. Do you agree or disagree with his last statement?

11. What do you think his central idea is?

12. What did you think about after you read this selection?

13. Would you want to try this kind of trip? Why or why not?

14. Have you had any experiences similar to Moore's?

15. Would you or have you ever treated a stranger as he was treated?

♦ VOCABULARY

Define the following words and then fill in the blanks in the paragraph which follows. Appropriate verb or noun endings have been supplied in parentheses.

benign [19]	phobia [10]
bigot [10]	psychotic [14]
cope [18]	rankle [17]
decade [12]	rebuff [17]
dissipate [10]	simultaneously [8]
distraught [13]	stomp [5]
fallacy [15]	strangle [5]
gruffly [17]	syndrome [15]
invariably [4]	tabloid [14]
lunatic [13]	wary [4]
paranoia [13]	

When Mika, a student from Finland, arrived at the airport in New York, he wasn't certain how to get to his new address. Since the _____(s) were full of headlines and pictures of crime in big American cities, he was _____ as he set out. First he asked a policeman how to find a taxi or bus into the city. The policeman responded _____, but pointed out the right location. While Mika was waiting for the taxi, he saw an old woman, who might have been a _____, dragging a shopping bag. As he stepped into the taxi, he thought to himself, "What if the driver takes me to the wrong part of town and leaves me!" After a few minutes, the driver put on some classical music, and turning _____ to Mika, smiled. "Are you coming to study in America?" he asked. The student's anxiety _____(ed), and he realized he had been suffering from _____. "Why yes," he said, "I'm from Finland and I've just arrived. How did you guess?" The driver responded, "I know that students _____ live at that address. I'm a student from Nigeria, but I've been here a long time, almost a _____." The new student asked many questions about how to _____ with life in the city as they found their way through the streets. When the driver dropped him off at the correct address, he said with a _____ expression on his face, "Don't be worried about life here. It's a _____ that everyone is too busy or too hostile in the city to help you. Just wait and see!"

♦ IDIOMS AND FIGURES OF SPEECH

Look back at the context of these expressions. Does it help you to understand their meaning? Then write a sentence of your own using them.

1. "Bring me to a sad end" [6]—result in failure or a bad result.
2. "Spell my doom" [6]—indicate that he was about to fail.
3. "Jam-packed" [9]—tightly packed.
4. "media overkill" [14]—excessive publicity in newspapers or on radio and TV.
5. "Whipped off" [17]—took off quickly

♦ JOURNAL ENTRIES

Begin a journal entry with one of the following:

If I could hitchhike across the United States, I would . . .

If I got lost in a big city, I would . . .

If I could plan a 3-month trip, I would go to . . .

Once when I was traveling, I . . .

◆ SMALL GROUP WORK

Divide into groups of 3–4 students and choose a recorder. The groups should come to a consensus about an idea related to Moore's essay. Are Americans a friendly people to strangers? Brainstorm aloud specific examples of situations in which Americans seem friendly and situations in which they do not seem friendly to strangers (5 minutes). Come to a consensus on whether the positive examples outweigh the negative ones. Report to the whole class on the results.

Follow-up Writing   Write a few paragraphs on whether the discussion in the small group changed or reinforced your original opinion on the question.

Paul Simon   *(1928–)*

Paul Simon is a U.S. Senator who has had a long career of public service, starting in the Illinois legislature in 1954, where he served until 1966. He was Lieutenant Governor of Illinois, taught at San-gamon State University and at the John F. Kennedy Institute at Har-vard, was elected to the U.S. Congress in 1974 and then to the U.S. Senate in 1984. He has written seven books. The following selection is taken from The Tongue-Tied American *and recounts some of the his-tory behind Americans' attitudes toward the study of foreign lan-guages. Americans are not known for their ability to speak other languages, and some people would argue that it is a major problem for us. This selection may give you some insight into the reasons for the problem.*

Before you read, write in your journal for 10 minutes about how you learned a second language.

Americanization Has Its Weaknesses

There is more than one reason for the lack of emphasis on foreign languages in the United States, but one word, *Americanization*, ex-plains a major part of it. That word speaks to this nation's strength and to its weakness.

The United States is the greatest amalgam of people of any single nation. The blending of our backgrounds into both a national culture and a diversity of cultures has not always been a smooth process, not always free of difficulty, but for all its minuses, on balance it has been a tremendous plus for the United States, and an example to other nations.

This Americanization process encouraged Italian, German, Armenian, Japanese, Nigerian, and other immigrants to be "American" in their attitude, culture, and citizenship. A heavily accented English, or strange clothing, or habits that did not fit completely into this new world were "deficiencies" they wanted their children to avoid. Their children went to school to become Americans. To promote this transition, the parents sometimes refused to speak their native tongue around the children; and the children were sometimes embarrassed if they did, and demanded that they speak in English. The last thing most of these parents wanted their children to learn in school was a foreign language. If someone asks the son of Italian immigrants if he speaks Italian, he will often deny it.

To speak another language has been a matter of shame, not of pride. 4
Even third, fourth, and fifth generation Americans are caught in this.
There is no sense that they have a resource, important to them personally and important to the nation. So we have this unusual, deep-seated
phenomenon: a historical cultural barrier to the learning of another
language in a land of great ethnic diversity.

Another reason for our present dilemma is our history of local control 5
of the schools. In almost all other nations, education curriculum and
policy are determined at the national level. Local control in the United
States applies to hiring teachers and administrators; it applies to building
the physical facilities—and it applies to shaping curriculum. There are
50,000 school districts in the fifty states. And no President of the United
States, no U.S. Secretary of Education, and no member of the U.S. Senate
or House of Representatives can tell even the smallest elementary school
in the nation that its curriculum must include any subject.

There have been times when a national need, or national passion, has 6
influenced the curriculum nationwide. During World War I, when anti-
German feeling was high, German language teaching virtually disappeared from schools all over the nation. After Sputnik's[1] ascent in 1957,
there was a sudden thrust forward in the teaching of sciences, and, to a
lesser extent, foreign languages. When there has been a perceived national need, ways to encourage curriculum change have emerged. When
we have wanted change, a financial "carrot"[2] has been available to
bring education more into line with national needs. A good example is
the Smith-Hughes Act, which established a federal subsidy of agricultural education and home economics. Soon after the passage, virtually every high school in the nation could offer these courses.

Foreign language study has been on a roller coaster,[3] but unfor- 7
tunately the general trend is more down than up. In 1979, approximately 17 percent of all high school students had studied a modern
foreign language, a slightly smaller percentage than in 1890. But there is
one major difference—in 1890, more than half of all high school students took Latin. Today, fewer than 1 percent study Latin or ancient
Greek. The Modern Language Association of America was established in
1883 because scholars found that the study of Latin and ancient Greek
had almost completely squeezed out modern language study at both the
high school and collegiate levels.

While language study appeared early in our history—missionaries 8
taught French to the Indians as early as 1604—modern languages have

---

[1] First satellite to orbit the earth, launched by the Russians.

[2] Incentive, from the expression, to dangle a carrot in front of a donkey.

[3] Meaning it rises and falls, like the amusement park ride called a "roller coaster."

usually been taught as "extras," things that enriched the student but had no part in the heart of the curriculum.

Language teaching followed the ethnic background of a community. One source notes that in 1895, nationally there were at least 3,000 elementary pupils enrolled in French classes and 23,000 in German classes, reflecting the immigrant background of the students. These students (and their parents) resisted the general trend toward abandonment of national heritage. The high point in percentages of high school students studying a foreign language appears to have been reached shortly before World War I. With the arrival of World War I, attempts to exclude "foreign" elements from the curriculum had great popular appeal. German, in particular, suffered. By 1922, the number of students who studied German had declined by 98 percent from 1915 levels. Some states attempted to ban the teaching of all foreign languages. Despite that, before World War II, 36 percent of high school students studied a modern foreign language.

During World War II, the national defense establishment found itself in desperate need of linguists. The academic community could not meet the need. Not only had the declining numbers of students resulted in a smaller academic base for foreign language study, but the skills developed were geared more to reading than to the practical needs of the nation's defense leaders. The War Department was compelled to move into the field of foreign language teaching quickly, with programs that differed drastically from the conventional academic approach. But after the war and by the time of Sputnik, foreign language enrollment had dropped to 20 percent; the Soviet space enterprise boosted enrollment up to approximately 24 percent. It was a brief respite. The percentage has gone downhill since that time, reaching an all-time low of less than 17 percent in 1979.

An additional factor militating against national curriculum priorities emerged during the Vietnam era. Students assumed near control of college curricula. American campuses came close to resembling battlegrounds with the violent eruptions at Kent State University in Ohio and Jackson in Mississippi[4] as the tragic climax to this period. On dozens of campuses, rebellious students occupied the president's office, or a dean's office. The slightest provocation sometimes erupted in chaos in the streets. Buildings were burned. Even campuses where violence did not erupt were affected by the turmoil elsewhere.

The curriculum became one of the most vulnerable pressure points. Students wanted fewer requirements for admission and for graduation.

9

10

11

12

---

[4] Kent State—Four students were killed by the Ohio National Guard during an antiwar demonstration. Jackson State College—two students were killed by police during a civil rights disturbance on May 14, 1970.

And part of the national reaction to Vietnam was an inward movement. Many school administrators, sensing the mood of the times and eager to be among the survivors, found it all too convenient to drop foreign language requirements.

The government nevertheless has been able to exert some influence   13
on foreign language study. A series of government programs has indirectly—and sometimes directly—fostered greater interest in foreign languages. Dr. Rose L. Hayden compiled a list of federal agency programs involved in international education for the American Council on Education; it turned out to be a seventy-six-page document. Unplanned and uncoordinated, these federal programs fill the needs and objectives of the separate agencies. While language requirements are not a part of most of these programs, some do have requirements such as: "Language proficiency sufficient to carry out the proposed study." Each of the programs has a fairly narrow focus, but all result secondarily in a greater appreciation for another culture. . . .

These programs have resulted in a tremendous reservoir of goodwill   14
for the United States among people in sensitive leadership positions in almost every country. Incomprehensibly, in 1974, the Nixon Administration recommended no funding at all for the Fulbright-Hays programs. Fortunately, Congress did not accept that suggestion. Nevertheless, Congress has sensed no great need to provide more adequate funding of international studies and foreign language programs. In fact, in a budget of more than half a trillion dollars, not much attention is paid to such studies. Indifference, rather than hostility, characterizes the congressional attitude. There has been enough support to keep most programs operating at a minimal level, but no more. . . .

The trend is unfortunately clear. These losses cannot be explained in   15
terms of a rational legislative and administrative response to a pressing national need. Rather, the foreign language program that has emerged is largely unplanned and meets only a small portion of the national need.

Constructing policy is a little like building a house. If you plan   16
carefully for it, there still will be problems. But if you build without planning, the problems are much greater. In foreign language policy, we have built without a plan, without asking what we are building or what we should build.

♦ COMPREHENSION/DISCUSSION QUESTIONS

1. This selection is excerpted from a chapter in Senator Paul Simon's book *The Tongue-Tied American*. Explain the play on words in the title.

2. What is the weakness of "Americanization" that Simon is concerned about?

3. What is the unusual phenomenon he refers to in paragraph 4?

4. How has "local control of schools" worked against foreign language study?

5. When was the high point of foreign language study in American high schools?

6. What factors have contributed to the decline of foreign language study?

7. What was the impact of the 1960s on foreign language study?

8. What does Simon mean when he writes, "Indifference, rather than hostility, characterizes the congressional attitude" [14].

9. Do you think Simon wants the federal government to play a larger role in promoting foreign languages? What tells you this?

10. How do you feel about the points Simon made?

11. Before you read this article, did you ever wonder why few American young people want to study foreign languages?

12. If you are going to live in the United States permanently, are you going to maintain your native language? Would you want your children to speak and read it also?

13. If you have a roommate or a spouse who also speaks several languages, how have you decided which language to speak together? Do you mix the two or use one language for one purpose and one for another? If you live in a multigenerational household, do the grandparents speak the same language as the grandchildren?

♦ VOCABULARY

Define the following words, paying particular attention to the meaning used in the context of the reading selection. Then fill in the blanks in the paragraph with the appropriate words. Once again, appropriate verb or noun endings have been supplied in parentheses.

amalgam [2]	linguist [10]
curriculum [5]	militate [11]
deficiency [3]	respite [10]

deep-seated [4]   subsidy [6]

dilemma [5]   transition [3]

enrich [8]   vulnerable [12]

ethnic [4]

America is made up of many _____ groups, all of whom have _____(ed) our culture. People who come here face a _____; should they push their children to speak nothing but English to speed up the _____ to the United States, or should parents help children to maintain their culture by speaking their native language at home? There is a _____ cultural pattern that _____(s) against preserving the native language beyond the first generation. Many people who are interested in languages other than English think this is unfortunate. They would like to see the federal government offer _____(ies) to the schools to teach foreign languages to English speaking students and to maintain languages for the new immigrants. Unfortunately, the _____ of the schools is not set by the federal government. Many people think that if Americans don't take the study of foreign languages more seriously, our businesses will be _____ in foreign competition. The time may have come for us to think beyond the great melting pot or _____ of peoples and languages and realize our need to preserve and promote the study of languages other than English.

♦ IDIOMS

Study the use of the following idioms in context; then try writing a sentence of your own using them.

1. "On balance" [2]—as a final choice between two almost equal positions.

2. "To a lesser extent" [6]—to a smaller degree or proportion.

3. "Gone downhill" [10]—declined.

4. "Pressing (national) need" [15]—an urgent need.

♦ JOURNAL ENTRIES

Write for 20 minutes in your journal on your own experiences in learning a new language.

♦ SMALL GROUP WORK

Divide into small groups of 3-5 students. Choose one of the following questions for discussion:

1. Do you think Americans are at a disadvantage because they don't speak foreign languages? Give specific examples of why or why not.

2. Should high schools, colleges, and universities require their students to study a foreign language? If so, what arguments would you use to convince the students that this is a good idea? If not, why not?

Brainstorm aloud, quickly, for 5 minutes while a recorder for each group takes notes. Spend another 5 minutes deciding as a group which are the three best ideas or examples. Reassemble as a whole class and have the recorders or another group member present the results to the whole class.

Follow-up Writing   Write several paragraphs in response to the original question. The written responses should be based on the discussion.

Otto Friedrich *(1929–)*

Otto Friedrich has held many jobs in publishing since he graduated from Harvard University. He has worked for United Press International, and at such publications as Stars and Stripes, The New York Daily News, Newsweek, The Saturday Evening Post, *and* Time. *He has contributed to a long list of magazines, which includes* Esquire, Mc-Calls, Reader's Digest, Harper's, *and* Yale Review. *In addition, he has written numerous children's books and adult novels. His most famous,* Decline and Fall, *published by Harper & Row in 1970, earned him the George Polk Memorial Award for the best book on journalism that year.*

This selection, from Time *magazine, discusses the changes in immigration patterns to the United States in recent years. You may already be aware of the changes the new immigrants are making in America. If not, it will be interesting for you to think about how a predominance of Hispanic and Asian immigrants will have a different impact on American culture than the predominantly European immigrants of the nineteenth century did.*

Before you read, write in your journal for 10 minutes on a recent immigrant you know or on what you think it must be like to be a new immigrant to the United States.

The Changing Face of America

Reina came from El Salvador because of "horrible things." She says 1
simply, "I got scared." When she finally reached Los Angeles and found a job as a housekeeper at $125 a week, her new employer pointed to the vacuum cleaner.[1] Vacuum cleaner? Reina, 24, had never seen such a thing before. "She gave me a maid book[2] and a dictionary," says Reina, who now writes down and looks up every new word she hears. "That's how I learn English. I don't have time to go to school, but when I don't speak English, I feel stupid, so I must learn. . . ."

Lam Ton, from Viet Nam, is already a U.S. citizen, and he did well 2
with a restaurant, the Mekong, at the intersection of Broadway and Argyle Street in Chicago. "When I first moved in here, I swept the sidewalk after we closed," he recalls. "People thought I was strange, but

---

[1] A machine for picking up dust from rugs and carpets.

[2] A book of instructions and vocabulary needed for housecleaning.

now everyone does the same." Lam Ton's newest project is to build an arch over Argyle Street in honor of the immigrants who live and work there. "I will call it Freedom Gate," he says, "and it will have ocean waves with hands holding a freedom torch on top. It will represent not just the Vietnamese but all the minorities who have come here. Just look down Broadway. That guy is Indian, next to him is a Greek, next to him is a Thai, and next to him is a Mexican."

They seem to come from everywhere, for all kinds of reasons, as indeed they always have. "What Alexis de Tocqueville[3] saw in America," John F. Kennedy once wrote, "was a society of immigrants, each of whom had begun life anew, on an equal footing. This was the secret of America: a nation of people with the fresh memory of old traditions who dared to explore new frontiers." It was in memory of Kennedy's urging that the U.S. in 1965 abandoned the quota system that for nearly half a century had preserved the overwhelmingly European character of the nation. The new law invited the largest wave of immigration since the turn of the century, only this time the newcomers have arrived not from the Old World but from the Third World,[4] especially Asia and Latin America. Of the 544,000 legal immigrants who came in fiscal 1984, the largest numbers were from Mexico (57,000 or more than 10%), followed by the Philippines (42,000) and Viet Nam (37,000). Britain came in ninth, with only 14,000. . . .

In addition to the half-million immigrants who are allowed to come to the U.S. each year, a substantial number arrive illegally. Estimates of the total vary widely. The Immigration and Naturalization Service apprehended 1.3 million illegal immigrants last year and guessed that several times that many had slipped through its net. . . .

The newest wave raises many questions: How many immigrants can the country absorb and at what rate? How much unskilled labor does a high-tech society need? Do illegals drain the economy or enrich it? Do newcomers gain their foothold at the expense of the poor and the black? Is it either possible or desirable to assimilate large numbers of immigrants from different races, languages and cultures? Will the advantages of diversity be outweighed by the dangers of separatism[5] and conflict?

When asked about such issues, Americans sound troubled; their answers are ambiguous and sometimes contradictory. In a *Time* poll taken by Yankelovich, Skelly & White Inc.,[6] only 27% agreed with the idea

---

[3] An eighteenth-century Frenchman who wrote about his impressions of Americans.

[4] The developing countries of Asia, Africa, and Latin America.

[5] Reference to separatist political movements, such as the Free Quebec movement in Canada.

[6] The findings are based on a telephone survey from April 30 to May 2 of 1,014 registered voters. The potential sampling error is plus or minus 3%. [Friedrich's footnote.]

that "America should keep its doors open to people who wish to immigrate to the U.S. because that is what our heritage is all about." Two-thirds agreed that "this philosophy is no longer reasonable, and we should strictly limit the number." Some 56% said the number of legal immigrants was too high, and 75% wanted illegal immigrants to be tracked down. On the other hand, 66% approved of taking in people being persecuted in their homelands.

"One of the conditions of being an American," says Arthur Mann, 7 professor of history at the University of Chicago, "is to be aware of the fact that a whole lot of people around you are different, different in their origins, their religions, their life-styles." Yet most Americans do not know exactly what to make of those differences. . . . Much of the concern comes from people who favor continued immigration, but who fear the consequences if a slowdown in the economy were to heighten the sense that immigrants, especially illegal ones, take jobs away from Americans. . . .

The number of newcomers is large in itself, . . . but their effect is 8 heightened because they have converged on the main cities of half a dozen states. Nowhere is the change more evident than in California, which has become home to 64% of the country's Asians and 35% of its Hispanics. Next comes New York, followed by Texas, Florida, Illinios and New Jersey. Miami is 64% Hispanic, San Antonio 55%. Los Angeles has more Mexicans (2 million) than any other city except metropolitan Mexico City, and nearly half as many Salvadorans (300,000) as San Salvador.

These population shifts change all the bric-a-brac,[7] of life. A car in Los 9 Angeles carries a custom license plate that says *Sie sie li*, meaning, in Chinese, "thank you." Graffiti[8] sprayed in a nearby park send their obscure signals in Farsi.[9] A suburban supermarket specializes in such Vietnamese delicacies as pork snouts and pickled banana buds. The Spanish-language soap opera *Tu o Nadie* gets the top ratings among independent stations every night at 8.

Such changes require adaptation not only in the schools and the 10 market place but throughout society. The Los Angeles County court system now provides interpreters for 80 different languages from Albanian and Amharic to Turkish and Tongan.[10] One judge estimates that nearly half his cases require an interpreter.

These changes do not represent social decline or breakdown. The 11 newcomers bring valuable skills and personal qualities: hope, energy,

---

[7] Small objects used for decoration.

[8] Words or pictures spray-painted onto public walls.

[9] Language spoken in Iran.

[10] Language spoken in, respectively, Albania, Ethiopia, Turkey, and Polynesia.

fresh perspectives. But the success stories should not blot out the fact that many aliens face considerable hardships with little immediate chance of advancement. Avan Wong, 20, came from Hong Kong in 1983 and hoped to go to college. She lives in the Bronx[11] with her aged father, commutes two hours by bus to a job of up to twelve hours a day in a suburban restaurant. "I don't even read the newspapers," she says. "You don't have time. Once you go home, you go to sleep. Once you get up, you have to go to work. The only thing I'm happy about is that I can earn money and send it back to my mother. Nothing else. You feel so lonely here." College is not in sight. . . .

Even with the best intentions on all sides, the question of how to fit all these varieties of strangers into a relatively coherent American society remains difficult. Linda Wong, a Chinese-American official of the Mexican-American Legal Defense and Education Fund,[12] sees trouble in the racial differences. "There is concern among whites that the new immigrants may be unassimilable," says Wong. "Hispanics and Asians cannot melt in as easily, and the U.S. has always had an ambivalent attitude toward newcomers. Ambivalent at best, racist at worst."   12

Many historians disagree. Hispanics, says Sheldon Maram, a professor of history at California State University at Fullerton, "are moving at about the same level of acculturation as the Poles and Italians earlier in the century. Once they've made it, they tend to move out of the ghetto and melt into the rest of society." Asians often have it easier because they come from urban middle-class backgrounds. "They are the most highly skilled of any immigrant group our country has ever had," says Kevin McCarthy, a demographer at the Rand Corp. in Santa Monica, Calif. . . .   13

How long, how complete and how painful the process of Americanization will be remains unclear. It is true that ethnic elitists have bewailed each succeeding wave of Irish or Germans or Greeks, but it is also true that the disparities among Korean merchants, Soviet Jews, Hmong tribesmen,[13] French socialites and Haitian boat people are greater than any of the U.S. or any other country has ever confronted. On the other hand, Americans are probably more tolerant of diversity than they once were. . . .   14

The question is not really whether the new Americans can be assimilated—they must be—but rather how the U.S. will be changed by that process.   15

---

[11] One of the boroughs of New York City.

[12] Organized in 1968, and based in San Francisco. They are dedicated to the protection of the rights of Hispanics in general and Mexican-Americans in particular. They have a scholarship fund to send Mexican-American students to law school and are responsible for most of the class-action law-suits filed on behalf of Mexican-Americans.

[13] From Cambodia.

♦ COMPREHENSION/DISCUSSION QUESTIONS

1. Why have immigration patterns changed since the 1960s?

2. How would you answer the question "Do newcomers gain their foothold at the expense of the poor and the black?" [5]

3. What reason is given for Americans' fear of the new waves of immigrants?

4. How are the new immigrants changing the face of America?

5. How did you respond to the last sentence?

6. Did this article provoke any particular emotions or memories for you?

7. Are you or any of your friends part of the new group of immigrants?

8. From what you have observed, are the large groups of Asian and Hispanic immigrants integrating themselves into the larger American culture or are they forming separate communities?

9. What do you think ought to be done to help new immigrants integrate themselves into the American culture?

10. Do you think America should have a complete "open door" policy regarding immigration? Why or why not?

♦ VOCABULARY

Define the words and then select those which are appropriate in the following passage.

acculturation [13]	disparity [14]
ambiguous [6]	diversity [14]
ambivalent [12]	elitist [14]
anew [3]	fiscal [3]
assimilate [5]	heighten [7]
bewail [14]	intersection [2]
coherent [12]	quota system [3]
confront [14]	perspective [11]
contradictory [6]	slowdown [7]
converge [8]	

The debate over who should be allowed to immigrate to the United States is beginning _____. Some people _____ the changes that were made in the _____ which allowed many more non-Europeans to come into the country. Those people are the _____(s) who want to preserve the dominant European background of the country. Some are worried about a _____ in the economy. But many other Americans have a different _____ on this situation. They know that the American culture benefits from the _____ of peoples who have formed the country. They also know that most ethnic groups become _____(ed) into the society by the third generation. Some Americans have _____ attitudes toward the newcomers; they want to welcome them to the land of opportunity, but they fear that if new groups form strong separate groups it will _____ the tensions in the society. Since these new immigrants are already here, the real question to ask is, in what ways will their process of _____ be the same or different from previous waves of immigration during the nineteenth century.

♦ IDIOMS AND FIGURES OF SPEECH

Study the use of these expressions in context. Then write a sentence of your own using them.

1. "Turn of the century" [3]—the early years of the century.

2. "Equal footing" [3]—on an equal basis.

3. "Slipped through its net" [4]—escaped detection.

4. "Gain a foothold" [5]—establish oneself, find a position.

5. "at the expense of" [5]—by taking away an opportunity from (someone else).

6. "tracked down" [6]—hunted, pursued.

♦ JOURNAL ENTRIES

Write for 20 minutes in your journal on one of the following:

an immigrant you know who is very successful

an immigrant you know who can't adjust to America

why immigrants come to America

♦ SMALL GROUP WORK

Choose a partner and brainstorm ideas on what is easy and what is difficult to adapt to in American culture (5 minutes). Reduce the lists to five items each and read them aloud to the class.

Follow-up Writing   Write several paragraphs on one of the ideas that came up during small group work that you had not thought about before.

WRITING TO INFORM

Before starting on the discussion of new types of writing, stop to think about the kind of reading you have just completed. What are some of the differences between the readings in Chapter 2 and those in this chapter?

You probably noticed that the readings in this chapter were not personal, descriptive, or narrative—they all were examples of what is called "expository prose": writing that attempts to inform or explain. It is the sort of writing we read every day in reports, essays, magazines, and books that are not fiction. It is also the sort of writing you will be asked to do in most of your classes and throughout your career.

Good expository writing informs, explains, or analyzes points in logical, clear, well-supported prose. In an essay, one of the most common forms of expository writing, the writer develops his or her main idea, the thesis, through examples, facts, and illustrations that will convince the reader of the validity of the writer's points. The word "essay" comes from the French *essai*, meaning an experiment or test, and it is good to keep in mind that the writer is trying out or testing a personal point of view or an opinion on a subject. It is the writer's obligation, however, to present supporting detail that will make the ideas believeable to the reader. Gary Moore's essay on "What America Is Really Like" is an example.

If the writing is primarily an accumulation of information, without opinions, then it is called a "report," not an essay. An article in a newspaper or an encyclopedia would be a good example of reporting and research. Much expository writing is a mixture of factual material with an analysis of the data which reveals a position taken or a personal point of view. Otto Friedrich's article, "The Changing Face of America" reports on immigration statistics, but note that it also provides some explanations of the impact that new immigrants are having on American society. Paul Simon's book is full of research on the foreign language crisis in America, but all the facts are presented as support for his opinion that the American government and the people should take language study more seriously. In other words, expository writing can range from the strictly factual to the well-supported or well-argued personal opinion. The readings in this chapter reflect such a range, with Gary Moore's piece being the most obviously personal essay and Friedrich's article being the most factual; but each selection is an example of expository writing.

The Summary: Restating the Main Points

One form of expository writing is the summary, which you will often be asked to write in making reports or in taking exams. Writing summaries is an excellent way to make certain you understand and can remember material you have been reading. The summary seems like such a simple skill—putting into shortened form the major ideas from someone else's writing—but, in fact, writing a summary is demanding. It depends first of all on your ability to read the original material well and understand it thoroughly. You must identify the main point or thesis, understand the difference between the major points and supporting detail, and restate these points in your own words.

A good summary should begin with a sentence that identifies the source, by title, author, and type of writing. Naturally, readers want to know the author and title, but they will also find it helpful to know that the summary is of a report, or an essay, or a magazine article, rather than guessing what type of writing the original was. The summary should also state at the beginning what the main point is, even if that does not come first in the original. As the writer of the summary, you must restate the main point in your own words before continuing to mention the other major points.

You may need to read the original piece several times, and then jot down a brief outline of the main ideas before writing your summary. The body of the summary should reflect the order in which the material was presented in the original, and you should not include the detail or support. Writing a summary is almost the opposite of drafting your own work as it was explained in Chapter 2. In your own writing, you must add detail to expand and clarify your descriptions or ideas; in summary writing, you remove the detail and restate only the main ideas.

The most difficult part of writing a summary is accurately restating the ideas *without using the exact phrases or sentences of the original*. Condensing and restating the main ideas of an expository piece or the main events of a narrative in your own words is called "paraphrasing." The easiest way to write a good paraphrase and avoid the danger of copying is to put the original piece away while you draft the summary. You may refer to it to clarify your thinking in revising the draft, but don't have it right there when you are writing. Remember to use your own sentence structure and vocabulary to express the ideas in the original piece.

This skill of paraphrasing is crucial in doing research for a report or research paper. The more you practice it by doing summaries of brief pieces of writing, the easier you will find it to do during a research project. It is important for you to understand just how seriously American instructors take the error of "plagiarism," which means using someone else's words or phrases without noting where they came from or who wrote them. The strong feelings against plagiarism which you will find expressed in most academic institutions comes from a strong Western tradition of pride in individual accomplishments, including authorship. This authorship is protected by copyright laws, and in a classroom by teachers who will respond very negatively to examples of plagiarism. Now is a good time to learn to paraphrase well, so you will avoid any possible problems.

A final point to remember is that a summary is not supposed to include your own judgments or conclusions about the original piece. Its purpose is to acquaint the reader in short form with the author's ideas, not the summary writer's opinions on those ideas.

Sample Student Writing

Here is an uncorrected summary of Simon's chapter, "Americanization Has Its Weaknesses." The writer followed some of the guidelines but not all. Read the summary and then answer the questions which follow.

"The word Americanization speaks to this nation's strength and its weakness"; this thesis is from The Tongue-Tied American written by Paul Simon. Immigrants sometimes refused to speak their native language around children. Children want parents to speak in English. The schools don't support these children to keep their native languages so that they easily forget. To speak another language has been a matter of shame, not of pride. Because of local control, government can't set the curriculum. The national need or passion has influenced the curriculum. Foreign language study goes up and down. The high point in the percentage of studying a foreign language at high school appears to have been reached shortly before World War I. In 1922 people got anti-German feeling, and then study of German declined by 98 percent from 1915 levels. During World War II, the War Department was compelled to teach foreign languages because of the need for linguists. After the War however, the enrollment dropped 20 percent. Soviet space enterprise sent the enrollment up. After that, the percentage has gone downhill. During the Vietnam era, students wanted fewer requirements, many schools dropped foreign language requirements. Congress doesn't show the interest or support the study of languages. They don't care about it. Language education in the United States would appear to be at a turning point. The federal government should support and encourage students to take a foreign language.

♦ DISCUSSION QUESTIONS

1. Has the writer accurately restated the main thesis?
2. Is the original adequately identified at the beginning?
3. Are the main points presented in the correct order?
4. Is this a good example of paraphrasing? Why or why not?
5. Are all the major points included?
6. Is too much or too little supporting detail included?
7. Does the writer include his or her own conclusions?

Now read another uncorrected summary and compare it to the preceding one.

The essay "Americanization Has Its Weaknesses" from the book The Tongue Tied American by Paul Simon is pointing out the reason how and why American falling behind in foreign languages. The United States has the greatest combination of people around the world. Many people have come to America with their own cultures, attitudes, and especially their own languages. Their children can not speak their native language because those parents refused to speak their language around the children. The children demanded to speak English. Paul Simon said that speaking another language is sort of like a shame to Americans. More or less he said that many people can not see the important of speaking another language to themselves or to the nation. One of the biggest problems is that the American school system is not under control of the federal government and so there are no dominant requirements throughout the nation school system. Foreign language study in America depends on the major events around the world. Simon gave some examples how wars was affected. One of the latest effect is the Vietnam Era. Simon said that during the Vietnam War, many student forced the school system to drop the foreign language requirement. This effect is still going on until today in a small number of school. The government has not done enough to improve the foreign language requirement. And also the government has not given enough fund to promote the study of foreign language.

◆ DISCUSSION QUESTIONS

1. Has the writer accurately restated the main thesis?

2. Is the original adequately identified?

3. Are the main points presented in the correct order?

4. Is this a good example of paraphrasing? Why or why not?

5. Are all the major points included?

6. Is too much supporting detail included?

7. Does the writer include his own conclusions?

8. On the basis of the answers to the preceding questions, is this a better summary than the other one? Why or why not?

9. Which of the two summaries needs more revision? Which needs only more editing?

◆ WRITING ASSIGNMENT

Write a draft of a summary of "What America Is Really Like," "The Changing Face of America," or another selection of your choosing.
Remember as you write:

1. Begin with the main idea of the original work, even if it is not stated at the beginning.

2. Identify the original work, including author, title and what type of writing it is (article, essay, chapter in a book, report).

3. Paraphrase, don't copy the phrases or sentences of the original; don't look at the original as you write; make certain your wording is different from the original.

4. Present each major point in the same order as the original.

5. Do not include much of the supporting detail.

6. Do not make your own conclusion or analysis of the material.

Once you have completed your draft, exchange it with a peer reviewer. If your peer reviewer has not read the original piece, you will need to attach a copy of it to the summary. It is impossible to judge how accurate the summary is if you don't know the original.

Questions a peer reviewer should ask about the summary (see peer review sheet 3 in Appendix A):

1. Does the first sentence clearly identify the original piece?

2. Is the major thesis restated at the beginning of the summary?

3. Has the writer put in the major points?

4. Is there anything missing or that doesn't belong in the summary?

5. Are the ideas presented in the same order as in the original?

6. Are there any places where the wording is too close to the original?

When you complete the peer review, revise your summary according to the feedback you have received, edit it as best you can, and then turn it in to your instructor. The instructor may want to read it as a draft and return it for further revision, in which case you will have another opportunity to revise and edit before turning in the final draft.

The Essay: Expressing Your Opinions

As was stated earlier, an essay is a form of expository writing through which the writer expresses opinions supported by facts, examples, statistics, illustrations, and/or logical arguments. It is a form you will be expected to use throughout your academic career, and the process of writing a good essay begins with the same techniques you used in writing either a description or a narrative, i.e., prewriting through drafting and revision.

Prewriting

When you start prewriting for an essay, you might get some idea for a topic by thinking back over the readings, looking at your journal entries, or thinking about a subject assigned by your instructor. If you don't have any good ideas, try some prewriting now. Some of the following suggestions may help, or the class as a whole might want to discuss possible topics drawn from class discussions.

Brainstorming   Choose one of the following and brainstorm for 5 minutes:

good and bad aspects of traveling alone

the dangers of America—real or unreal?

the advantages of being bilingual

Americanization—what does it mean?

helping immigrants—how could Americans do more?

Freewriting   Choose one of the following and write nonstop for 10–15 minutes:

what you would explain to a new foreign student about Americans

how you would convince an American student to study a foreign language

how you would plan for a trip across America

how you think the "new immigrants" will change American culture

Drafting and Revising

Once you have done some prewriting and it is time to begin drafting, you may still feel that you don't have much to say. Remember that ideas will come to you through the writing process itself. This is why various prewriting activities and a discovery draft are helpful. Or, depending on the topic, you may be brimming over with good ideas before you even get started on a draft. Whichever is the case, think about several points as you begin the drafting process: your purpose, the thesis or main point, the audience, and organization and development.

Purpose   Since this chapter introduces you to the essay, you should ask yourself how its purpose or purposes differ from those of descriptive or narrative writing you did in Chapter 2. One of the broadest purposes for an essay is to inform the reader. Assume, then, that for writing done in this chapter, you will start with the broad purpose of explaining a topic to your reader. Other purposes for essays, analysis and persuasion, for instance, will be studied in the following chapters.

If your purpose is to inform and provide your audience with an explanation, how should you begin? You might use one of several strategies. You could include a definition of something, as Simon does of the word "Americanization." Or you could define through many examples what "America Is Really Like." You might trace the history of an event or the process of change, as in "The Changing Face of America." Being clear about your purpose helps you to decide what to include in your essay and what strategies you will use in developing it. The pre-writing ideas listed above were all good ones for generating this sort of essay.

Although you may have a purpose in mind when you begin, it is easy to forget the purpose and just wander from idea to idea in the first draft. When writing the second draft, you must reconsider what you have written, leaving out some parts and adding others to maintain a consistent purpose.

Sample Student Writing

As an example, read the following draft written by a student who didn't find anything in the topics from this chapter that interested her. She knew she was supposed to write an essay that would explain something, so she decided to get started by writing a discovery draft about something she knew very well: advertising. She had worked for an advertising agency in Brazil before coming to the United States. As she began writing, she didn't have any clear sense of where she would go with the essay, but she began by writing down all her ideas on creating an advertisement.

Draft 1

The process of creating an advertisement is fascinating to me.   1

It's incredible how much time, energy and money is been spent in advertising today, and sometimes just to have a one time ad in a magazine or a 30 seconds TV commercial.   2

It's amazing how someone with a creative mind can make so many people believe and live, according with what he paid or showed.   3

Each day, lists of new products or things in general are seen, and to make the buyers know about them, better advertisements need to be shown to catch the consumer's attention and make them change their minds.   4

Each advertisement created depends on what you're going 5
to see, how much money you want to spent, to whom it is
made for, how much it will cost, where this is going to be
sold.

Vision is the strongest of the senses and it makes a vital 6
factor in consumers acceptance.

Cultural, national and economic factors have great influ- 7
ence in advertisement. New fashions have been created to
help sell something new.

The client—the one who is paying for your work—some- 8
times is the first obstacle you have. Sometimes he or she has
a straight mind, "Only the traditional!" Sometimes he has an
idea of his own and he doesn't accept anything different,
even if the idea he has, is the worst for his business. Sometimes he leave the project in your hands, but let you know
about it in the last minute. It's something like: "I want it for
yesterday, and I want the best you can do."

Private life is something you can have but only if the work 9
is finished, because there are thousands of dollars been
spent.

Regina Prestefelippe

♦ DISCUSSION QUESTIONS

1. Does the first sentence imply that the purpose is to explain a
   process or to explain why creating an advertisement is fascinating? Is there a difference between these two purposes?

2. Which purpose do the ideas the writer has written down tend to
   support?

Now read the second draft, which was written to clarify the purpose.
Which purpose dominates in the second draft? Note all the ideas that
have been left out of the second draft.

Draft 2

The process of creating an advertisement is fascinating to 1
me. I can say it's hard work, but it's so diversified that when
I can see it finished and approved by everybody, it's so de-
lightful that I can forget every hour of sleep I have missed.

That was the first thing I had to learn when I decided to   2
work with advertising—my time would belong to the company. Private life was something I could have, but only if the
work was finished. I had never had time to do one thing at a
time. There were always three or four advertisements to be
finished at the same hour, and sometimes, at the same day. I
learned how to be organized by the hardest way—I had no
choice.

To create each advertisement, first I needed to know about   3
what I was going to sell, and how much money I could spend
on it. Then, I had to know what kind of ad the client wanted,
if it was for TV, radio, newspaper, magazine, outdoor, new design for a package. With all that information I could start re-
searching about the competitors, and what they were doing
to promote their products. After that, I had to do another research, related to the consumers—for whom the product was
made, how much it would cost, where it was going to be sold.
This research had to be done every time, because cultural,
national and economic factors have great influence on advertising. Sometimes, new fashions had to be created to help sell
something new.

After that, I could start working together with the writer.   4
We were like a team, because we depended on each other
ideas. When the first three or four drafts were done, I had to
get at least one approved, in order to continue my work. If I
was succeded in that first step, I could decide how to finish
the ad. The next step was to find out what kind of material to
be used, places and actors (if needed), voices (if it was for the
radio), photographers, illustrators.

It was a merry-go-round every time, but when the results
were positives, it was worth the efforts.

♦ DISCUSSION QUESTIONS

1. Does this draft have a clear purpose? What is it?

2. What are some of the differences between draft 1 and 2?

3. Do those differences make this a better draft? Why or why not?

4. Do you think she could have kept some of the detail from draft 1? Where could she have put it?

Note that this is not a final draft, so there are still many points to be revised and edited.

Thesis   A thesis, a main point or opinion, is central to writing an essay, but your precise thesis may not be clear to you until you have written at least one draft. You may start out thinking that you know what your main point will be, but the writing of the essay will often lead you in new directions or make you think about your subject in different ways. It is useful to start with a tentative thesis, but keep in mind that you probably will change it after you have completed a draft. What is important to understand in writing an essay is that a *thesis is not a statement of fact*; it is a statement that expresses an opinion, a judgment, or a position on an issue which could be questioned or debated from another point of view.

To illustrate the difference between your topic, facts about your topic, and a thesis, consider the following examples.

1. *Topic*: programming on public television
   Facts: (1) Public television does not use normal commercials. (2) It broadcasts many cultural and children's programs. (3) It also broadcasts news. (4) I am going to write about public TV.
   Thesis: Public television in America is better than commercial television because the programs are freer from control by large corporations.

2. *Topic*: the American melting pot
   Facts: (1) Various waves of immigrants have come to the U.S. since the early 19th century. (2) Some immigrant groups, like the Italians and Irish, settled primarily in eastern cities. (3) The melting pot is a metaphor used to describe the American society.
   Thesis: The idea of the melting pot won't be true any longer because the new immigrants are not predominately European.

♦ DISCUSSION QUESTIONS

1. Do you understand the difference between the facts and the thesis in each example?

2. Note especially fact 4 in example 1. You may think that writing such a sentence at the beginning of your essay is stating your thesis. In fact, you would only be announcing your topic. Your reader expects to read a statement, a thesis, that gives an idea of what your main point will be, not just your topic.

3. Complete the following exercise with ideas drawn from the readings in this chapter.

    (A) Topic:
           Fact(s):

           Thesis:

    (B) Topic:
           Fact(s):

           Thesis:

Sample Student Writing

As you write, it will become clearer to you what it is that you really want to say. This is what is meant by developing a thesis. Here, for instance, is how one student started a first draft. He thought he would start off directly with a thesis.

> Arranging for a trip is very important, so the person can enjoy his time. I mean by arranging a trip, that the person should get a visa for the country he is going to visit and get some information about the famous places and the tourist activities in that country.
>
>   Abdullah Almaimanee

When he completed the draft, he realized he had written very specifically about problems he had encountered and how not being prepared spoiled part of his vacation. So when he revised, he added more information about what his essay would cover and a more precise thesis statement at the end of his first paragraph, which avoids starting off abruptly with the thesis as the first sentence.

> Arranging for a trip is very important so that the traveler can enjoy his time. The person should get a visa for the countries he is going to visit and get some information about the famous places and the tourist activities in those countries. He should plan an itinerary and make some reservations for hotels, if the places are very popular with tourists. Thinking

about many details like how much money to take and the way to travel help the traveler prepare. It might be fun to make a trip at the last minute, but going without making arrangements might cause some problems and spoil the trip.

Here is another example of the beginning of a first draft in which the first paragraph was especially confused.

Draft 1

Money is a problem in the world today. Many people use money to do or buy thing that they want. In the world today money is the most powerful substance. There are people who need money to live everyday life, and others use money to make them richer. With money one can order the other to do what they want. Money can create war because the countrys in the world want to make their countrys stronger by using money to buy the weapon or make the weapon by using money.

For example, I used money to pay for my education. In the beginning I didn't have any money to pay for my education, and I know I had to look for money by studying hard so I can get the scholarship from the schools that I want to be in. All my hard work had pay off for me. I got the scholarship from the school and some money from the government. I still don't have enough to pay for the school, so I have to borrow money from the bank to pay for the education.

In this world money was everything for most people. For example, the poor people work very hard for their money and still do not have enough to pay the rent, buy food or buy new clothes on the other hand the rich people can afford anything they wants because they use money to make money like putting it in the bank and getting interest and using the money to buy or make bigger things so that can sell and make more money. The rich people can do many things with their money and anyway they like to make more.

Minh Mai

◆ DISCUSSION QUESTIONS

1. Why does the reader have difficulty understanding what the writer's main point is?

2. Look at the first paragraph and underline the repetitions.

3. What makes the first paragraph vague?

After some thought about how confused the opening was, the student decided to try a more interesting first and second paragraph that would lead up to a clear thesis. His introduction is still quite broad, because it tries to track the development of money systems from the beginning of time, but by the end of the second paragraph he was able to clarify where he was going in the essay. Note where the thesis is.

Draft 2

Long ago, no one needed money. People grew their own food or hunted it. They made their own clothing and shelter. As time went on, some persons found that they could do a certain job better than their neighbors. They began to spend their time doing that one job. They then exchanged the things they produced for other things they needed but did not make themselves. To avoid some of the problem of barter, people began to accept certain object in exchange for any product. These object served as the first money. Then China invented the first paper money. Paper money, unlike gold and silver coins, had little value of its own. But it could be exchanged for valuable metals. 1

As time went on, people used the method of handling or exchanging goods buy using money. In the beginning money did not play an important part of a human life but now people use money in many different ways, and it becoming a problem in the world today. Many people use the money system to make themselves rich, and other people still work very hard to support their family. Although money is a problem for some people, many put money to good use. . . . 2

[Then the writer continued with the paragraph about paying for his education and other points on the good and bad uses of money.]

Audience   Remember what was said in Chapter 2 about identifying characteristics of your audience that will influence choices you make as a writer. Since you are now writing to inform, you should try to judge whether your audience will have some general information about the topic or have none at all and make the appropriate adjustments. Also, you must keep in mind the attitudes and backgrounds of your audience. For instance, a Japanese student writing about her language (see entire essay on p. 154 ff.) mentioned in an early draft that Japanese ranked with several other major world languages in importance. The class, which was her audience, had more Spanish-speaking students in it than any other language group, so they were quick to notice that she had left Spanish off her list of important languages. She corrected this in the next draft out of respect for her audience. That is just one example of how an awareness of your audience will determine your choice of words (level of vocabulary) and how you develop certain points.

Look back at the three readings in this chapter and answer the following questions:

> Who do you think the intended audience is for each one?
>
> Would one or two of these readings appeal to a specific audience rather than a general one?
>
> How educated would the audience need to be for each one?

Organization and Development   An important consideration while you are drafting and revising is the organization of your thoughts, because an essay should have a clear beginning, middle, and end. You probably already know that an essay should have an introduction, body paragraphs, and a conclusion. Specific examples of how to improve introductions and conclusions, how to determine the best order for your paragraphs, and how to revise for unity and coherence will be found in Chapter 4, so we will not go into those points here.

For now, keep in mind that you should get your reader involved in the subject by writing an interesting introduction, and you should not stop your essay abruptly. The last paragraph should bring your thinking to a conclusion and draw out the implications of your essay for the audience. The most natural order to use in arranging the body paragraphs is a historical or chronological one (first to last) for narratives and essays describing a process. In descriptive writing, order can be highly varied. You might use a spatial order–front to back, top to bottom, or right to left. In writing a definition of something, there is no ''natural'' order but you might give background information first and then current examples, as the writer does in the last essay in this chapter. Or, you might start off with an example and follow with the various explanations of the term you want to define. In other words, it is up to you to decide on the best order for your paragraphs. One simple way to revise for order is to ask yourself whether the paragraphs follow well from one to the next, or what would happen if you changed their order.

Look back at the three readings in this chapter and answer the following questions:

> In what order are the ideas presented in each one?

> Can you think of a different order for each that would also have been effective?

In addition to overall structure, another aspect of organization is development, which you studied in Chapter 2, in the discussion of the use of detail, examples, and illustrations. These are part of all expository writing, no matter what the purpose is, and with each assignment you should concentrate on using ever more precise detail and appropriate examples.

Before doing revision, you should ask your peer reviewer and instructor whether they think you have enough detail to support your points. One way for you to know this is to ask whether everything is clear or where they want to know more about something (see peer review sheet 4, in Appendix A). There may also be instances where you have too much detail, which then detracts from your main ideas or causes your reader to get lost in a minor point.

◆ WRITING ASSIGNMENT

Once you have some ideas that seem promising to you, write an answer to the following questions:

> What is the topic you want to write on?

> Why do you want to write about this topic?

> What is your purpose?

> What are you going to say about the topic?

> What characteristics of your audience should you keep in mind?

> What do you think your thesis will be?

Exchange this with a partner in class and discuss each other's answers. With your partner's help, decide whether the topic and your knowledge of it are appropriate for an essay written to inform or explain. It may help you to discuss several examples aloud in front of the whole class, so that the instructor can comment on whether the topic, the purpose, and the tentative thesis work well together.

Once this exercise has been completed and you feel you understand what the assignment is, write a full draft. Review Chapter 2, especially pp. 51–55, if you need help in getting from your prewriting to drafting. Remember that as you draft, you can stop at any time to do any form of prewriting you want in order to generate more ideas.

Exchange this draft with a partner in class and do a peer review, asking the following questions (peer review 4):

What did you think was most interesting?

What is the purpose?

What is the thesis?

Are there any places where you want to have more information?

Are there any parts that are not related to the thesis?

Look over your peer reviewer's comments and ask any questions you have. Revise this draft according to the peer reviewer's comments and hand both the peer review sheet and your draft to the instructor. Once the instructor has commented on the draft, in writing or during a conference, begin your final revisions. You may want to take the draft to a writing center for further help at this point, if you have one available to you.

Editing the Essay

Now you can begin the process of editing. In Chapter 2 you were asked to concentrate especially on subject-verb agreement, verb forms, and verb tenses. In addition to checking especially for those problems, this time, concentrate on sentence fragments, comma splices, and run-ons. Your instructor will explain those terms, if you are not certain what they mean.

Sample Student Writing

Here is an example for the class to use as a group editing exercise.
Look especially for fragments, comma splices, and run-ons as well as spelling errors.

If I could plan a 3-month trip, I would go to Europe. Beginning the trip with Rome and Greece, because of its very different scenes. Also the people and the customs are different from those that we usually see that's why it should be a great and different experience for me.

Europe has the magic and beauty from the ancient world. This is a world only known to me through history books and movies. For example, Greece and Rome especially are art centers to which all Europe looks. Pantheons, sculptures, statues, and other ruins of Roman cities are example of this big, valuable collection of antique art. Because at that time Rome dominated Europe, it represents almost all of ancient civilization.

Using the term civilization remind me that it was a culture based on humanism, a system of thought interested in the development of human capacities but including a cult of divinities. Something that is even more interesting to me is the pagan face of this civilization, characterized by the greedy and common people. Can you imagine participating in a roman party with dancers and abundance of food and wine? A place where everything is luxurious and revolves around the emporer and his friends. I will be fascinated but lost at the same time.

After visiting every museum and important piece of art in Rome, it would be good to take a cruise along the Mediterranean Sea. There is nothing like a cruise to get relax. Relaxation is what I am going to need after visitng every museum and beautiful place in Rome and Greece. I don't know much about the night life in these places but it surely be good or at least with a good companion. A two weeks trip over the Greek Islands will be perfect, because it has the beauty of the islands itself and all these monuments as background. The environment and climate of an island are great. I have a passion for the water and the smooth sea breeze, it will be a place with sophisticated beauty.

Turkey is another place that I would like to visit on my trip, so at the end of this first month in Rome and Greece, and the last three weeks visiting the coast of the Mediterranean Sea, my next port is Turkey. Once there a turkish bath will be perfect to get ready to continue visiting more and more places. I am planing to go shopping in this area because I want to buy a persian carpet. I dont care how long it took me to find the right persian carpet, it has to be the one of my dreams. It has to be pretty because it's going to be the essential furniture in my living room and nobody better step on it with shoes on. The final weeks of my trip will be spend in Italy.

By this time I know that this three month trip is going to be almost impossible to me, because is not easy to afford it. But all these remote places have a unique beauty that I would like to see one day, a day not too far from today.

Luis Alonso

The Final Draft

Once your draft is returned to you, you will be ready to finish up your own essay by working on the editing by yourself with help from a writing center tutor or with help from a partner in class. Once you have finished the editing, neatly write or type a final draft for your instructor. Follow the guidelines for submitting final drafts outlined by your instructor, and don't forget to do one last proofreading. You are responsible for mistakes, even if they are typographical ones made by your typist.

Sample Student Essay for Writing to Inform

Here is an example of a short essay in two drafts. Read draft 1 and comment on it yourself before reading the peer reviewer's comments. Can you add to the reviewer's comments? Notice how the writer tries to develop the second draft in response to the peer reviewer's comments.

Draft 1

WHAT IS A REAL ATHLETE?

Today when it's so popular to be in good physical shape it's interesting to think about what a real athlete is. In the last ten years has the participation in sport activities increased enormous. It began with the jogging wave which rinse over us and caused some kind of jogging hysteria. After the jogging wave came the bodybuilding, and now we are up in the middle of the workout and body work. But are the people who participate in those trendy activities real athletes? Of course some of them are, but alot of them are not. Most of them are just practising because its modern and because everyone else does it. They have the right assessories and equipments but they have forgotten the heart.

A real athlete loves his sport and will never think about   2 start with something else. He is one whit his sport, and the sport affect him so much so it's a way of being.

I think its good that its modern to participate in different   3 sport activities but it can be dangerous for the specific sport if too many trends affect people in the sport. Because when a new sport introduces as the right one, a lot of people will leave the sport they are participating in now and start with the new one. That's why every sport need pure athletes who don't care about trendsetters and other circumstances, just because they love their sport. My conclusion is that every sport needs real athletes for survive.

Niclas Karlsson

Draft 2

Today, when it's so popular to be in good physical shape,   1 it's interesting to think about what a real athlete is. In the last ten years the participation in sport activities has in- creased enormous. It began with the jogging wave which washed over us and caused some kind of jogging hysteria. After the jogging wave people started to be interested in bodybuilding, aerobics and workouts. But are the people who participate in those trendy activities real athletes? Of course, some of them are, but alot of them are not. Most of them are just practicing because its modern, and because everybody else does it. They have the right equipment and accessories, but they have forgotten the most important, the heart.

A real athlete loves his sport, and it's no superficial love,   2 it's deeply rooted in his soul. He has grown up with a specific sport, and he know the history and the rules. He wants to

Peer Review 4
Writing to Inform

Writer: *Niclas Karlsson*
Peer Reviewer: *Ivan Fernandez*

1. What did you think was most interesting?

I like the topic. The first paragraph is good.

2. What is the purpose?

to explain what is an athlete

3. What is the thesis?

A real athlete loves his sport and will never think about start with something else.

4. Are there any places where you want more information?

the middle doesn't have any examples. Maybe write more about what new sports have a bad effect on old ones. Give more detail on what he's saying in second paragraph

5. Are there any parts that are not related to the thesis?

no

make influence on the sport in the future, contribute to giving it good renown, and a lot of participators. He gets many good side effects for his love of the sport. He doesn't smoke, he drinks a minimal doze of booze and his whole life-style affects in many positive ways his interest.

I think it's good that it's popular to participate in different sport activities, but it can be dangerous for the specific sport

3

if too many fads affect the people in the sport. I mean, if a new sport is introduced as the in thing, many of the people who are not real athletes will leave the activity they carry on now for the new one. It can be a death blow for the hole sport, and for those people who have invest money in the activity. I can, as an example, tell you about the skateboard wave in Sweden. As the demand on skateboards and appliances increased, shops grew up as mushrooms from the earth. The municipalities built up skateboard houses where interested people, most young, could meet and carry on their favorite activity. These investments cost a lot of money, but they thought it was well used money because a lot of the young people had something to do. After about one and a half year was it not fun any more, and many of the people didn't want to use skateboard anymore. The result was that the shops filed petitions and the municipalities lost a lot of money. The big problem was that the sport missed the real athletes, significant actors, who could take care about the sport, and try to stop the downward trend, it died out in two years.

My conclusion is that every sport needs real athletes for 4 survive. People who don't care about trendsetters and any other circumstances who affect human being of today. Their love for the sport is strong enough to avoid any kind of influence.

◆ DISCUSSION QUESTIONS

1. What are the major revisions?

2. Is this draft better? If so, why?

3. What is the essay's organization? What is the purpose of each paragraph?

4. Note that the thesis is still in the second paragraph? Do you think this is effective?

5. How has the second paragraph been changed?

6. Does the third paragraph relate well to the thesis?

7. Notice that as the writer adds more material, he naturally makes more mistakes, but they can be corrected with a thorough editing in the next draft.

The instructor read draft 1, the peer review sheet, and draft 2, then commented on the improvements in development. For this particular assignment, the instructor made only a few comments on draft 2 that would lead to further revision and concentrated on assisting the writer with editing by suggesting a few more idiomatic expressions and by pointing out grammar and usage errors. If you do not recognize the abbreviations the instructor has used, refer to the instructor's marks sheet in Appendix B.

This is what draft 2 looked like when it was returned to the writer.

Draft 2

(with instructor's marks)

Today, when it's so popular to be in good physical shape, it's interesting to think about what a real athlete is. In the last ten years the participation in sport activities has increased enor-

good intro   mous. It began with the jogging wave   *adv.*   which washed over us and caused some kind of jogging hysteria. After the jogging wave people started to be interested in bodybuilding, aerobics and workouts. But are the people who participate in those trendy activities real athletes? Of course, some of them are, but alot of them are not. Most of   *sp*   them are just practicing because its   *sp*   modern, and because everybody else does it. They have the right equipment and accessories, but they have forgotten the most important, the heart.

A real athlete loves his sport, and it's no superficial love, it's deeply   *c.s.*   rooted in his soul. He has grown up with a specific sport, and he know the   *agr.*

history and the rules. He wants <u>to</u> <u>make</u> influence on the sport in the future, contribute to giving it good renown, and a lot of <u>participators</u>. He gets many good side effects for his love of the sport. He doesn't smoke, he drinks a minimal <u>doze of booze</u> and his whole life-style affects in many positive ways his interest.

to have

look up the noun for the verb "participate"

amount of alcohol

    I think <u>its</u> good that it is popular to participate in different sport activities, but it can be dangerous for the specific sport if too many trends affect people in the sport. I mean, if a new sport <u>introduce as the in thing</u>, <u>alot</u> of people who are not real athletes will leave the activity they carry on now for the new one. It can be a death blow for the <u>hole</u> sport, and for those people who have <u>invest</u> money in the activity. I can, as an example, tell you about the skateboard wave in Sweden. As the demand <u>on</u> skateboards and appliances increased, shops grew up as mushrooms from the earth. The municipalities built up skateboard houses where interested people, most young, could meet and carry on their favorite activity. These investments cost a lot of money, but they thought it was well used money because a lot of the young people had something to do. After about one and a half year <u>was it not</u>

sp

is introduced as the latest thing

sp
verb form

good additions for detail

WW

could you divide this into several paragraphs and expand?

word order

fun any more, and many of the people
didn't want to use skateboard anymore. The result was that the shops
filed petitions and the municipalities
lost a lot of money. The big problem   (vb)
was that the sport <u>missed</u> the real ath-   *was missing*
letes, significant actors, who could
take care about the sport, and try to
stop the downward tren<u>d,</u> it died out   *c.s.*
in two years.

My conclusion is that every sport
needs real athletes for <u>survive</u>. People   *survival frag.*
who don't care about trendsetters and
I don't understand. Could you be more specific? any other circumstances who affect
human bein<u>g</u> of today. Their love for
the sport is strong enough to avoid
any kind of influence.

In the third draft, the writer did some editing but not much revision,
perhaps because he did not yet understand how thoroughly most writers
revise their work, adding and deleting paragraphs, and reordering the
material before it is given a final editing.

Rather than reading his corrections, write out a third draft yourself,
doing the necessary editing and noting where you would make revisions
if it were your essay. Consider also how you could make changes to
avoid the sexism reflected in his constant use of "he" for the athlete.
Aren't there great female athletes as well?

Chapter Four

THE AMERICAN WAY
Writing to Analyze

Writing represents a unique mode of learning—not merely valuable, not merely special, but unique.

—Janet Emig

Richard Rodriguez   (1944–)

Richard Rodriguez, son of Mexican-American parents, received his B. A. from Stanford University and his M. A. from Columbia University. Rather than pursuing his original intention to have a career in teaching, he turned down offers from universities in order to take other jobs and do freelance writing. He has held a Fulbright Fellowship and a National Endowment for the Humanities Fellowship for study on Renaissance British literature. He won the Christopher Award in 1982 for Hunger of Memory: The Education of Richard Rodriguez, *in which he speaks against bilingual education as an official policy.*

The following is an article originally published in Harper's *magazine in 1984. The title refers to traditional America—the America dominated by white Anglo-Saxon Protestant values fostered by the early British settlers. Rodriguez speaks here of all the diversity that recent immigrants have brought to our culture and suggests that diversity is the true "America" more than the melting pot ever was. This is an especially challenging reading because of Rodriguez' rich vocabulary and his use of figures of speech.*

Before you read, write for 10 minutes in your journal on what you think "America" means. Then as you read, jot down questions you have about the meaning of specific portions of the text.

Does America Still Exist?

For the children of immigrant parents the knowledge comes easier. America exists everywhere in the city—on billboards, frankly in the smell of French fries and popcorn. It exists in the pace: traffic lights, the assertions of neon,[1] the mysterious bong-bong-bong through the atriums[2] of department stores. America exists as the voice of the crowd, a menacing sound—the high nasal accent of American English.   1

When I was a boy in Sacramento (California, the fifties), people would ask me, "Where you from?" I was born in this country, but I knew the question meant to decipher my darkness, my looks.   2

---

[1] Glowing neon signs used in advertising meaning here that advertising assaults the senses or surrounds everyone.

[2] A signal that echoes through the large entry or central floor of department stores.

My mother once instructed me to say, "I am an American of Mexican   3
descent." By the time I was nine or ten, I wanted to say, but dared not
reply, "I am an American."

Immigrants come to America and, against hostility or mere loneli-   4
ness, they recreate a homeland in the parlor, tacking up postcards or
calendars of some impossible blue—lake or sea or sky. Children of
immigrant parents are supposed to perch on a hyphen between two
countries. Relatives assume the achievement as much as anyone. Relatives are, in any case, surprised when the child begins losing old ways.
One day at the family picnic the boy wanders away from their spiced
food and faceless stories to watch other boys play baseball in the
distance.

There is sorrow in the American memory, guilty sorrow for having   5
left something behind—Portugal, China, Norway. The American story is
the story of immigrant children and of their children—children no
longer able to speak to grandparents. The memory of exile becomes
inarticulate as it passes from generation to generation, along with wedding rings and pocket watches—like some mute stone in a wad of old
lace. Europe. Asia. Eden.

But, it needs to be said, if this is a country where one stops being   6
Vietnamese or Italian, this is a country where one begins to be an
American. America exists as a culture and a grin, a faith and a shrug. It is
clasped in a handshake, called by a first name.

As much as the country is joined in a common culture, however,   7
Americans are reluctant to celebrate the process of assimilation. We
pledge allegiance to diversity. America was born Protestant and bred
Puritan, and the notion of community we share is derived from a
seventeenth-century faith:[3] Presidents and the pages of ninth-grade
civics readers[4] yet proclaim the orthodoxy: We are gathered together—
but as individuals, with separate pasts, distinct destinies. Our society is
as paradoxical as a Puritan congregation: We stand together, alone.

Americans have traditionally defined themselves by what they re-   8
fused to include. As often, however, Americans have struggled, turned in
good conscience at last to assert the great Protestant virtue of tolerance.
Despite outbreaks of nativist frenzy,[5] America has remained an immigrant country, open and true to itself.

[3]Reference to the Protestant settlers of America, especially Puritans, who left Europe
for religious freedom.

[4] Civics is a study of government in the American public schools.

[5] Highly emotional reactions on the part of long-time settlers, usually Anglo-Saxon,
against more recent immigrants.

Against pious emblems of rural America—soda fountain, Elks hall,[6] 9
Protestant church, and now shopping mall—stands the cold-hearted
city, crowded with races and ambitions, curious laughter, much that is
odd. Nevertheless, it is the city that has most truly represented America.
In the city, however, the millions of singular lives have had no richer
notion of wholeness to describe them than the idea of pluralism.[7]

   "Where you from?" the American asks the immigrant child. "Mex- 10
ico," the boy learns to say.

   Mexico, the country of my blood ancestors, offers formal contrast to 11
the American achievement. If the United States was formed by Protestant individualism, Mexico was shaped by a medieval Catholic dream of
one world. The Spanish journeyed to Mexico to plunder, and they may
have gone, in God's name, with an arrogance peculiar to those who
intend to convert. But through the conversion, the Indian converted the
Spaniard. A new race was born, the *mestizo,*[8] wedding European to
Indian. José Vasconcelos, the Mexican philosopher, has celebrated this
New World creation, proclaiming it the "cosmic race."

   Centuries later, in a San Francisco restaurant, a Mexican-American 12
lawyer of my acquaintance says, in English, over *salade niçoise,* that he
does not intend to assimilate into gringo[9] society. His claim is echoed by
a chorus of others (Italian-Americans, Greeks, Asians) in this era of
ethnic pride. The melting pot has been retired, clanking, into the museum of quaint disgrace, alongside Aunt Jemima and the Katzenjammer
Kids.[10] But resistance to assimilation is characteristically American. It
only makes clear how inevitable the process of assimilation actually is.

   For generations, this has been the pattern. Immigrant parents have 13
sent their children to school (simply, they thought) to acquire the
"skills" to survive in the city. The child returned home with a voice his
parents barely recognized or understood, couldn't trust, and didn't like.

   In eastern cities—Philadelphia, New York, Boston, Baltimore—class 14
after class gathered immigrant children to women (usually women) who
stood in front of rooms full of children, changing children. So also for
me in the 1950s. Irish-Catholic nuns. California. The old story. The
hyphen tipped to the right, away from Mexico and toward a confusing
but true American identity.

   [6] The Elks are a secret fraternity whose members get together for social functions in a
building called a lodge or hall.

   [7] A condition where many religious, ethnic, and racial groups coexist harmoniously.

   [8] Latin American name for people who are half native Indian and half European.

   [9] Derogatory term for an American.

   [10] Aunt Jemima: picture of an old black woman on boxes of pancake mix. Katzenjammer Kids: an American comic strip that has run since 1897.

I speak now in the chromium American accent of my grammar school 15
classmates—Billy Reckers, Mike Bradley, Carol Schmidt, Kathy O'Grady.
. . . I believe I became like my classmates, became German, Polish, and
(like my teachers) Irish. And because assimilation is always reciprocal,
my classmates got something of me. (I mean sad eyes; belief in the Indian
Virgin; a taste for sugar skulls on the Feast of the Dead.[11] In the blending,
we became what our parents could never have been, and we carried
America one revolution further.

"Does America still exist?" Americans have been asking the question 16
for so long that to ask it again only proves our continuous link. But
perhaps the question deserves to be asked with urgency—now. Since the
black civil rights movement of the 1960s, our tenuous notion of a
shared public life has deteriorated notably.

The struggle of black men and women did not eradicate racism, but it 17
became the great moment in the life of America's conscience. Water
hoses, bulldogs, blood—the images, rendered black, white, rectangular,
passed into living rooms.

It is hard to look at a photograph of a crowd taken, say, in 1890 or in 18
1930 and not notice the absence of blacks. (It becomes an impertinence
to wonder if America *still* exists.)

In the sixties, other groups of Americans learned to champion their 19
rights by analogy to the black civil rights movement. But the heroic
vision faded. Dr. Martin Luther King Jr. had spoken with Pauline[12]
eloquence of a nation that would unite Christian and Jew, old and
young, rich and poor. Within a decade, the struggles of the 1960s were
reduced to a bureaucratic competition for little more than pieces of a
representational pie. The quest for a portion of power became an end in
itself. The metaphor for the American city of the 1970s was a committee: one black, one woman, one person under thirty . . .

If the small town had sinned against America by too neatly defining 20
who could be an American, the city's sin was a romantic secession. One
noticed the romanticism in the antiwar movement—certain demonstra-
tors who demonstrated a lack of tact or desire to persuade and seemed
content to play secular protestants. One noticed the romanticism in the
competition among members of "minority groups" to claim the status
of Primary Victim. To Americans unconfident of their common identity,
minority standing became a way of asserting individuality. Middle-class
Americans—men and women clearly not the primary victims of social
oppression—brandished their suffering with exuberance.

[11] Mexican version of a Roman catholic festival on All Saints Day (November 1).

[12] Refers to the apostle Paul in the Bible.

The dream of a single society probably died with *The Ed Sullivan* 21
Show.[13] The reality of America persists. Teenagers pass through big-city
high schools banded in racial groups, their collars turned up to a uni-
form shrug. But then they graduate to jobs at the phone company or in
banks, where they end up working alongside people unlike themselves.
Typists and tellers walk out together at lunchtime.

It is easier for us as Americans to believe the obvious fact of our 22
separateness—easier to imagine the black and white Americas proph-
esied by the Kerner report[14] broken glass, street fires)—than to recognize the reality of a city street at lunchtime. Americans are wedded by
proximity to a common culture. The panhandler[15] at one corner is
related to the pamphleteer at the next who is related to the banker who
is kin to the Chinese old man wearing an MIT sweatshirt. In any true
national history, Thomas Jefferson begets Martin Luther King Jr. who
begets the Gray Panthers.[16] It is because we lack a vision of ourselves
entire—the city street is crowded and we are each preoccupied with
finding our own way home—that we lack an appropriate hymn.

Under my window now passes a little white girl softly rehearsing to 23
herself a Motown obbligato.

◆ COMPREHENSION/DISCUSSION QUESTIONS

1. What do you think the author means by his title?

2. What is the definition of America or Americans that is implied in
   his first paragraph?

3. Why do you suppose he "dared not" say he was American when
   he was a child?

4. What is the cause of the sorrow he refers to in paragraph 5?

5. Explain "America exists as a culture and a grin, a faith and a
   shrug. It is clasped in a handshake, called by a first name" [6].

6. What is amusing about the first sentence of paragraph 12?

---

[13] A popular T.V. variety show in the 1950s.

[14] Report of the Kerner commission, appointed by President Johnson to look into U.S.
racial relations (1968).

[15] Beggar.

[16] A group of politically active older citizens; the name was imitative of the Black
Panthers, a radical black group.

7. What does "the melting pot" mean? Why does Rodriguez say it has been retired [12]?

8. In paragraph 14, Rodriguez refers again to the hyphen, a figure of speech he used in paragraph 4. Can you explain the meaning of the first and second references?

9. What does "Americans are wedded by proximity to a common culture" mean?

10. Why do you think he says it is easier for Americans to think of themselves as separate than as united?

11. Rodriguez says we are so preoccupied with ourselves as individuals that we don't have one national song. In fact, we have several. His final image is a reference to music. What is Motown? What is an obbligato? Could this be our national song? If so, how is it connected to the point he has been making throughout his essay?

12. Rodriguez is describing cultural attitudes of the 1980s, not earlier periods of American history. In what ways does Rodriguez think attitudes toward ethnic identity are different now? (Refer to paragraph 16 for one clue.)

13. Did you have any particular feelings about this selection?

14. Did anything Rodriguez wrote about relate to your own experience?

♦ VOCABULARY

Define the following words, paying particular attention to the meaning in the context of the reading selection. In your definitions, underline any synonyms of the vocabulary word that you think could be used in the original sentence. For example, "tenuous" is used in paragraph 16. It means "problematic, open to question, weak." Either "problematic" or "weak" could be used in the original sentence.

arrogance [11]	brandish [20]
assertion [1]	chromium [15]
atrium [1]	decipher [2]
beget [22]	emblem [9]
billboard [1]	exile [5]

exuberance [20]   proximity [22]

hyphen [4]   reciprocal [15]

inarticulate [5]   secession [20]

mute [5]   wad [5]

nasal [1]

♦ FIGURES OF SPEECH

Study and explain the following expressions.

1. "The memory of exile becomes inarticulate as it passes from generation to generation, along with wedding rings and pocket watches—like some mute stone in a wad of old lace" [5].

2. "We pledge allegiance to diversity" [7].

3. "We stand together, alone" [7].

4. "I speak now in the chromium American accent of my grammar school classmates . . ." [15].

5. "Within a decade, the struggles of the 1960s were reduced to a bureaucratic competition for little more than pieces of a representational pie" [19].

6. "The metaphor for the American city of the 1970s was a committee: one black, one woman, one person under thirty . . ."[19].

♦ JOURNAL ENTRY

Write for 20 minutes about your reactions to Rodriguez' essay. You might, for instance, think about whether you agree with some of the characteristics he mentioned as typical of Americans or whether you believe Americans should be more concerned or less concerned about their ethnic heritage.

♦ SMALL GROUP WORK: CONSENSUS BUILDING

Divide into small groups of 3–4 students. Choose a recorder and then brainstorm aloud for 5 minutes on what phrases best describe what you think most new immigrants or foreigners (whether you are one or not) believe is true about "America" (whether it is true or not). Remember to listen without criticism to everyone's ideas while the recorder jots down key words. Then spend 10 minutes reducing the list to the five phrases everyone can agree upon.

When the small groups come together as a whole class, have each recorder put the five phrases on the board. Then the class should try to come to a consensus on five from the combined lists. Spend a few more minutes discussing whether the characteristics are true or not.

Follow-up Writing   Write a few paragraphs on why or how people in other countries have gotten certain impressions of America that may not be true.

William J. Fulbright   *(1905–)*

Former U.S. Senator, William J. Fulbright, holds his B. A. degree from Oxford University (England) as well as an M. A. from Oxford and an LL.B. (law degree) from George Washington University. He taught law there and practiced in Washington, D.C. He was a United States Senator from Arkansas from 1945 until 1974, and was best known as chairman of the powerful Senate Committee on Foreign Relations. He co-sponsored the Fulbright-Hayes Act that helped to create prestigious Fulbright Fellowships for faculty and student exchanges between the United States and nations throughout the world.

This selection is taken from Fulbright's book, The Arrogance of Power, *written in 1966. At the beginning of this portion, he refers to three great American politicians. Abraham Lincoln, the president who presided at the time of the Civil War, signed the Emancipation Proclamation (1863) abolishing slavery in this country. Adlai Stevenson, a Senator from Illinois, was never president, although he ran for the office several times. He was known for his advocacy of liberal and humane causes. Theodore Roosevelt (not to be confused with Franklin D. Roosevelt) was president from 1901 to 1909, an era when the United States was just beginning to emerge as a powerful nation in world politics. His foreign policy was based on the assumption that our form of government is superior and that we have an obligation to spread our influence and protect democracy in the Western Hemisphere.*

Before you read, write for 10 minutes in your journal on whether you think America has a right, a duty, or no business interfering with another nation's government.

The Two Americas

There are two Americas. One is the America of Lincoln and Adlai   1
Stevenson; the other is the America of Teddy Roosevelt and the modern superpatriots.[1] One is generous and humane, the other narrowly egotistical; one is self-critical, the other self-righteous;[2] one is sensible, the other romantic; one is good-humored, the other solemn; one is inquiring, the other pontificating;[3] one is moderate, the other filled with

[1] Those who are excessively patriotic.

[2] Someone who believes he or she is always right.

[3] Preaching.

passionate intensity; one is judicious and the other arrogant in the use of power.

We have tended in the years of our great power to puzzle the world by presenting to it now the one face of America, now the other, and sometimes both at once. Many people all over the world have come to regard America as being capable of magnanimity and farsightedness but no less capable of pettiness and spite. The result is an inability to anticipate American actions which in turn makes for apprehension and a lack of confidence in American aims.

The inconstancy of American foreign policy is not an accident but an expression of two distinct sides of the American character. Both are characterized by a kind of moralism, but one is the morality of decent instincts tempered by the knowledge of human imperfection and the other is the morality of absolute self-assurance fired by the crusading spirit. The one is exemplified by Lincoln, who found it strange, in the words of his second Inaugural Address, "that any man should dare to ask for a just God's assistance in wringing their bread from the sweat of other men's faces,"[4] but then added: "let us judge not, that we be not judged." The other is exemplified by Theodore Roosevelt, who in his December 6, 1904, Annual Message to Congress, without question or doubt as to his own and his country's capacity to judge right and wrong, proclaimed the duty of the United States to exercise an "internal police power" in the hemisphere on the ground that "Chronic wrongdoing, or an impotence which results in a general loosening of the ties of civilized society, may in America . . . ultimately require intervention by some civilized nation . . ." Roosevelt of course never questioned that the "wrongdoing" would be done by our Latin neighbors and we of course were the "civilized nation" with the duty to set things right.

After twenty-five years of world power the United States must decide which of the two sides of its national character is to predominate—the humanism of Lincoln or the arrogance of those who would make America the world's policeman. One or the other will help shape the spirit of the age—unless of course we refuse to choose, in which case America may come to play a less important role in the world, leaving the great decisions to others.

The current tendency is toward a more strident and aggressive American foreign policy, which is to say, toward a policy closer to the spirit of Theodore Roosevelt than of Lincoln. We are still trying to build bridges to the communist countries and we are still, in a small way, helping the poorer nations to make a better life for their people; but we are also involved in a growing war against Asian communism,[5] a war which

[4] A reference to Lincoln's distaste for slavery.

[5] The Vietnam War.

began and might have ended as a civil war if American intervention had not turned it into a contest of ideologies,[6] a war whose fallout is disrupting our internal life and complicating our relations with most of the world.

Our national vocabulary has changed with our policies. A few years 6 ago we were talking of détente[7] and building bridges, of five-year plans in India and Pakistan, or agricultural cooperatives in the Dominican Republic, and land and tax reform all over Latin America. Today these subjects are still discussed in a half-hearted and desultory way but the focus of power and interest has shifted to the politics of war. Diplomacy has become largely image-making, and instead of emphasizing plans for social change, the policy-planners and political scientists are conjuring up "scenarios" of escalation and nuclear confrontation and "models" of insurgency and counter-insurgency.

The change in words and values is no less important than the change 7 in policy, because words *are* deeds and style *is* substance insofar as they influence men's minds and behavior. What seems to be happening, as Archibald MacLeish[8] has put it, is that "the feel of America in the world's mind" has begun to change and faith in "the idea of America" has been shaken for the world and, what is more important, for our own people. MacLeish is suggesting—and I think he is right—that much of the idealism and inspiration is disappearing from American policy, but he also points out that they are not yet gone and by no means are they irretrievable:

> . . . if you look closely and listen well, there is a human warmth, a human meaning which nothing has killed in almost twenty years and which nothing is likely to kill. . . . What has always held this country together is an idea—a dream if you will—a large and abstract thought of the sort the realistic and the sophisticated may reject but mankind can hold to.[9]

The foremost need of American foreign policy is a renewal of dedica- 8 tion to an "idea that mankind can hold to"—not a missionary idea full of pretensions about being the world's policemen but a Lincolnian idea expressing that powerful strand of decency and humanity which is the true source of America's greatness.

---

[6] Sets of beliefs of an individual, a country, or a culture; can have a negative connotation that implies rigid thinking.

[7] A lessening of tensions, especially between the U.S. and Russia.

[8] American poet and dramatist (1892–1982).

[9] Archibald MacLeish, Address to the Congress of the International Publishers Assoc., May 31, 1965 [Fulbright's note].

♦ COMPREHENSION/DISCUSSION QUESTIONS

1. What are the two faces of American policy according to former Senator Fulbright?

2. Who is it that has "an inability to anticipate American actions" (paragraph 2)?

3. What is the difference between the two words "moralism" and "morality," used in paragraph 3?

4. Explain ". . . one is the morality of decent instincts tempered by the knowledge of human imperfection and the other is the morality of absolute self-assurance fired by the crusading spirit" (paragraph 3).

5. Do you think that America's entry into World War II and her entry into Vietnam could illustrate each type of morality on the part of the American government? Why or why not?

6. Why does Fulbright refer to our world power having existed for twenty-five years at the time he wrote this?

7. A footnote said that "the growing war against Asian communism" was a reference to the Vietnam War. In what way was this war a "contest of ideologies?"

8. What change in American foreign policy seems to worry Fulbright the most?

9. Who do you think Archibald MacLeish means by "the sophisticated"? Why would they reject a dream which mankind could hold to?

10. What does Fulbright want American foreign policy to be?

11. Do you think he is writing for a well-educated audience? Why?

12. How would his ideas affect decisions that will be made in Washington about the Middle East or Central America?

13. Can you think of any examples of the two faces of the American character showing in recent American actions in the world?

14. Are there any aspects of current American foreign policy that worry you?

♦ VOCABULARY

Define the following words, paying particular attention to their meaning in context. In defining the words, use at least one synonym which could be used in the sentence from the reading selection (a thesaurus will be useful for this exercise).

conjure [6]	impotence [3]
desultory [6]	inconstancy [3]
egotistical [1]	insurgency [6]
escalation [6]	irretrievable [7]
exemplified [3]	magnanimity [2]
fallout [5]	moralism [3]
hemisphere [3]	pontificating [1]
humane [1]	scenario [6]
humanism [4]	spite [2]
ideology [5]	strand [8]
imperfection [3]	strident [5]

◆ JOURNAL ENTRY

Write for 20 minutes in your journal on your interests in politics. Is it a boring or a very interesting subject to you? Do you know much about international politics? Would you want to be a politician? Why or why not?

◆ SMALL GROUP WORK: CONSENSUS BUILDING

Divide into small groups of 3–4 students and choose a recorder. Then brainstorm two lists: one of the positive qualities of Americans' way of relating to other countries and the other of the negative. List quickly everything that anyone in the group mentions without discussion or criticism (5–7 minutes). Then the group should reduce the list by consensus to the five most "typical" (or substitute another word) qualities on each of the two lists (5–7 minutes). The recorders from each group should present the results, and the class as a whole should discuss any differences in the lists and come to a consensus on a list of five qualities (10 minutes).

Follow-up Writing Write a few paragraphs on what is most positive or most negative about America's relationship to other nations. Include why this quality is the best or the worst.

William Ouchi   (1943–)

William Ouchi was born in Honolulu and has taken an active interest in Asian/American relations. Educated at Stanford University and the University of Chicago, he is now the director of Convergent Techs Corporation and serves on the Board of Directors of Leadership Education for Asian-Pacifics. After years of research and collaborative study, he published Theory Z: How American Business Can Meet the Japanese Challenge, *which he followed up a few years later with* The M-Form Society: How American Teamwork Can Recapture the Competitive Edge.

The following is an excerpt from Ouchi's very popular book, Theory Z. Ouchi describes differences between Japanese and American management styles that have led to the Japanese winning at a game that some think Americans invented, i.e., high productivity in business.

Before reading the selection, write in your journal for 10 minutes on anything you know about Japanese culture or Japanese products.

Japanese and American Work Ethics

Perhaps the most difficult aspect of the Japanese for Westerners to comprehend is the strong orientation to collective values, particularly a collective sense of responsibility. Let me illustrate with an anecdote about a visit to a new factory in Japan owned and operated by an American electronics company. The American company, a particularly creative firm, frequently attracts attention within the business community for its novel approaches to planning, organizational design, and management systems. As a consequence of this corporate style, the parent company determined to make a thorough study of Japanese workers and to design a plant that would combine the best of East and West. In their study they discovered that Japanese firms almost never make use of individual work incentives, such as piecework[1] or even individual performance appraisal tied to salary increases. They concluded that rewarding individual achievement and individual ability is always a good thing.

In the final assembly area of their new plant, long lines of young Japanese women wired together electronic products on a piece-rate

[1] Being paid for individual items produced.

system: the more you wired, the more you got paid. About two months after opening, the head foreladies[2] approached the plant manager. "Honorable[3] plant manager," they said humbly as they bowed, "we are embarrassed to be so forward, but we must speak to you because all of the girls have threatened to quit work this Friday." (To have this happen, of course, would be a great disaster for all concerned.) "Why," they wanted to know, "can't our plant have the same compensation system as other Japanese companies? When you hire a new girl, her starting wage should be fixed by her age. An eighteen-year-old should be paid more than a sixteen-year-old. Every year on her birthday, she should receive an automatic increase in pay. The idea that any of us can be more productive than another must be wrong, because none of us in final assembly could make a thing unless all of the other people in the plant had done their jobs right first. To single one person out as being more productive is wrong and is also personally humiliating to us." The company changed its compensation system to the Japanese model.

Another American company in Japan had installed a suggestion sys-   3
tem much as we have in the United States. Individual workers were encouraged to place suggestions to improve productivity into special boxes. For an accepted idea the individual received a bonus amounting to some fraction of the productivity savings realized from his or her suggestion. After a period of six months, not a single suggestion had been submitted. The American managers were puzzled. They had heard many stories of the inventiveness, the commitment, and the loyalty of Japanese workers, yet not one suggestion to improve productivity had appeared.

The managers approached some of the workers and asked why the   4
suggestion system had not been used. The answer: "No one can come up with a work improvement idea alone. We work together, and any ideas that one of us may have are actually developed by watching others and talking to others. If one of us was singled out for being responsible for such an idea, it would embarrass all of us." The company changed to a group suggestion system, in which workers collectively submitted suggestions. Bonuses were paid to groups which would save bonus money until the end of the year for a party at a restaurant or, if there was enough money, for family vacations together. The suggestions and productivity improvements rained down on the plant.

One can interpret these examples in two quite different ways. Per-   5
haps the Japanese commitment to collective values is an anachronism that does not fit with modern industrialism but brings economic success

---

[2] Rather than foremen or forewomen.

[3] A formal, typically Japanese form of address.

despite that collectivism. Collectivism seems to be inimical to the kind of maverick[4] creativity exemplified in Benjamin Franklin, Thomas Edison, and John D. Rockefeller.[5] Collectivism does not seem to provide the individual incentive to excel which has made a great success of American enterprise. Entirely apart from its economic effects, collectivism implies a loss of individuality, a loss of the freedom to be different, to hold fundamentally different values from others.

The second interpretation of the examples is that the Japanese collectivism is economically efficient. It causes people to work well together and to encourage one another to better efforts. Industrial life requires interdependence of one person on another. But a less obvious but far-reaching implication of the Japanese collectivism for economic performance has to do with accountability.   6

In the Japanese mind, collectivism is neither a corporate or individual goal to strive for nor a slogan to pursue. Rather, the nature of things operates so that nothing of consequence occurs as a result of individual effort. Everything important in life happens as a result of teamwork or collective effort. Therefore, to attempt to assign individual credit or blame to results is unfounded. . . .   7

The *shinkansen* or "bullet train"[6] speeds across the rural areas of Japan giving a quick view of cluster after cluster of farmhouses surrounded by rice paddies. This particular pattern did not develop purely by chance, but as a consequence of the technology peculiar to the growing of rice, the staple of the Japanese diet. The growing of rice requires the construction and maintenance of an irrigation system, something that takes many hands to build. More importantly, the planting and the harvesting of rice can only be done efficiently with the cooperation of twenty or more people. The "bottom line" is that a single family working alone cannot produce enough rice to survive, but a dozen families working together can produce a surplus. Thus the Japanese have had to develop the capacity to work together in harmony, no matter what the forces of disagreement or social disintegration, in order to survive.   8

Japan is a nation built entirely on the tips of giant, suboceanic volcanoes. Little of the land is flat and suitable for agriculture. Terraced hillsides make use of every available square foot of arable land. Small homes built very close together further conserve the land. Japan also suffers from natural disasters such as earthquakes and hurricanes. Tradi-   9

---

[4] A dissenter, someone who does not abide by the rules.

[5] Franklin (1706–1790), printer, writer, diplomat, and inventor; Edison (1847–1931), inventor in field of electricity; Rockefeller (1839–1937), capitalist and founder of the Standard Oil Company.

[6] High-speed train.

tionally homes are made of light construction materials, so a house falling down during a disaster will not crush its occupants and also can be quickly and inexpensively rebuilt. During the feudal period until the Meiji restoration of 1868, each feudal lord sought to restrain his subjects from moving from one village to the next for fear that a neighboring lord might amass enough peasants with which to produce a large agricultural surplus, hire an army and pose a threat. Apparently bridges were not commonly built across rivers and streams until the late nineteenth century, since bridges increased mobility between villages.

Taken all together, this characteristic style of living paints the picture of a nation of people who are homogeneous with respect to race, history, language, religion, and culture. For centuries and generations these people have lived in the same village next door to the same neighbors. Living in close proximity and in dwellings which gave very little privacy, the Japanese survived through their capacity to work together in harmony. In this situation, it was inevitable that the one most central social value which emerged, the one value without which the society could not continue, was that an individual does not matter.   10

To the Western soul this is a chilling picture of society. Subordinating individual tastes to the harmony of the group and knowing that individual needs can never take precedence over the interests of all is repellent to the Western citizen. But a frequent theme of Western philosophers and sociologists is that individual freedom exists only when people willingly subordinate their self-interests to the social interest. A society composed entirely of self-interested individuals is a society in which each person is at war with the other, a society which has no freedom. This issue, constantly at the heart of understanding society, comes up in every century, and in every society, whether the writer be Plato, Hobbes, or B. F. Skinner.[7] The question of understanding which contemporary institutions lie at the heart of the conflict between automatism[8] and totalitarianism[9] remains. In some ages, the kinship group, the central social institution, mediated between these opposing forces to preserve the balance in which freedom was realized; in other times the church or the government was most critical. Perhaps our present age puts the work organization as the central institution.   11

In order to complete the comparison of Japanese and American living situations, consider flight over the United States. Looking out of the window high over the state of Kansas, we see a pattern of a single   12

---

[7] All writers of social utopias. Plato (427–347 B.C.), *The Republic*; Thomas Hobbes (1588–1679), *Leviathan*; B. F. Skinner (1904–), *Walden Two*.

[8] Ability to function independently of outside influence; function without conscious control.

[9] Government by total control of the state over individual.

farmhouse surrounded by fields, followed by another single homestead surrounded by fields. In the early 1800s in the state of Kansas there were no automobiles. Your nearest neighbor was perhaps two miles distant; the winters were long, and the snow was deep. Inevitably, the central social values were self-reliance and independence. Those were the realities of that place and age that children had to learn to value.

The key to the industrial revolution was discovering that non-human 13 forms of energy substituted for human forms could increase the wealth of a nation beyond anyone's wildest dreams. But there was a catch. To realize this great wealth, non-human energy needed huge complexes called factories with hundreds, even thousands of workers collected into one factory. Moreover, several factories in one central place made the generation of energy more efficient. Almost overnight, the Western world was transformed from a rural and agricultural country to an urban and industrial state. Our technological advance seems to no longer fit our social structure: in a sense, the Japanese can better cope with modern industrialism. While Americans still busily protect our rather extreme form of individualism, the Japanese hold their individualism in check and emphasize cooperation.

♦ COMPREHENSION/DISCUSSION QUESTIONS

1. How would you describe the difference between the American and Japanese systems of management?

2. Do you think the Japanese compensation system mentioned in the first example is a good one?

3. What is the difference between "collectivism" and "individual incentive"?

4. Why does Japanese collectivism seem to work?

5. How has geography influenced the character of the two nations?

6. Give some examples that would support Ouchi's statement that "A society composed entirely of self-interested individuals is a society in which each person is at war with the other, a society which has no freedom" [11].

7. What does he mean by a conflict between automatism and totalitarianism [11].

8. Do you think it is true that "the work organization" or our workplaces should be the place where this conflict is worked out?

9. Restate the first sentence in paragraph 13 in your own words.

10. What associations do the words "collective values" bring to your mind? Do you think that "collectivism" has a negative connotation for some Americans? Why?

11. Did anything about this reading surprise you?

12. Thinking of examples from your own life, when is your work better accomplished as an individual and when is a collective system of work better?

13. Do you agree that the Japanese are better adapted to the industrial state?

14. From what you have read, do you think you would like to work for a Japanese company? Why or why not?

♦ VOCABULARY

Define the following words, paying particular attention to their meaning in context. Underline the synonyms in your definition which you think could be substituted for the vocabulary word.

accountability [6]	inimical [5]
amass [9]	interdependence [6]
anachronism [5]	inventiveness [3]
appraisal [1]	irrigation [8]
arable [9]	mediate [11]
disintegration [8]	orientation [1]
homogeneous [10]	self-reliance [12]
incentive [1]	

♦ IDIOMS

Study the meaning and use of the following idioms in context. Then try to write a sentence of your own using them.

1. "A good deal" [7]—very

2. "Bottom line" [8]—actually a figure of speech from accounting, meaning the last figure on a balance sheet that tells whether there is a positive or negative balance in the account.

3. "A catch" [13]—a trick or something unexpected.

4. "In check" [13]—under control.

♦ JOURNAL ENTRY

Write in your journal for 20 minutes on your reactions to the reading selection. Do you think the Japanese collectivism would work in the United States? Should we try it? Would you like to work under such a system?

♦ SMALL GROUP WORK

Let's assume for the sake of this exercise that a major problem has developed at your school, and the students have been asked to help solve it. It is a political problem—a student organization with a small number of members has invited a well-known businessman onto the campus to speak on the issue of exporting American technology. Unfortunately, he has just been arrested and charged by the police with possessing drugs. The president of the school has heard about this, and he objects, saying that the Board of Trustees (the name given at most American colleges and universities to those who govern the institution and help it raise money) will think this man has a bad character and should not be given an audience. The president suggests that the students surely could find someone to speak on the same issue who would be less controversial. The student organization refuses to cancel the invitation, saying that the man is innocent until proven guilty and that his knowledge in business has nothing to do with his personal life. Several other student organizations object because they think student activity fees should not be used for this speaker. The faculty demands that the man's freedom of speech be protected.

Now, your task is to brainstorm a solution that will make everyone happy—the president, the trustees, the student organization, and the other students. Divide into small groups of 3–4 students and brainstorm some solutions. After the initial 5 minutes of brainstorming, narrow the ideas down to one solution, taking no more than another 5 minutes. Reassemble and have the recorders present the solution to the whole class. Allow some time for discussion of these solutions.

Follow-up Writing   Write at least a paragraph or two discussing whether you could have come up with a better solution by brainstorming alone. If so, why? If not, why not? After the follow-up writing is completed, the instructor might ask several of the students to share their writing aloud and then discuss the connection between their answers and the Ouchi selection.

WRITING TO ANALYZE

In Chapter 3, we discussed purpose and suggested that it would determine your strategy in writing. To explain a subject, you chose to define it, describe it as a process, and/or categorize it in some way. In this chapter, since we are looking specifically at how to write an essay which *analyzes* a subject, you will want to think about several other strategies.

To analyze means to break a subject into parts for the purpose of explaining its causes and results, or how it compares or contrasts with something else. An analysis might answer the questions "in what way," "why," or "how." Consider, for example, the readings in this chapter. Richard Rodriguez answers the question "Does America Still Exist?" by analyzing different parts of the immigrant experience and by comparing the myth of assimilation with the reality of cultural diversity. William Fulbright analyzes American foreign policy by dividing it into two parts ("faces") and contrasting them. William Ouchi analyzes why the Japanese management style is successful by showing examples of collectivism, comparing it to American practices, and locating a cause for the development of the style in Japanese geography and cultural values.

As each of these writers illustrates, there are many ways to write an analysis. If, for instance, you wanted to write on something related to American sports, you might analyze what causes Americans to put so much money into sports. You could take the psychology of sports in America, the impact of T.V. broadcasting of major league sports, and the players' salaries as separate parts of the issue and analyze which are causes and which are results. Or, you might want to take one of these aspects and compare it to or contrast it with sports in another country. You will read several different examples of analysis in the following pages. One of the student essays compares educational opportunities in Brazil to those in the United States; another analyzes why spoken Japanese is easy to learn by discussing various parts of the language; and another contrasts life in Vietnam and America.

Whatever the strategy, when you are ready to begin your essay, the same techniques described in earlier chapters for drafting are used. The first step, then, is to do some prewriting, unless you want to use ideas you generated in your journal entries or from class discussions of the readings and small group work.

Prewriting

Brainstorming   Jot down words and phrases for five minutes on one of the following:

> the immigrant experience in the 1980s—what is different?

Americans as "police" of the world

how to resolve a particular political situation that worries you

competitiveness vs. cooperation—pros and cons

Or proceed with a discovery draft, if you already have in mind an idea, experience, event or phenomenon you want to analyze.

Mapping: Visualizing Connections   Another form of prewriting is called mapping. You start with one word in the middle of a page and then see how many ideas come to you as branches off that central idea. In "mapping" out each new idea, you are able to push your thinking further, and the map creates a pattern of relationships between major and minor ideas that is helpful in organizing your essay. (See the example of mapping below.)

Take an idea you had while reading one of the selections in this chapter, and create a map of related ideas. Think in terms of analyzing the relationship between parts of the idea.

MAPPING

◆ SMALL GROUP WORK

Write answers to the following questions about the ideas you have for the essay:

What is the topic you want to write on?

Why do you want to write about this topic?

What is your purpose?

What are you going to say about the topic?

What do you think your thesis might be?

Get together with a partner and discuss the answers each of you has given about your own topics. Help each other to clarify whether the purpose is to separate the topic into parts that can be analyzed by one or more of the strategies mentioned above. Then ask your partner, "What do you want to know about this subject?" His or her response should give you some additional ideas on what to include in your essay. Perhaps your partner's questions will suggest the need to look up some additional information on your topic.

◆ WRITING ASSIGNMENT

Take the prewriting and notes from the preceding discussion with your partner and write a full first draft. Your instructor will tell you the desired length for this draft. As you work on it, keep in mind your purpose, your audience, and your tentative thesis. Then save this draft until you have read the following section.

Drafting and Revising: Organizing Your Draft

In Chapter 3, the overall organization of an essay—the introduction, body, and conclusion—were mentioned so that you could keep that organization in mind as you were drafting. In the section that follows, methods of writing a good introduction and conclusion, as well as how to order your paragraphs, will be explained more fully.

You should keep in mind that early drafts are often not well organized because our minds do not necessarily function in a perfectly organized fashion. In fact, if the first draft is at all typical of most writers' drafts, then it reflects the way the writer was thinking, not necessarily the way the writing must be organized to make a reader understand. In the first draft we produce "writer-based" texts. This early writer-based draft is usually perfectly clear to the writer but may not be clear, logical, or even interesting to the reader. It must be turned into a "reader-based" text with thought given to leading the reader into the essay, making points clear through a logical, well-organized structure that ends up by making connections between points and drawing out the implications of the essay. In other words, we write first for ourselves, trying to put our thoughts into words, then we must reorganize those thoughts into a structure that will be understandable to someone else. One of the first considerations is to introduce the subject matter to the readers in a way that will make them want to read your essay and prepare them for what follows.

Introductions: Creating Interest   Read the following student essay comparing higher education in a developing country and in the United States. (Student writing is uncorrected.)

Sample Student Writing
EDUCATION IN BRAZIL

Education is considered an essential field by all govern- 1
ments in the world. Without education, one nation cannot become richer and improve the living conditions of its people. But to a nation that is still growing, its priorities are various, and the money the government has needs to be divided among those priorities. That gives a contrast that I think is shared by all the still growing nations—the necessity to give its people the education they deserve and the lack of money to make it possible.

Do you want to continue reading? Why or why not?

My country, Brazil, is one of those nations that believes 2
and tries, as much as possible, to give its people the necessary education. Brazil is a big country. It has good universities, but there are only a few in the whole country, compared with the number of students that are able to enter in a college. That makes it difficult for every Brazilian student to find a place in one, and very expensive too.

At the beginning of the year, there are selective tests in 3
each of those universities. In some cities, like Sao Paulo and Rio de Janeiro, almost 200,000 students (other cities have

less than that) take those tests to apply for one of the 3,500 places (or around that) that each university can offer. Some majors, such as medicine, have 35–45 applicants for each place available. That situation sometimes makes the really capable people nervous, and they fail once, twice, even more until they succeed or give up. Those who are lucky to get those places have their dreams to become someone one day started there, but less than a half go further than one year because of the expenses. The majority need to work to pay the tuition, books and accomodation, and when they start working, they don't find time to study, or the job they get does not cover the expenses of the university life and their own survival. Only the ones who can afford it, go through to the end, or they choose to go to a university in a foreign country.

One of the most demanded of [sought after] countries is the United States of America because of its high technology and great variety of majors. Of course, I cannot forget to mention the great number of colleges that exist. Everybody has a place in a school, if they wants to. The only thing that will say what school one can apply to is their grades in high school. Like everything in this world, school costs money, but students can ask for a scholarship to help them pay the expenses (it can be as an athlete, as an Army officer, or if they have a job, the company will pay for them, etc.) Anyway, all students are capable of finding the monetary help they need to continue their studies. Another important contrast is that almost every school in the United States has dormitories where the students can live, without worrying about increasing their expenses with rentals of any kind. But the most important of all is the fields of study that the universities cover. With the technology and knowledge that the United States has, its universities can offer any kind of matter you can think about.

The great difference between studying in one of the two countries is that the United States is richer than Brazil. Consequently, it has better conditions to offer to its people; new discoveries, new methods, and everything will be brought to the students up to date, even if those students are from a foreign country.

♦ DISCUSSION QUESTIONS

1. Look carefully at the introduction in the preceding example.

   Does it set a scene or introduce the subject?

   Does it include a clearly stated thesis?

   Does it make you want to read the essay? Why or why not?

2. If the answer is yes to each one of these questions, then the introduction is a good one. This particular introduction is adequate but not outstanding. Can you make some suggestions for improving it?

There are other ways to introduce an essay. An illustration or some interesting, specific facts are good for catching the reader's interest. The introduction may start out with a precise or narrow focus and broaden to the thesis (the opposite of the model above). Compare two drafts of another student essay whose writer tried to make her introduction more interesting in the second draft.

Draft 1

THE EFFECTS OF MUSIC

There are many both abstract and concrete objects in the environment that influence people's different feelings. One of these "objects," in this case an abstract one, is almost always surrounding us, although we sometime doesn't notice it—music. Different kind of music creates different kind of feelings, or effects, in people. Music can make us feel sentimental, happy or even irritated. Or it can make the person's already existing emotion stronger. 1

Do you want to keep reading? Why or why not?

First of all, we must all, most surely, have been in the situation when we turn on the radio and hear a tune that in- 2 stantly makes us feel happy or maybe sentimental. The feelings we get occur because we have heard the tune, or another tune very much alike this one, in connection to a certain feeling we had the last time we heard it. Lets say a girl won a price [prize] in a contest, and she got very happy. When she received the price, they played a tune for her. The next time she heard the tune, maybe on the radio, she felt happy because it reminded her of the happy moment she had before.

Music can also make us feel irritated in certain situations. 3 That is if music is disturbing us when we are trying to concentrate and focus our minds on something else. A good example of that situation is when students, living in dorms, are trying to study a subject in his or her own room. At the same time their neighbors, or sometimes their roommate wants to listen to music. It usually doesn't matter what kind of music it is—it makes you irritated anyway, because it is played in the wrong situation. But there are exceptions. Some people can mentally shutout the music and concentrate on their task, without getting irritated.

Finally music can, besides putting people in certain feel- 4 ings, make an already existing emotion or feeling stronger. A person that, for the moment, is feeling sad, can get even more sad if he or she listens to "sad" music. "Sad" music is usually music that has a slow rhythm and is tuned in the minor key. People attending a funeral can often describe the sad feeling increasing when the funeral music is played. On the other hand, people that are feeling happy for some reason, can get even more happy if they listen to "happy" music. That is usually the opposite of "sad" music, fast rhythm and tuned in the major key. An example of that is people dancing and enjoying themselves at a party. A "happy" tune is played and everybody starts smiling and feel the emotion of increasing exhilaration inside them as they move to the rhythm of the tune.

As we can see, there is a very strong correlation between 5 music and the way we feel at the moment. Music can bring us up and down on a emotion-curve like a yo-yo, depending on what kind of music it is, and in what kind of situation it is being played.

Annika Svensson

Draft 2

MUSIC AND MOODS

The little baby girl is lying in her cradle babbling with joy, as she listens to the noise of the rattle, that she is holding in her little hand. Her mother is joyfully singing one of her old favourite tunes that is playing on the radio, while she is cooking dinner. At the same time, the husband is silently growling something about, why it never can be quiet when he wants to read the paper. People's feelings are often influenced by objects both abstract and concrete in the environment. One of these "objects," in this case an abstract one, is almost always surrounding us, although we sometimes don't notice it—music. Different kinds of music creates different kinds of feelings, or effects, in people. Music can make us feel sentimental, happy or even irritated. Or it can make the person's already existing emotion stronger.

What is different about this introduction?
As you continue reading, watch how the example in the introduction is referred to again throughout the essay.

First of all, we must, most surely, all have been in the situation when we turn on the radio and hear a tune that instantly makes us feel happy or maybe sentimental. The feeling we get could depend on whether we have heard the tune, or another tune very much like this one, before in connection with a certain feeling we had the last time we heard it. Let us say that the mother, in the early illustration, was dancing to a tune by Sinatra with her husband for the first time when she heard it. Standing by the radio in the kitchen, maybe a year later, she hears the tune again. She reminds herself of the happy moment she had that specific time, and that makes her feel happy.

Music can also make us feel irritated in certain situations, 3 such as, when we are trying to concentrate and focus our minds on something else. A good example of that situation, with "disturbing" music, is when students, living in dorms, are trying to study in his or her own room. At the same time, their neighbors, or sometimes their roomate, wants to listen to music. The husband in the early illustration, was obvious irritated. He couldn't concentrate on his reading because of all noise around him. His wife was singing and his little child was playing with her rattle. It usually doesn't matter what kind of music it is—it makes you irritated anyway because it is played in the wrong situation. But some people get more disturbed, and irritated, by music like heavy metal and hard rock than by, for example, a ballad of a classic music composer. There are also some people that mentally can shut out the music and concentrate on their task without getting irritated and annoyed.

Finally, music can, besides put people in certain moods, 4 make an already existing emotion, or feeling stronger. A person that, for the moment is feeling sad, can get even more sad if he or she listens to "sad" music. "Sad" music is usually expained as music with slow rhythm and tuned in the minor key. Some pieces of classical music are played in this way, for example Mozarts "Concerto in A for clarinet." But there are also many modern pop-music tunes that seem to be made just to make us feel even more sad if we already feel sad and moody. I am thinking of all songs about broken hearts and unhappy love. "Sad" music is also the music played at funerals. People attending a funeral can often describe the sad feeling as increasing, when the music is being played. On the other hand, people that are feeling happy for some reason, can get even more happy if they listen to "happy" music. "Happy" music is usually the opposite of "sad" music—fast rhythm and tuned in the major key. An almost perfect example of that kid of music is carneval music, which the word itself makes us think about color, joy, movements and happiness. At a carneval almost everybody is happy and laughing. When the carneval music is being played the people get even more happy because they feel the emotion of increasing exhilaration inside themselves as they move to the rhythm and listen to the music. The little baby in the cradle was playing with her rattle and the sound of the rattle made the happy baby even more happy. It may have sound like a mini-carneval to the little girl.

As we can see, there is a very strong correlation between   5
music and the way we feel at the moment. Music can bring us up and down on an emotion-curve like a yo-yo, depending on what kind of music it is, and in what kind of situation it is being played.

♦ DISCUSSION QUESTION

Do you think the introduction to draft 2 is better? Why or why not?

Note as you work on your revisions that an introduction should

◊ Get the reader interested in what will follow.

◊ Provide background for the topic or provide some specific example or illustration (facts, a short narration or description, a quotation, or a question).

◊ Clearly state the thesis—preferably not as the first sentence but usually toward the end of the first paragraph; if not there, then in the second or third paragraph depending on the length of the essay.

◊ Let the reader know at least something about the major points to be discussed.

Order: Arranging Your Paragraphs   While writing your discovery draft or during the early stages of prewriting, you will decide on your purpose and your tentative thesis, which may naturally imply some order for your body paragraphs. In Chapter 3, for instance, you read about chronological order—the most natural order for an essay describing a process—and about other possibilities for different types of writing. For an analysis there are many choices.

Comparison and Contrast   If you want to compare or contrast two subjects, you can choose to discuss one of them completely, then discuss the other one. Or, you may want to discuss points of comparison or contrast by taking up examples from both subjects together as you compare them point by point. For example, if the topic is education in your home country and in the United States, the organization of your paper might look like either [A] or [B]:

[A]

I. Introduction

II. University in your country
    A.   Who attends
    B.   What it costs
    C.   What majors are offered
    D.   Where students live

III. University in the United States
    A.   Who attends
    B.   What it costs
    C.   What majors are offered
    D.   Where students live

IV. Conclusion

[B]

I. Introduction

II. Who attends university in your country and in the United States.

III. What are the costs of a university education in both countries.

IV. Where do university students live while attending university in each of the countries

V. Conclusion

Each section identified by a Roman numeral might be one paragraph or more. What is important is to note the two different patterns of organization and to think about following one rather than mixing them. The sections might be arranged in several different ways. In other words, the writer can decide, for the preceding example, what difference it makes whether the student body or the costs are described first. It is always a good idea to leave the best or most powerful points until the end of the essay, but if there is no "natural" order, the writer must decide what order is most effective in making certain points or for a certain audience.

◆ DISCUSSION QUESTIONS

1. Does the Fulbright essay follow a pattern?

2. Which pattern does the student essay on education in Brazil follow?

3. In the student paper, did the writer take up the same points for both sides in showing the contrast between them?

4. What would have been the effect if the writer had reversed the two body paragraphs?

Cause and Effect   If you are writing an analysis of causes and effects, you need to decide which you want to emphasize, the causes or the effects. You might briefly explain a situation and then devote most of the paper to analyzing the effects (or results). You might do the opposite by spending most of your time discussing the causes. One way to order the paragraphs after you have decided upon the emphasis is to lead up to the most important points. In other words, you may go from least to most important causes, or perhaps the simplest to the most complex effects, so that the reader is given the strongest impression toward the end of your essay.

◆ DISCUSSION QUESTIONS

1. Look back at the essay on music. This is clearly an essay analyzing effects. What is the order of the paragraphs?

2. Do you think the order shows any sort of progression? Is it an acccptablc order?

3. What would happen if the order were changed?

Since writing is a process of discovering what you want to say, it is not always possible or even useful to try to outline it all in advance. It is much better to review carefully what you have written in a first draft and then revise to clarify the order. Organizing an essay is not just a matter of labeling the ideas in a mechanical way, such as "the first reason," "the second reason," and "in conclusion"—each at the beginning of a paragraph. In fact, most essays written like that are boring. Eliminating the obvious and overused labels for your points, however, does not mean eliminating good organization for your essay. You should be aware that jumping around from one point to another will confuse and irritate your reader. So in revising for order, think about the reader. Ask yourself:

◇ What will make this essay clearer to the reader?

◇ What will make the reader understand what I think is important?

◇ Is there any particular reason why I have put this paragraph before this other one?

◇ What would happen if I moved it?

Unity, Coherence, and Transitions   Finding a good order for the paragraphs is not the only way to make your writing clear and well organized. You must consider whether there is unity and coherence. These terms relate primarily to the organization of a paragraph, but obviously, the paragraphs themselves need to be related to each other in a way that makes the entire essay clear.

Unity in a paragraph means that the sentences are related to one major idea supported by facts, details, or illustrations of that particular idea. If the paragraph wanders from one idea to another, as if the writer simply recorded the sentences in the order they came into his or her mind, then the paragraph lacks unity. If all the sentences seem to be at the same level of generalization, instead of a generalization supported by specifics, then it is not a well-organized paragraph; it is a collection of separate ideas.

Coherence in sentences, paragraphs, and essays is the logical flow of ideas—the weaving together of major and minor points—in a way that makes clear to the reader the relationship among the parts. Coherence is reinforced by the careful use of *transitions*, those words, phrases, or even sentences that clarify the connections between one idea and the next. For instance, pronouns are used to refer back to previously mentioned nouns; demonstrative adjectives (this, that) and relative pronouns (who, which, what) refer forward or backward; adverbs (now, later, sooner, etc.) establish time sequences; conjunctions and coordinators (and, but, so) create relationships such as contrast or addition; subordinators (because, since, although) connect and make one idea subordinate to another; and numerical adjectives or nouns (first, one) obviously enumerate.

These are just a few examples of words that can be used as transitions. In fact, almost any word could be a transition; it is the word's *use* in context that makes it a transition from one part to another. Likewise, a whole sentence or even a paragraph can function as a transition if its primary function is to demonstrate the relationship between what precedes and what follows.

Sample Student Writing

To see how one student made an effort to reorganize her essay in order to correct problems of unity and coherence, look at the following drafts.

Draft 1

MY LANGUAGE

Japanese is considered one of the easier languages for a be- 1
ginner to approach.

The Japanese language has its own peculiar sentence 2
structure and writing system and has little common with
other language of the the world. The language has served as
an important medium of expression for the literature, writings, and other cultural achievements made by Japanese people during their long history.

It has a simple pronounciation scheme and few exceptions 3
to grammatical rules. Restrictions on sentence structure are
not severe. Probably the most difficult aspect of the language
is the reading and writing of Kanji characters.

It uses written characters of more than one type, Kanji, 4
Hiragana, Katakana characters and Roman letters. The number of character used is large. There are about 3,000 commonly used Kanji characters, 46 Hiragana and 46 Katakana
characters. Sentence can be written either vertically or horizontally. In constructing a sentence, the speaker has freedom in choosing the order of the words. It is difficult for
foreigners to understand that many words are pronounced
the same but have different means. Also the same thing or
idea can often be expressed with a number of different
words.

The Japanese themselves, however, are not good at speak- 5
ing foreign languages, therefore they understand the problems of the foreigner and will make efforts to understand
him even if he makes mistakes.

Because of the many differences between it and other lan- 6
guages, Japanese tends to be considered difficult. In fact,
spoken Japanese is not difficult at all. Many foreign visitors
master the language well enough for their daily needs after
only a year's stay.

♦ DISCUSSION QUESTIONS

1. Does this draft start with an introduction?

2. Does she need to develop certain places with more detail?

3. What transitions are used? Where are some needed?

4. Is there an apparent order to the paragraphs?

Read the second draft, noting the comments in the margins. The comments written on the left point out changes from draft 1. The instructor's comments on the right ask questions about the organization and especially the unity of the paragraphs.

Draft 2

a new introduction In terms of the number of people who use the language and the high level of their linguistic culture, Japanese ranks side by side with English, Russian, Chinese, French, German and Arabic as one of the major languages of the world.   1

Japanese is considered one of the easier languages for a beginner to approach. The Japanese language has its own peculiar sentence structure and writing system and has little in common with other language of the world.   2

thesis + former (2) The language has served as an important medium of expression for the literature, writings and other cultural achievements made by Japanese people during their long history.   *is this related to the first 2 sentences?*

It has a simple pronunciation scheme and few exceptions to grammatical rules. Restrictions on sentence structure are not severe. *unity?*

Probably the most difficult aspect of the language is the reading and writing of Kanji characters.   *does this sentence belong here?*   3

It uses written characters of more   4

than one type, Kanji, Hiragana, Katakana characters and Roman letters. The number of character used is large. There are about 3,000 commonly used Kanji characters including the 1,850 "daily use" characters, 46 Hiragana and 46 Katakana characters. Sentence can be written either vertically or horizontally. In constructing a sentence, the speaker has freedom in choosing the order of the words. The

is this related to "characters"?

way Japanese is spoken differs somewhat depending on whether the speaker is a man or a woman, an adult or a child. Also the speaker must choose his words considering the relationship between himself and the person he is speaking to.

new detail

It is difficult for foreigners to understand that many words are pronounced the same but have different means. Also the same thing or idea can often be expressed with a number of different words.

The Japanese themselves, however, are not good at speaking foreign languages, therefore they understand the problems of the foreigner and will make efforts to understand him even if he makes mistakes.

5

Because of the many difference between it and other languages, Japanese tends to be considered difficult. In fact, spoken Japanese is not difficult at all. Many foreign visitors mas-

6

ter the language well enough for their
daily needs after only a year's stay.

Now read draft 3. The comments on the left point out changes made
in organization. Answer the questions which follow the draft. (Student
writing has not been fully corrected.)

Draft 3

changed for audience In terms of the number of people
who use the language and high level of
its linguistic culture, Japanese ranks
side by side with English, Spanish,
Russian, Chinese, French, German

moved from old #2 and Arabic as one of the major languages of the world. The Japanese lan-
guage has served as an important
medium of expression for the extensive literature, writings and other
cultural achievements made by Japanese people during their long history.

1

Japanese is considered one of the   *tr*
easier languages for a beginner to approach. The Japanese language has its
own peculiar sentence structure and
writing system and has little in com-

from old #3 mon with other languages. It has a
simple pronounciation scheme and
few exceptions to grammatical rules.
Restrictions on sentence structure are
not severe. Sentence can be written ei-

from old #4 ther vertically or horizontally. In constructing a sentence the speaker has a
lot of freedom in choosing the order of
the words.   *tr*

2

Japanese uses written characters of
more than one type—Kanji, Hiragana,
Katakana characters and Roman letters. There are about 3,000 commonly
used Kanji characters including the
1,850 "daily use" characters, 46
Hiragana and 46 Katakana characters. Japanese has borrowed a large
number of words from other languages. The oldest and largest group
of borrowed words is from China.
Around the fourth century AD, the
Chinese writing system was introduced to Japanese with social systems, religion, arts and crafts. The
origin of Kanji characters are these
Chinese words. However, as the meanings assigned to most of the Chinese
words used in Japanese are different
from the original Chinese meanings
around the early eighth century, people remade Kanji characters into simple shaped characters called Kana.
Hiragana and Katakana are the same
but differs from its shapes.

The way Japanese is spoken differs
somewhat depending on whether the
speaker is a man or a woman, an adult
or a child. For example, there are numerous words meaning "I" and each
speaker refers to himself using the
one that is most appropriate for his
situation. Also the speaker must
choose his words considering the rela-

tionship between himself and the person he is speaking to. It is difficult for foreigners to understand that many words are pronounced the same but have different meanings. *tr* HASHI means bridge but it also means chopsticks. Japanese can tell the difference by hearing a tone of the words. Also, the same thing or idea can be expressed with a number of different words. *tr*

new detail [It is a requirement for Japanese to take English at junior high and high school, but many people don't have much opportunities to speak to English speakers. Japanese people can write and understand but are not good at speaking, therefore they understand the problems of the foreigner and will make efforts to understand him even if he makes mistakes.

5

Because of the many differences between it and other languages, Japanese tends to be considered difficult. In fact, spoken Japanese is not difficult at all. Many foreign visitors master the language well enough for their daily needs after only a year's stay.

6

♦ DISCUSSION QUESTIONS

1. Do you think the organization and unity of this draft are better?

2. Underline all the transitions. You will notice that more were needed (indicated by "tr" in the margin). Read this draft aloud and you will hear that many of the sentences are rather short, which means the writer could have combined a few and used a

few more transitions to smooth out the jumps from sentence to sentence and paragraph to paragraph.

3. What additional transitions would you suggest?

Conclusions: Ending Strongly   Look back at the conclusion to the student essay on Brazilian education on p. 144. Does it restate or summarize the points in the essay? Do you think it should? The best conclusions may restate a few major ideas, but it is more important for the conclusion to draw implications from the thesis and place the essay back into a broader context. The writer's purpose in the essay on education was to analyze educational opportunities, and she had begun by mentioning the question of monetary priorities in developing countries. It is a good idea to come back to that idea in the conclusion, although she has not said anything more precise than that the United States is a richer country. She may have run out of ideas or be tired of her essay at this point. The conclusion to the essay on music is similar. It is very brief, and, although the writer tries out a new figure of speech to capture what she has been describing ("it's like a yo-yo"), the conclusion seems a bit mechanical. It may be difficult to keep up your enthusiasm for your topic in order to write a good conclusion; but the conclusion should be considered one of the most important parts of the essay, rather than as something to be written as an afterthought.

♦ WRITING ASSIGNMENT

Compare the conclusions to the essay on the Japanese language, the one at the end of this chapter, and the one for the essay at the end of Chapter 6 (pp. 275–6).

Describe what happens in each conclusion.
Is one is more effective than the other?
Why?

Consider also Rodriguez' conclusion to "Does America Still Exist?" It is a simple sentence, not an elaborate paragraph, but it presents a powerful image illustrating, through a depiction of cultural assimilation, the whole point of the essay. Consider also the way Fulbright has concluded. From writing about the history of American foreign policy, he moves to predicting what is needed for the future. He refers back to the expression "an idea that mankind can hold to" from the MacLeish quotation and ties it to the side of the American character that he claims is the "true source of America's greatness." His long sentence makes us think back over what he has analyzed and then asks us to think about "greatness" as we project ourselves into the future. Therefore, he leaves us with an inspiring thought.

In writing a conclusion, it will help to ask yourself as you are looking back over your first draft, What is the importance of what I wrote? Why should anyone care about this? What do I want my reader to think about after finishing my essay? If your conclusion can answer at least one of those questions then it should be a good one.

In short, a good conclusion should:

◊ Tie together the major ideas of the essay.

◊ Draw implications from the material.

◊ Place the specific points developed back into a larger context.

Improving Your Editing

In editing your next-to-last draft, you need the help of your instructor or a writing center tutor to correct idiomatic expressions. You will get some practice by studying the changes made in drafts of the student writing in this text. Learning idiomatic English is not a matter of memorizing lists of expressions, and there are no rules to follow about idioms. The best way for you to improve that aspect of your English is to listen carefully to English spoken by educated speakers and to watch carefully in your reading. In other words, paying serious attention to the way people express themselves in speech and in writing will, over the course of months and years, bring you to a good command of standard English. There are no three-day cures with guaranteed results in regard to idioms.

To sharpen your editing skills further, go over each of the last drafts of the student writing in this chapter. As a class, look for idiomatic expressions that are not quite correct. Grammar and usage, of course, are elements that you can train yourself to correct on your own. So look for spelling errors and problems with verbs and sentence boundaries (run-ons, comma splices, and fragments), and add to your search a check of pronoun reference and number (nouns singular or plural) as appropriate. In the third draft of the essay on Japanese, correct any errors and suggest some transitions.

◆ WRITING ASSIGNMENT

Take the draft that you completed after doing the prewriting (pp. 141 ff).

Exchange it with a partner and fill out peer review sheet 5 (found in Appendix A). After you have discussed each other's papers, start to work on a revised draft, taking into consideration your partner's comments and the discussions in this chapter on revising for organization.

Cut up your draft into paragraphs and experiment with rearranging them in different orders. If you are working on a word processor, rearrange them and print out different versions.

Once you have decided on the order, give the second, revised draft to your instructor. After you have had a conference or received the instructor's comments, start on the third draft. In doing the editing on this draft, pay particular attention to your verbs and transitions. Follow whatever suggestions your instructor has given about points that you need to work on in your editing, and schedule another appointment in the writing center or with your instructor, if needed.

When you feel that you have revised and edited as much as possible, prepare a final draft and bring it to class. Exchange your paper with a partner and do a final proofreading. If your partner finds any mistakes, correct them neatly, if you must turn in the paper immediately.

Sample Student Essay for Writing to Analyze

Now read a final example of a student essay in three drafts which will illustrate some of the decisions related especially to organization that a student writer makes. A peer review sheet and discussion questions follow each draft. The assignment was for students to consider what they would gain or lose if they immigrated to the United States. This Vietnamese student knows precisely why she made the choice she did.

Draft 1

WHAT WILL AN IMMIGRANT GAIN OR LOSE
IN COMING TO AMERICA?

Since 1975 the Communist Revolution had been take over Vietnam. The communist governed Vietnam, and they took the Vietnamese freedom. People tried to escape. I was one of those people. I have left Vietnam, and I came to America about three years ago. I think I have gain more than I lost while I am living in America.   1

I have to set down my pain that I have living far away from my parents. I came to a strainge country and I do not know how to speak English. I have to start to get use to the American customs and weather. Beside those events that I had lose, I also found some other events that I think are so important to me. It is also the reason that I left my country, such as freedom, education, my dreams and my future.   2

The Communist have controlled all the Vietnamese life and   3
freedom. People can buy certain amount of food that the government decide to sell depending on the number of people in
each family. I can not choose what I wanted to buy. I can only
buy what they sell. Some families do not have enough food to
eat. They have to buy at a black market with triple price. In
this country I can buy anything I want to. Except I have to
have some money, but I can earn it. Most people in Vietnam
are unemployed. People have land, they can plant rice and
vegetables, but the government collect two-thirds of what
they harvested. People just have enough food to eat. I can not
have more education in Vietnam than in America. The Vietnam government said "Education is not important, work is
important." The students had to work for them several hours
a week. The school hours shorter in Vietnam than in America. In Vietnam student attend either morning or afternoon.

With the education I can get, I may not have good future   4
and my dreams may not come true. Student that graduate
from college in Vietnam and they have a job their salary may
not be enough for them to spend. My dreams are to get most
education I can (I like school) become good daughter, wife
and mother. I have many sisters, and I want to help them and
my parents, but my salary just enough for me if I graduated
from Vietnam. I may get better job and my salary may be
higher in America, so I can help my parents and sisters.

Bichnga Do

♦ DISCUSSION QUESTIONS

1. What comments would you make about this draft?

2. What do you think of the reviewer's comments?

Following her instructor's advice, Bichnga went to the writing center
for some help with revising in response to the peer reviewer's comments and for help with verb tenses. She tried to do some editing along
with the revisions in writing draft 2. You will notice, however, that in
several places she has made a second mistake in correcting the first one.
That occurs for several reasons. One is that any tutoring session or
conference cannot possibly cover everything the student might want to

Peer Review 5   Writer: *Bichnga Do*
Writing to Analyze   Peer Reviewer: *Carmen Fernandez*

What do you think is most interesting?

> I like the description of things in Vietnam. It is very sad she had to leave her parents.

What is the purpose?

> to analyze why she left Vietnam —she wants to say she has gained by coming here

What is the thesis?

> "I think I have gain more than I lost while I am living in America"

How is the essay organized? Make a brief outline of major points.

> intro — thesis
> body —
>   what she left — what she gained
>   food and education
>   future job —money

Does it have a good introduction and conclusion?

> intro ok because it gives background information
> I wanted to read more. I don't think any conclusion.

Does the organization need any revision?

> Separate paragraphs on food and education
> add conclusion
> maybe add more development in each part

discuss. Also, in this writing center, student tutors are not allowed to write on the papers. Sometimes the student writer doesn't remember exactly how to make the correction or misunderstands what has been discussed. The same thing occurs in a conference with an instructor. It is discouraging, but it is a normal part of the process. You can help avoid that situation by trying to write down very quickly all the corrections you discuss that seem new or the slightest bit confusing. You can also use your English handbook to check on punctuation rules, verb forms, etc. to verify that the changes you make are correct.

Now read Bichnga's second draft. The comments on the left point out revisions.

Draft 2

WHAT I GAINED IN COMING TO AMERICA

In 1975, the Communist revolution took over Vietnam. They have remained in Vietnam ever since. The Communist controll all aspects of Vietnamese life. People tried to escape. I was one of those people. I have left Vietnam, and I came to America about three years ago. I think I have gained more than I have lost while I am living in America.

1

Although I have to set aside my pain which comes from living far away from my parents. I came to a strange country, and I did not know how to speak English. I had to get used to the American customs and weather. Except for the people and the language that I have leave. I also found some other things that are very important to me are freedom, education, my dreams and my future. These are also

2

the reasons that I left my country.

The Communists have controlled all 3
Vietnamese life and freedom. The people could buy certain amounts of food
that the government decided to sell depending on the number of people in
each family. People can not choose
what they wanted to buy. People can
only buy what they sell. Some families
do not have enough food to eat. They
have to buy at a black-market with
triple price. In America, I can buy
anything I want to but I have to have
some money, but I can earn it. Most
Vietnamese are unemployed. People
have land; they can plant rice and vegetables, but the government collects
two-thirds of what they harvest. People just have enough food eat.

break into
new
paragraph

With the Communist controll sys- 4
tem I can not get more education in
Vietnam than in America. The communist said "Education is not important, but work is." The students had
to work for school several hours a
week. The school hours shorter in
Vietnam than in America. In Vietnam
students attend either morning or afternoon. Each student attend about
four and half hours a day. They start
at 7:00 till noon for the morning
classes and they attend from 1:00 till
5:30 for the afternoon classes. They

new
informa-
tion

new *inform* *ation* attend six days a week, but Thursday is work day. In America every student attends full times, they do not have to work for school, and they attend five day a week. American school also have more school equipments than Vietnam.

With the education I can get in Vietnam, I may not have good future, and my dreams may not come true. Students that graduate from college in Vietnam and they have a job. Their salary may not be enough for them to spend. My dreams are to get most education I can (I like school), become good daughter, wife, and mother. I have many sisters, and I want to help them and my parents but my salary just enough for me if I graduated from Vietnam. I may get better job and my salary may be higher in America so I can help my parents and sisters. My *new* *sentence* life will be better in America than in Vietnam.

5

♦ DISCUSSION QUESTIONS

1. In revising, did she follow the advice of the peer reviewer?

2. What do you think of the changes she made?

3. Does she have a conclusion?

4. What else do you think she should have revised?

5. Do you think she should have combined the first two paragraphs? Why or why not?

6. Is the order of the paragraphs good? Why or why not?

♦ EDITING EXERCISE

Here are some changes Bichnga made:

[1] the first sentence

[2] the first sentence—what has happened here?
    strainge > strange
    to get use to > to get used to
    besides those events > except for the people and language

[3] people can buy > could buy—is this a good change?
    I can buy only > people—why?
    Why keep "I" later in the paragraph?
    In this country I can buy . . . I can earn it > In America . . . earn
    it—are these good corrections?
    people have land, they can plant > people have land; they can
    plant

[4] work for them > work for school

[5] second and third sentences—what happened here?

Read over the draft again and comment on what needs further revision
and what needs to be edited. (The instructor did this with Bichnga
before asking her to work on draft 3.) Then read her third draft.

Draft 3

WHAT I GAINED IN COMING TO AMERICA

In 1975, the Communist Revolution took over Vietnam.   1
They have remained in Vietnam ever since. The Communists
controlled all aspects of Vietnamese life. People tried to escape. I was one of those people. I have left Vietnam, and I
came to America about three years ago. I think I have gained
more than I have lost since I have come to America.

Although I have gained much, I have to set aside my pain   2
which comes from living far away from my parents. I came to
a strange country, and I did not know how to speak English.
I had to get used to the American customs and weather, except for the people and the language that I have left. I also
found some other things that are very important to me, such
as freedom, education, my future, my dreams. These are also
the reasons that I left my country.

The Communists <u>controlled</u> all Vietnamese life and free- 3
dom. The people <u>could buy</u> certain amounts of food that the
government decided to sell depending on the number of <u>mem-
ber</u> in each family. For instance <u>I</u> could not choose what I
wanted to buy. I could only buy what they <u>sale.</u> Some families do not have enough food to eat; they have to buy food at a
black-market at triple the price. In America I can buy anything I want to, but I have to have some money. I can earn it
easier here than in Vietnam. Most Vietnamese are unemployed. If people have lands they can plant rice and vegetables, but the government collects two-thirds of what they
harvest. People just have enough food to eat.

The people have difficulties with money and food. They 4
also have a hard time with the educati<u>on for their</u> child. With
the Communist <u>controll</u> system, I cannot get more education
in Vietnam than in America. The Communists said "Education is not important, but work is." The students had to work
for school several hours a week. The school hours <u>is</u> shorter
in Vietnam than in America. In Vietnam students attend either morning or afternoon. Each student attends about four
and a half hours a day. They <u>start at 7:00 AM until</u> noon for
morning classes and from 1:00 PM until 5:30 PM for afternoon classes. They attend six days a week, but Thursday is a
work day. In America every student attends full time. They
do not have to work for school, and they attend five days a
week. American schools also have more equipment for labs
and other activities than schools in Vietnam do.

With the education I <u>can get</u> in Vietnam, I <u>may not have a</u> 5
good future, and my dreams <u>may not</u> come true. When the
students are graduated from a college and have a job in Vietnam, their salary may not be enough for them. My dreams
are to get the most education I can, become a good daughter,
wife, and mother. I have many sisters, and I want to help
them and my parents. If I graduated from a university in
Vietnam and <u>have</u> a job, my salary would be just enough for
me. I may <u>get better</u> job and my salary may be higher in
America, so I can help my parents and my sisters.

Although I have many problems with the langu<u>age and</u> I 6 am very sad to be far away from my parents, I am glad I came to America. Here I can go to school and get a good job in the future. My life will be better in America than in Vietnam.

◆ DISCUSSION QUESTIONS

1. Look at the revisions in paragraph 3. Do you think they are good?

2. What is the purpose of the first two sentences in paragraph 4?

3. What do you think of the conclusion now?

4. Is there anything else you think she should have revised?

◆ EDITING EXERCISE

1. Most of Bichnga's time went into editing this draft. Note her changes:

    [1] controll > controlled

    [2] first sentence

    [3] have controlled > controlled
    people have land > If people have land

    [4] can not > cannot
    communist > Communists
    four and half > four and a half
    Thursday is work day > Thursday is a work day
    full times > full time
    times, they do not > time. They do not
    school > schools
    school equipments > equipment for labs
    than Vietnam > than schools in Vietnam do

    [5] have good future > have a good future
    the second sentence
    to get most education > to get the most education
    delete (I like school)
    next to last sentence

Look at all the underlined places in draft 3. The major problem is in the sequence of verb tenses. Correct the verbs and any other errors you find.

♦ WRITING ASSIGNMENT

You have been studying the skills of revision and editing throughout this chapter by looking at someone else's writing. Now you can apply those skills to your own draft. If, by chance, you are not interested in completing the draft you have been working on, here is a reminder of the steps you should follow to start over on another topic.

◇ Prewrite to generate ideas and decide on a tentative thesis.

◇ Write a discovery draft to find out what you want to say; think about purpose and audience before you write.

◇ Rewrite carefully reconsidering your purpose, your audience, your thesis, and the order of your ideas.

◇ Do a peer review in class or in the writing center (use peer review sheet 5).

◇ Revise for clarity of thesis, organization (including a good introduction and conclusion), and development.

◇ Hand in a revised draft for the instructor's comments, or have a conference with the instructor.

◇ Go to the writing center, if possible, for a peer tutoring session.

◇ Revise and edit a final draft, paying particular attention to unity, coherence, and transitions.

◇ Exchange papers with someone for a final proofreading, or do your own proofreading very carefully.

◇ Hand in the essay for evaluation if you are certain it is in final form.

Chapter Five

MAKING CHOICES
Writing to Form a Judgment

The art of writing is the art of applying the seat of the pants to the seat of the chair.

—*Mary Heaton Vorse*

Lewis Thomas   *(1913–)*

Lewis Thomas graduated from Princeton University and Harvard Medical School. He taught medicine at several universities before becoming, first, dean of the School of Medicine at New York University, and then dean of Yale University's Medical School. From 1973 to 1980 Thomas was president of Memorial Sloan-Kettering Cancer Center in New York City. During his career, Thomas wrote extensively; he had a monthly column in the New England Journal of Medicine *and published papers, poems, essays, and books such as* Lives of a Cell *(1974), which was awarded the National Book Award for Arts and Letters.* The Medusa and the Snail: More Notes of a Biology Watcher, *from which the following essay is taken, was published in 1979. He has subsequently published* The Youngest Science: Notes of a Medicine-Watcher *(1985) and* Late Night Thoughts on Listening to Mahler's Ninth *(1986).*

In this essay, Thomas surprises us with his approach to what machines should do for us. Since he is a master of irony, you must read carefully for sudden turns in his thinking or contrasts between what he sets you up to think and what he is actually proposing.

Before reading this selection, write in your journal for 10 minutes on whether you think we learn from making mistakes.

To Err Is Human

Everyone must have had at least one personal experience with a computer error by this time. Bank balances are suddenly reported to have jumped from $379 into the millions, appeals for charitable contributions are mailed over and over to people with crazy-sounding names at your address, department stores send the wrong bills, utility companies write that they're turning everything off, that sort of thing. If you manage to get in touch with someone and complain, you then get instantaneously typed, guilty letters from the same computer, saying, "Our computer was in error, and an adjustment is being made in your account." 1

These are supposed to be the sheerest, blindest accidents. Mistakes are not believed to be part of the normal behavior of a good machine. If things go wrong, it must be a personal, human error, the result of fingering, tampering, a button getting stuck, someone hitting the wrong key. The computer, at its normal best, is infallible. 2

I wonder whether this can be true. After all, the whole point of computers is that they represent an extension of the human brain, vastly 3 improved upon but nonetheless human, superhuman maybe. A good computer can think clearly and quickly enough to beat you at chess, and some of them have even been programmed to write obscure verse. They can do anything we can do, and more besides.

It is not yet known whether a computer has its own consciousness, and it would be hard to find out about this. When you walk into one of those great halls now built for the huge machines, and stand listening, it is easy to imagine that the faint, distant noises are the sound of thinking, and the turning of the spools[1] gives them the look of wild creatures rolling their eyes in the effort to concentrate, choking with information. But real thinking, and dreaming, are other matters.

On the other hand, the evidences of something like an *unconscious*, equivalent to ours, are all around, in every mail. As extensions of the human brain, they have been constructed with the same property of error, spontaneous, uncontrolled, and rich in possibilities.

Mistakes are at the very base of human thought, embedded there, feeding the structure like root nodules. If we were not provided with the knack of being wrong, we could never get anything useful done. We think our way along by choosing between right and wrong alternatives, and the wrong choices have to be made as frequently as the right ones. We get along in life this way. We are built to make mistakes, coded for error.

We learn, as we say, by "trial and error." Why do we always say that? Why not "trial and rightness" or "trial and triumph"? The old phrase puts it that way because that is, in real life, the way it is done.

A good laboratory, like a good bank or a corporation or government, has to run like a computer. Almost everything is done flawlessly, by the book, and all the numbers add up to the predicted sums. The days go by. And then, if it is a lucky day, and a lucky laboratory, somebody makes a mistake: the wrong buffer[2], something in one of the blanks, a decimal misplaced in reading counts, the warm room off by a degree and a half, a mouse out of his box, or just a misreading of the day's protocol. Whatever, when the results come in, something is obviously screwed up, and then the action can begin.

The misreading is not the important error; it opens the way. The next step is the crucial one. If the investigator can bring himself to say, "But even so, look at that!" then the new finding, whatever it is, is ready for snatching. What is needed, for progress to be made, is the move based on the error.

Whenever new kinds of thinking are about to be accomplished, or new varieties of music, there has to be an argument beforehand. With

---

[1]In this case, the reels of computer tape.

[2]Chemical used to neutralize a reaction.

two sides debating in the same mind, haranguing, there is an amiable understanding that one is right and the other wrong. Sooner or later the thing is settled, but there can be no action at all if there are not the two sides, and the argument. The hope is in the faculty of wrongness, the tendency toward error. The capacity to leap across mountains of information to land lightly on the wrong side represents the highest of human endowments.

It may be that this is a uniquely human gift, perhaps even stipulated in our genetic instructions. Other creatures do not seem to have DNA[3] sequences for making mistakes as a routine part of daily living, certainly not for programmed error as a guide for action.   11

We are at our human finest, dancing with our minds, when there are more choices than two. Sometimes there are ten, even twenty different ways to go, all but one bound to be wrong, and the richness of selection in such situations can lift us onto totally new ground. This process is called exploration and is based on human inability. If we had only a single center in our brains, capable of responding only when a correct decision was to be made, instead of the jumble of different, credulous, easily conned clusters of neurones[4] that provide for being flung off into blind alleys, up trees, down dead ends, out into blue sky, along wrong turnings, around bends, we could only stay the way we are today, stuck fast.   12

The lower animals do not have this splendid freedom. They are limited, most of them, to absolute infallibility. Cats for all their good side, never make mistakes. I have never seen a maladroit[5] clumsy, or blundering cat. Dogs are sometimes fallible, occasionally able to make charming minor mistakes, but they get this way by trying to mimic their masters. Fish are flawless in everything they do. Individual cells in a tissue are mindless machines, perfect in their performance, as absolutely inhuman as bees.   13

We should have this in mind as we become dependent on more complex computers for the arrangement of our affairs. Give the computers their heads, I say; let them go their way. If we can learn to do this, turning our heads to one side and wincing while the work proceeds, the possibilities for the future of mankind, and computerkind, are limitless. Your average good computer can make calculations in an instant which would take a lifetime of slide rules[6] for any of us. Think of what we could gain from the near infinity of precise, machine-made miscomputa-   14

---

[3]Deoxyribonucleic acid, genetic material in the cell.

[4]Nerve cells.

[5]French for clumsy.

[6]An instrument used in logarithmic calculations.

tion which is now so easily within our grasp. We would begin the solving of some of our hardest problems. How, for instance, should we go about organizing ourselves for social living on a planetary scale, now that we have become, as a plain fact of life, a single community? We can assume, as a working hypothesis, that all the right ways of doing this are unworkable. What we need, then, for moving ahead, is a set of wrong alternatives much longer and more interesting than the short list of mistaken courses that any of us can think up right now. We need, in fact, an infinite list, and when it is printed out we need the computer to turn on itself and select, at random, the next way to go. If it is a big enough mistake, we could find ourselves on a new level, stunned, out in the clear, ready to move again.

♦ COMPREHENSION/DISCUSSION QUESTIONS

1. This essay starts with an assumption about the normal behavior of machines. What is it?

2. In what respect do we tend to think of computers as superior to humans?

3. Does Lewis Thomas believe computers are like human minds? In what way?

4. What is unexpected about his description of the "property of error" in paragraph 5?

5. How does Thomas reverse our normal thinking about the nature of error?

6. Explain the examples he gives of what happens in a lucky laboratory (paragraph 8).

7. Explain the last sentence in paragraph 10.

8. What does he mean when he says that "fish are flawless?" As a biologist, Thomas surely knows that this is not literally true. Yet, what is the truth in his statement?

9. Summarize Thomas' final point about what we should expect computers to do for us.

10. What did you think about after you finished reading this essay?

11. Have you ever had trouble because of a computer error? Describe what happened.

12. Can you think of a little or big error you have made that led to a very positive outcome?

13. What do you think might happen in academic courses if the instructor emphasized how productive it is to make mistakes?

14. Do you think you learn from making mistakes in your writing? If yes, give some examples.

♦ VOCABULARY

Define the following words, paying particular attention to their meaning in context. Write sentences of your own using each word or several in one sentence.

credulous [12]	knack [6]
chess [3]	nodules [6]
decimal [8]	nonetheless [3]
embedded [6]	programmed [3]
fallibility [12]	protocol [8]
flawlessly [8]	stipulate [11]
haranguing [10]	tamper [2]
infallible [2]	wince [14]
jumble [12]	

♦ IDIOMS

Study the use of the following idioms in context; then try writing a sentence of your own using them.

1. "Trial and error" [7]—trying and making mistakes.

2. "Screwed up" [8]—slang expression for messing up or ruining something (might be considered inappropriate by some instructors for you to use in writing).

3. "Con" [12]—to trick.

4. "Into blind alleys, up trees, down dead ends" [2]—clichés meaning to take a wrong direction

5. "Out into blue sky" [12]—to be off in dream land, impractical.

6. "Stuck fast" [12]—stopped.

7. "Turn on itself" [14]—attack itself or reverse directions.

8. "Out in the clear" [14]—free of constraints.

◆ FIGURES OF SPEECH

Study the use of the following figures of speech. Can you explain the comparisons being made?

1. ". . . and the turning of the spools gives them the look of wild creatures rolling their eyes in the effort to concentrate, choking with information" [4].

2. "We are built to make mistakes, coded for error" [6].

3. "With two sides debating in the same mind, harranguing, there is an amiable understanding that one is right and the other wrong" [10].

4. ". . . dancing with our minds . . ." [12].

5. "Give the computers their heads, I say . . ." [14].

◆ JOURNAL ENTRY

Write for 20 minutes in your journal about your reactions to this essay. You might want to comment on Lewis Thomas' style of writing—did you like it or not?

◆ SMALL GROUP WORK

Divide into groups of 3–4 students and brainstorm silently, as individuals, on some ideas about the value of computers that you might want to write about. Here are a few ideas:

Why are computers useful for writers?

Are any important values threatened by the accumulation of personal information in computer data banks?

What is the value of computer courses for students majoring in disciplines other than computer science?

What would be some good uses of computers in the future?

After the individual brainstorming (5 minutes), each student should try to write a tentative thesis for an essay, and then share it with the others in the group. The students should respond to each other's theses by telling the writer what they, as readers, would like to read about that topic.

Follow-up Writing   Write a few paragraphs on your topic to keep in your idea file.

Norman Cousins (1915–)

*Norman Cousins was an influential editor of major American pub-
lications, including the* New York Evening Post, Current History, *and*
Saturday Review, *where he was executive editor from 1942 to 1971 and
from 1975 to 1978. He is well known for championing many liberal
causes, especially those pertaining to education. Later he received attention for his story of healing himself from what was diagnosed as a
terminal illness* (Anatomy of an Illness as Perceived by the Patient,
*1979). During his career, he has received nearly fifty honorary docto-
rates. Currently he is Professor of Medical Humanities at UCLA.*

This selection, one of his last editorials in Saturday Review, *expresses
his commitment to the value of liberal education, i.e., that sort of
education which broadens the mind and develops the person more than
training the individual for a specific skill.*

Before you read the selection, write in your journal for 10 minutes
about what courses you believe you and other students should study
during your college career.

How to Make People Smaller Than They Are

Three months ago in this space the [editorial column of *Saturday*   1
Review] we wrote about the costly retreat from the humanities on all the
levels of American education. Since that time, we have had occasion to
visit a number of campuses and have been troubled to find that the
general situation is even more serious than we had thought. It has
become apparent to us that one of the biggest problems confronting
American education today is the increasing vocationalization of our
colleges and universities. Throughout the country, schools are under
pressure to become job-training centers and employment agencies.

The pressure comes mainly from two sources. One is the growing   2
determination of many citizens to reduce taxes—understandable and
even commendable in itself, but irrational and irresponsible when connected to the reduction or dismantling of vital public services. The
second source of pressure comes from parents and students who tend to
scorn courses of study that do not teach people how to become attrac-
tive to employers in a rapidly tightening job market.

It is absurd to believe that the development of skills does not also require the systematic development of the human mind. Education is being measured more by the size of the benefits the individual can extract from society than by the extent to which the individual can come into possession of his or her full powers. The result is that the life-giving juices are in danger of being drained out of education. 3

Emphasis on "practicalities" is being characterized by the subordination of words to numbers. History is seen not as essential experience to be transmitted to new generations, but as abstractions that carry dank odors. Art is regarded as something that calls for indulgence or patronage and that has no place among the practical realities. Political science is viewed more as a specialized subject for people who want to go into politics than as an opportunity for citizens to develop a knowledgeable relationship with the systems by which human societies are governed. Finally, literature and philosophy are assigned the role of add-ons—intellectual adornments that have nothing to do with "genuine" education. 4

Instead of trying to shrink the liberal arts, the American people ought to be putting pressure on colleges and universities to increase the ratio of the humanities to the sciences. Most serious studies of medical-school curricula in recent years have called attention to the stark gaps in the liberal education of medical students. The experts agree that the schools shouldn't leave it up to students to close those gaps. 5

The irony of the emphasis being placed on careers is that nothing is more valuable for anyone who has had a professional or vocational education than to be able to deal with abstractions or complexities, or feel comfortable with subtleties of thought or language, or to think sequentially. The doctor who knows only disease is at a disadvantage alongside the doctor who knows at least as much about people as he does about pathological organisms. The lawyer who argues in court from a narrow legal base is no match for the lawyer who can connect legal precedents to historical experience and who employs wide-ranging intellectual resources. The business executive whose competence in general management is bolstered by an artistic ability to deal with people is of prime value to his company. For the technologist, the engineering of consent can be just as important as the engineering of moving parts. In all these respects, the liberal arts have much to offer. Just in terms of career preparation, therefore, a student is shortchanging himself by shortcutting the humanities. 6

But even if it could be demonstrated that the humanities contribute nothing directly to a job, they would still be an essential part of the educational equipment of any person who wants to come to terms with life. The humanities would be expendable only if human beings didn't have to make decisions that affect their lives and the lives of others; if the human past never existed or had nothing to tell us about the present; 7

if thought processes were irrelevant to the achievement of purpose; if creativity was beyond the human mind and had nothing to do with the joy of living; if human relationships were random aspects of life; if human beings never had to cope with panic or pain, or if they never had to anticipate the connection between cause and effect; if all the mysteries of mind and nature were fully plumbed; and if no special demands arose from the accident of being born a human being instead of a hen or a hog.

Finally, there would be good reason to eliminate the humanities if a free society were not absolutely dependent on a functioning citizenry. If the main purpose of a university is job training, then the underlying philosophy of our government has little meaning. The debates that went into the making of American society concerned not just institutions or governing principles but the capacity of humans to sustain those institutions. Whatever the disagreements were over other issues at the American Constitutional Convention,[1] the fundamental question sensed by everyone, a question that lay over the entire assembly, was whether the people themselves would understand what it meant to hold the ultimate power of society, and whether they had enough of a sense of history and destiny to know where they had been and where they ought to be going. 8

Jefferson was prouder of having been the founder of the University of Virginia than of having been President of the United States. He knew that the educated and developed mind was the best assurance that a political system could be made to work—a system based on the informed consent of the governed. If this idea fails, then all the saved tax dollars in the world will not be enough to prevent the nation from turning on itself. 9

♦ COMPREHENSION/DISCUSSION QUESTIONS

1. What type of higher education is Cousins criticizing?

2. Why is that type more popular now?

3. Cousins seems to use ''humanities'' and ''liberal arts'' interchangeably throughout this essay. Are they the same?

4. What sort of attitude do people have now toward the humanities?

5. Restate and explain the second sentence in paragraph 3.

6. Why do doctors, lawyers, and business executives need the humanities? What are the specific talents, such as ''the engineering of consent'' that he is refering to?

---

[1]Convened in 1787 when the colonies were designing a constitution.

7. Explain "The humanities would be expendable only if human beings didn't have to make decisions that affect their lives and the lives of others . . . ." [7].

8. What is the connection between studying the humanities and a "functioning citizenry?" [8]

9. How does concluding with the reference to Thomas Jefferson help Cousins tie two points together?

10. Do you agree with any or all of his points about the value of a liberal arts education?

11. Have you taken many humanities or liberal arts courses? If so, what do you think their value is?

12. Do you think colleges and universities should try to convince students to study the humanities more and worry less about job preparation? Why or why not?

♦ VOCABULARY

Define the following words, paying particular attention to their meaning in context. Then write a sentence using each word or two words.

bolster [6]	organism [6]
dank [4]	pathological [6]
dismantle [2]	plumb [7]
employment agency [1]	shortchanging [6]
irrelevant [7]	vocationalization [1]

♦ IDIOMS AND FIGURES OF SPEECH

Study the use of the following expressions in context. Try to explain the comparisons in the figures of speech.

1. "Have occasion" [1]—have the opportunity.

2. ". . . literature and philosophy are assigned the role of add-ons" [4]

3. "The result is that *the life-giving juices are in danger of being drained out of education.*" [3]

4. ". . . abstractions that carry dank odors." [4]

♦ JOURNAL ENTRY

Write in your journal for 20 minutes on the type of higher education that you think would be best for yourself. You might think about why you have chosen a specific school to attend or why you are planning to study a certain field.

♦ SMALL GROUP WORK

Divide into small groups of 3–4 students and try to find some specific examples to illustrate the statements in paragraph 7, starting with "The humanities would be expendable only . . . if the human past never existed or had nothing to tell us about the present" and continuing to the end of the paragraph. For example, you might say, "Since the past obviously does exist, we must study it and learn from it; i.e., if we don't know what Hitler said and did, then we may not recognize the dangers of other racist speakers and movements." The group should explain each of Cousin's statements and find an example for each one. After 10 minutes of work, the group should report its findings to the whole class; then the class members can help one another discuss anything that remains unclear.

Follow-up Writing   Write a few paragraphs summarizing the discussion, adding any further ideas that might have developed after the discussion.

Margaret Robinson (1937–)

Margaret Robinson is a graduate of the University of Vermont and has an M.A. from the University of Wisconsin. Her short stories have appeared in Redbook, Mademoiselle, Cosmopolitan, Seventeen, Fiction Network, *and the* Pennsylvania Review. *Her first novel,* Arrivals and Departures *was published in 1981, and a second one,* Courting Emma Howe, *will appear in 1988. She is currently teaching part-time at Widener University in Chester, Pennyslyvania, and she reports that she is still happy living in Swarthmore.*

In this selection, which was originally published in the Philadelphia Inquirer *(1984), she writes of her childhood in rural Connecticut, her experiment with city living in New York, and her decision to live in the classic American place—the suburbs.*

Before you read, write for 10 minutes in your journal about what images you have of people who live in the suburbs of an American city.

Why I Live in the Suburbs

Because my father loved growing up in rural Vermont and wanted his   1
children to experience something comparable, I spent my early years, if not in deep country, then certainly in a rural area. Our eastern Connecticut town—in most states the designation would be "township"—was characterized by small, not very prosperous dairy farms. During what used to be called the "formative" years of my life, we lived up a hill on a steep dirt road with a rocky goat pasture across the way and no other people at all. The narrow valley at the bottom of the hill, where there was a mill pond and an abandoned mill, was called the Pink Ravine. It got its name from the abandoned graveyard down the road from our house which was planted with a carpet of moss pinks.[1] For a small child, it was a time of wild and solitary adventure: the shadowy barn, trees and sky, burdock[2] and jewelweed,[3] and, like an island in the middle of the overgrown fields, a mowed patch on which sat our house. When I was six, we moved closer to civilization, but by then the twig had been bent.

Civilization was a black-topped[4] road where we had a few neighbors   2
but still no street lights or sidewalks. Across the road: woods. Behind

[1]Flower (genus *Dianthus*).

[2]A weedy plant with thistles.

[3]Flower with seed pods that burst open upon touching.

[4]Asphalt road covering.

our house: woods, fields, a brook and more woods. The brook was lined with skunk cabbage, cowslips (which my father once picked and cooked for dinner), poison ivy, and woodbine. . . .[5]

My father, who would have liked a cow or at least a couple of pigs, made do with a large vegetable garden. In addition to the usual peas, beans, tomatoes, and sweet corn, he raised asparagus, rhubarb, and a wide variety of leaf lettuce. He tended a long perennial bed, backed by forsythia bushes and filled with iris, poppies, lilies, primroses, lupin, heliotrope, and phlox. . . .[6]   3

Our water came from a shallow well covered by a slab of concrete and some scratchy juniper[7] in the front yard. You could tug aside the slab, look down into the well, and see a glint. Sometimes—an exciting event to children—the well went dry, which meant we could accompany our father to haul water, cold and silvery in ten-gallon milk cans, and could bathe in the fascinating bathtubs of neighbors. Lots of people kept chickens. The family across and up the road had a flock and sold us eggs; and in those early days, the bird for Sunday dinner was bought at the coop[8] with its feathers and innards[9] intact. Occasionally the Black Angus cattle in the meadow up the road would break through their fence. You'd be walking home in the dark when a hunk of the dark would first move and then moo. We'd wake up to find the lawn covered with cow flops.[10]   4

There was no train and scarcely any bus, at least not a bus that went anywhere you'd want to go. Six days a week my father drove close to an hour to work in Hartford, but nobody else's father did, and the verb *commute* was not part of our lexicon. Because my mother wanted to expose us to the arts, we were taken occasionally to the city for cultural events: an exhibit of paintings at the Wadsworth Atheneum, a concert by the symphony, *Hansel and Gretel* performed by the students of the Hart School of Music. Twice a year we kids were shepherded to the dentist and then to a restaurant on Front Street near the river where we celebrated surviving the ordeal with a pizza as big as a wagon wheel, thin, crisp, and covered with absolutely everything. It was not fast food. We waited a long time for it—six months, not counting the endless minutes in the booth at Pepi's Green Bottle. It was as exotic as a cockatoo[11] and in every way wonderful.   5

[5]All wild plants.

[6]All flowering plants; consult a large dictionary for descriptions and pictures.

[7]A type of evergreen bush.

[8]Small house or cage for birds.

[9]The intestines, lungs, etc.

[10]A euphemism for cow dung.

[11]A bird in the parrot family.

But our daily life was strictly countrified. My sisters and I walked to   6
the four-room grammar school, which is what the elementary school
was called, up the Gurleyville Road, through some woods, along
Willowbrook Road and Dog Lane, across a couple of fields, over a
brook, through more fields, and finally along a path on the weedy bank
above the main drag, Route 195. . . .

At three o'clock we dawdled home, exploring the water, dirt, bugs,   7
rocks, dogs, and other kids along the way. I chanted the multiplication
tables while stepping only on stones, never on dirt, on the path down
from Willowbrook to our road. Once in the fall a friend and I came
home at dusk through those woods armed with big sticks to fend off
"the wildcat." On the way to play with another friend on a summer day
I walked into those woods and first heard, in the sense of absorbed into
my bones, the hot, lazy buzz of cicadas.[12] And in those same woods I felt
the initial jolt of sexual excitement when a "new boy" named Brian
condescended to walk and flirt with me. That was thirty years ago, but
if the Brian I remember, cute and cocky, with straight brown hair and a
sidelong smile, were to walk in the door this minute, I would feel just as
I did then, scared, embarrassed, and intensely thrilled.

We lived eight miles from the nearest hospital, movie theater, high   8
school, supermarket, liquor store, and drugstore, but we children did
not feel deprived. In warm weather, we built dams in the brook. In cold
weather, we built forts in the snow. My mother, who hated her childhood in rural Vermont, had frequent attacks of cabin fever.

As a child, I loved it. When I grew up—maybe it was the lure of the   9
pizza—I couldn't wait to get away.

In getting away, I lived in a couple of small cities and then for five   10
years took up residence in the Big Apple[13] itself, right there in Manhattan
on the West Side, where the lights are never turned off and the subways
run all night and if you have enough money, you can buy anything. The
Sunday *Times* on Saturday night. Fresh strawberries in winter. A
nymphet[14] of any race. Tickets to a first-run Broadway show. Anything,
if you have the cash.

One thing I discovered about living in New York was that it conferred   11
an instant identity. I traveled in Europe the first summer after I moved to
Manhattan and quickly learned not to reply, "Storrs, Connecticut,"
when asked, "Where are you from?" "Storrs, Connecticut" produced a
look of unhappy bafflement. But when you told foreigners you were
from New York, it was as though you had given them a gift. New York!
Of course! Everybody knows New York! I didn't mention that I couldn't

---

[12]An insect that creates a high-pitched droning noise.

[13]New York City.

[14]Young girl.

afford it, or that I'd been hassled on the street, had my car repeatedly vandalized, my apartment robbed. It was a summer trip, and I'd forgotten how the winter wind off the Hudson[15] whipped up 104th Street as though it were a wind tunnel, blowing grit into your eyes and cold into your ribcage. The day I liked best in New York was the fall evening when the lights went out. The elevators stopped, the subways stopped, the neon stopped. Factories, presses, and automatic doughnut fryers—everything ground to a halt. A full moon rose over Central Park, and in my apartment building, the neighbors came from behind their triple-locked doors holding candles.

Eventually, like many country mice who run away to the city but find they can't stay, I wound up in the suburbs, and an unfashionable suburb of an unfashionable city at that. Mention Scarsdale, Cambridge, or Menlo Park and there's instant recognition. Shaker Heights and Silver Springs[16] are known and have a classy ring. Say you live in Swarthmore, outside Philadelphia, and even Americans say, "Where?" | 12

If they're acquainted with Philadelphia, they recover with, "Oh, yes, that's on the Main Line," [17] but it isn't. If they're unacquainted with Philadelphia, they'll ask what it's near. Chester? you say hopefully, making your statement sound like a question. A blank look. Between Philadelphia and Wilmington, Delaware, you say. Ahhh—Wilmington is on the map. Then, if they're really polite or trying to butter you up, they'll ask how to spell it. | 13

Ever since I moved to the suburbs, and quite by chance to this particular suburb, I have been fending off the jibes of urban and rural friends alike. The suburbs, it seems, have a bad rep. They're instant mashed potatoes: bland, tasteless, formless. Suburbanites are smug, mediocre, fearful, racist. They eat hamburger helper and wear white socks.[18] That's the city point of view. To rural folk, suburbanites are soft. They barbeque in the backyard and have waistline flab. They don't have calluses or boots. They drink contaminated water and breathe polluted air and buy vegetables swathed in plastic wrap. They buy corn at the supermarket! They wouldn't know how to kill and dress a rabbit or how to milk a goat. | 14

"How can you live so far out?" one set of friends asks, while the other wonders, expressions of scorn, concern, and disbelief on their faces, "How can you live so far in?" The answer probably lies by the brook | 15

[15]The Hudson River.

[16]All well-known suburbs of major cities.

[17]A series of suburbs along a railroad line in Philadelphia where wealthy, very well-established families live.

[18]It is considered in poor taste for a man to wear white socks (unless he's dressed for sports).

running from the mill pond and down through the Pink Ravine, where my father showed my sister and me, as his mother had showed him in East Hardwick, Vermont, how to pinch lightly the plump pods of jewel-weed to make them burst, exploding their brown seeds in all directions. That moment by the brook—one of many that my father gave his children—was magical.

As I grew up, I became aware, as young people do, of other less idyllic 16 aspects of my hometown. Storrs was dominated by Republican Protes-tants who took their churchgoing seriously. The parents of the Catholic kids in my class held the blue-collar jobs. There were no blacks and scarcely any Jews. The town was dry[19] and there was among the par-ents of my friends much disapproval of strong drink and strong lan-guage. . . .

My parents were not pious or narrow in their views and—thank 17 God—they drank and occasionally swore. To my best friend in high school, my folks were the ultimate in sophistication because they once, when she came to dinner, served her a seafood Newburg,[20] which she had never had before, and it actually contained sherry! But still I remember as a teenager the tediousness of summer vacations with no place to go, no way to get there, and nothing to do except the things I had always done which were suddenly no longer interesting. Despite close ties to my family, I couldn't stay. So, starting with college, I went away to seek my fortune, wanting something more, wanting at first only to use strong language and have red wine and pizza close at hand.

When I drive through the Pink Ravine today, where the road is still 18 unpaved and "our" house still stands very much alone, I get the creeps if I think about actually living there. The dark damp of that valley and the isolation of the house seem awful to me. My mother's influence—"It's a big world," she often used to say—was as strong as my father's. I never want to be more than half an hour from a good orchestra, a museum, Chinese food. But the jewelweed seeds were sown in the soil of my psyche when I was maybe four years old. I still stop, on my walks in early fall along the creeks of Swarthmore, to pinch the pods lightly and watch them explode, and that act is deeply, irrationally satisfying. I see my niece do the same thing on her way to school, because my grandmother taught my father and my father taught his children and my sister has taught my niece that popping jewelweed pods is, simply, one of the things you do.

We are, for better or worse, what we were. Jewelweed doesn't grow 19 in Center city. And so I live in the suburbs.

---

[19]Had voted not to sell or serve alcohol.

[20]A dish made usually with lobster in a cream sauce seasoned with sherry.

◆ COMPREHENSION/DISCUSSION QUESTIONS

1. What are the three environments that Robinson is comparing in her essay?

2. What did she especially like about the rural setting of her "formative" years?

3. What was the difference between her father's and her mother's influence on her?

4. Why did she run away to the city?

5. What didn't she like about living in New York?

6. Why is she criticized for living in the suburbs?

7. What are the stereotypes about it? Do you think they are accurate?

8. Now that she is an adult, what does she realize about the environment she grew up in?

9. In what way do the suburbs reflect the combination of values her parents gave her?

10. Was anything in your childhood similar to Robinson's?

11. Do you agree with her about the limitations of a rural environment?

12. Which of the three environments would you prefer to live in?

◆ VOCABULARY

Define the following words, paying particular attention to their meaning in context. Write sentences of your own, using one or more of he words at a time.

bland [14]	exotic [5]
callus [14]	flab [14]
Catholic [16]	formative [1]
cocky [7]	glint [4]
commute [5]	grit [11]
condescend [7]	hassled [11]
countrified [6]	hunk [4]
dawdled [7]	idyllic [16]

intact [4]	perennial [3]
Jew [14]	pod [15]
jibe [14]	psyche [18]
lexicon [5]	sherry [17]
mediocre [14]	slab [4]
mow [1]	smug [14]
neon [11]	solitary [1]
ordeal [5]	sophistication [17]
ostentatiously [16]	swathed [14]

♦ IDIOMS

Study the use of the following idioms in context. Then write a sentence using each one. Those marked with an asterisk are colloquial or slang expressions.

1. "Make do" [3]—get along with, manage.

2. "*Main drag" [6]—main street.

3. "*Cabin fever" [8]—feeling of being closed in.

4. "Grind to a halt" [11]—come to a stop.

5. "*Butter up" [13] — flatter someone.

6. "*Classy ring [12]—sound fancy or sophisticated.

7. "*Bad rep" [14]—bad reputation.

8. "*Strong drink" [16]—alcoholic beverages.

9. "*Strong language" [16]—swearing.

10. "Close ties" [17]—close relationships.

11. "Close at hand" [17]—nearby, convenient.

12. "*Get the creeps" [18]—have an uneasy feeling.

♦ FIGURES OF SPEECH

Study the following figures of speech and then comment on how appropriate they are to the rest of her essay.

1. ". . . but by then the twig had been bent" [1].

2. "Civilization was a black-topped road . . ." [2].

3. ". . . a pizza as big as a wagon wheel . . ." [5].

4. "It was as exotic as a cockatoo . . ." [5].

5. ". . . I'd forgotten how the winter wind off the Hudson whipped up 104th street as though it were a wind tunnel . . ." [11].

6. "Eventually, like many country mice who run away . . ." [12].

7. "But the jewelweed seeds were sown in the soil of my psyche when I was maybe four years old" [18].

♦ JOURNAL ENTRY

Write for 20 minutes in your journal on the best place you have ever lived or where you would like to live.

♦ SMALL GROUP WORK

Divide into small groups of 3–4 and brainstorm a list of criteria for a good living environment (5 minutes). After listing the qualities, come to a consensus on the five most important ones. Be prepared to justify the choice to the class (10 minutes). When the class reassembles, a spokesperson for each group will present the results. If there are major differences in the qualities that the groups have selected, the class should rank-order the top ten. A short discussion could then be held on where we are most likely to find those qualities (15–20 minutes).

Follow-up Writing Write a few paragraphs on the three most important qualities for a good environment and why they are important.

WRITING TO FORM A JUDGMENT

By now you have written many drafts and several final compositions with a variety of purposes. You have described, narrated, explained, and analyzed a subject. Another common purpose in writing is to express your judgment or evaluation of something. We make informal judgments in our conversations and casual writing every time we say we like or dislike something or justify a choice we have made. But how do you defend your preferences in movies, places to live, or academic majors when someone challenges those choices? You must come up with the value or values they represent to you, i.e., you judge them by some criteria that others should be able to understand and see as valuable, even if they don't accept the choices or values for themselves. You know that you don't get very far in a conversation if you can't defend your judgments with anything better than "Oh I just like it!" The challenge in writing to express a judgment is to find the criteria, or standards to support your evaluation.

In "To Err is Human," Lewis Thomas is trying to describe and justify a quality of the human mind that he thinks is superior. He talks about the value of human mistakes by pointing out the great discoveries that happen in a laboratory when mistakes are made; he points to the limitations of lower animals who do not routinely make mistakes and therefore remain locked in inevitable patterns of behavior. He tries to convince us that we should design computers to make errors occasionally, and this idea is based on his judgment that error is positive.

Norman Cousins' essay expresses his evaluation of two different types of education, the vocational and the liberal. He credits the humanities and liberal education in general with providing students with certain valuable abilities—a sense of history, an ability to deal with other people, logical thinking, and knowledge of the American political system that allows them to be functioning members of a democracy. These are the criteria by which he judges higher education, and they are obviously desirable qualities that are hard to dispute, even if you remain convinced that the primary purpose of a college degree is to get you a high-paying job.

In "Why I Live in the Suburbs," Robinson defends her choice of a place to live by describing her childhood in rural Connecticut, her brief stay in New York City, and the advantages of that midway point between city and country that Americans call suburbs. Think back to that reading. Do you remember what values the country seemed to hold for her? What was the appeal of the city? Why was her mother bored in the country? What were the limitations of the country that she could understand when she became an adult? What are the values of both country and city that are combined in the suburbs? Note that Robinson's very detailed descriptions make her point as much, if not more, than her own analytical comments about the various places she has lived. As with most forms of writing, detail makes the piece much more convincing than any number of broad statements could. But analysis of the facts or experiences is also crucial to show the reader what the meaning is for the writer.

In any sort of evaluation or judgment, the criteria inevitably have an element of subjectivity, i.e., they are based upon individual perceptions more than on empirical evidence (gained through observation and measurement). What is good, beautiful, or important to one person is not necessarily so to another. There may be a consensus among many people that certain values, such as truth, friendship, or freedom are "good," but we often disagree over the definition of those large value terms. For instance, what are the criteria for a good essay? Neat handwriting? Wide margins? A cute title? You would not expect your instructor to evaluate you primarily on that basis. You would, however, accept the criteria of mature ideas, good development and organization, and well-constructed sentences, even if you might wonder whether the instructor applies the criteria too rigorously.

You cannot expect your reader to automatically accept your judgments as if they were based on some absolute, indisputable standard. But you can expect your reader to read, understand, and be tolerant of your judgments *if* you make the standards by which you make the judgment clear and support them well with appropriate examples, whether facts or illustrations. There should be a balance in your essay between the statements you make expressing your judgment of the topic and the supporting material which will justify the standards you are using.

Prewriting

Brainstorming   Brainstorm for 5–10 minutes on one of the following ideas:

the value of a certain "accident" or "mistake" you once made

what makes a particular city good to live in

the value of courses in literature, philosophy, or another humanities discipline

the value of business courses

the good aspect of living in the dorms vs. living in an apartment (or the opposite point of view)

how you would justify your choice to live in _____ (a specific location)

Mapping   See the example of a map on "the value of higher education." Take one of your own ideas from the small group work following the readings and create a map to expand those ideas.

Small Group Work   Take one of the ideas that you have generated in one of the previous prewriting exercises. Assume that your purpose is to form a judgment or write an evaluation of that subject. Now think about a tentative thesis and write it down. Get together with a partner and discuss your purpose and your thesis. In working with your partner, ask whether the thesis expresses a judgment or makes an evaluation. The key here is to express a value judgment, i.e., to use a word or words in the thesis which clearly indicate an opinion on the value of this subject. You and your partner should help each other to clarify your tentative thesis.

♦ WRITING ASSIGNMENT

Once you have decided on a topic to form a judgment or to evaluate, write a first draft keeping in mind what you have learned in previous chapters about purpose, a thesis, audience, development, and organization. Hold this draft until you read the following section.

Drafting and Revising

Establishing Criteria: Clarifying Your Judgment   If you thought carefully about your subject, purpose, and a tentative thesis, you probably started off with a clear judgment, for instance, "Computer courses are the most exciting ones in the curriculum," "Criminality is

MAPPING EXAMPLE

the worst problem in Puerto Rican society today," "*West Side Story* was a great American musical." Now the difficult part starts: how do you justify that statement? Where do you come up with criteria for your judgment, and what do you use to support it?

As is most often the case, the best way to begin is to write the first draft to get as many ideas on paper as possible, then reconsider what you have written. Is it really a judgment of the subject, or does your draft remain merely an analysis or explanation of the subject?

Look at the first draft of an essay on crime in Puerto Rico.

Sample Student Writing

Draft 1

According to the public opinion criminality is the worst problem of Puertorican society today. If you visit Puerto Rico and examine through the daily newspaper you will arrived to the same conclusion. On the last ten years Puerto Rico has been shaken with a wave of criminality never seen before. It looks incontrollable, no matter the efforts of the goverment and community directed to controlled this situation. Let see what statistic indicators show.

For the year 1982 in Puerto Rico were reported to the police department 96,739 felony crimes. The island population for that year was of 3,154,675 inhabitants. This mean that for each 100,000 inhabitants about 3,065 felony crimes were committed. If you compare figure of the year 1982 with years 1985 you will see the magnitude of the criminality problem in Puerto Rico. For the year of 1985 the number of felony crimes reported to the Police Department amounted to 115,939. That make 3,420 felony crimes showed the high criminal activity incidence. These statistic figures suggested that something has been happening in Puerto Rico during the last years.

Since the year 1950 Puerto Rico has been changing from an agricultural society to an industrial community. A great economic and urban development have been taking place. There is a large number of factories all through out the island. Popular metropolitan areas have displaced the traditional small town. In these metropolitan areas there are many luxurious hotel with their gambling places that running without control. On the other hand Puerto Rico has received more than 75,000 Cuban and Dominican immigrants. More than 20% of the working force of the island is unemployed. The addicts population has been estimated in more than 100,000 and in the year 1985 about 2,717 persons were arrested for violation of the controlled substances law in which 1,637 were smugglers.

In addition to all these facts Puerto Rico has one of the higher population density in the world. In 1980 federal census figured a population for the island of 3,196,520 inhabitants that make a population density of 924.1 inhabitants per square miles. Also the island is geographically located in the mid-way of south and north America. Everybody know that that mean for the business of drug traffic.   4

All those facts gives a reasonable and logical base to understand the reasons for a such high criminal activity in Puerto Rico. The island is victim of its economic progress, urban development and geographical location. Something must be done to win the battle against this high criminal activity in Puerto Rico.   5

José Jimenez

♦ DISCUSSION QUESTIONS

Note that the essay begins directly with the thesis, but the writer may place it differently in the next draft. The thesis does express a value judgment because it says that criminality is the *worst* problem in Puerto Rican society. *Worst* is the value term that clearly signals a judgment or evaluation. Now look at each paragraph.

1. What is the main point of each one?

2. Do these paragraphs support the opinion that criminality is the "worst" problem or do they analyze the causes of the problem?

3. If the essay is primarily an analysis of causes, then what should the writer do? How could he prove his original thesis?

José seemed to have trouble when he was asked to prove that it is the worst problem. His response was simply, "It's my opinion." He was facing the problem of finding appropriate criteria. To help him get past a temporary block, the instructor suggested that he think about the fact that the word "worst" implies a comparison. What other problems does his society have that are not as bad? What makes one social problem worse than another?

Then the class did a group brainstorming and came up with the following suggestions.

What makes one social problem worse than another one?

> number of people affected
>
> cost to public
>
> impact on personal safety
>
> corruption of youth

Here is how he began to use some of these suggestions in the second draft.

Draft 2

Some Puertorican think that the worst problems of Puerto 1
Rico are political and economic ones. But they are wrong; according to public opinion criminality is the worst problem of Puertorican society today. If you visit Puerto Rico and examine the daily newspaper you will arrive at the same conclusion. In the last ten years Puerto Rico has been shaken with a wave of criminality never seen before. It looks uncontrollable, no matter the efforts of the government and community directed to control this situation. Let's see what statistic indicators show.

For the year 1982 in Puerto Rico 96,739 felony crimes 2
were reported to the police department. The island population for that year was of 3,154,675 inhabitants. This means that for each 100,000 inhabitants about 3,065 felony crimes were committed. If you compare figure of the year 1982 with year 1985 you will see the magnitude of the criminality problem in Puerto Rico. For the year of 1985 was 115,939. That makes 3,420 felony crimes showed the high criminal activity incidence. These figures suggest that something has been happening in Puerto Rico during the last years.

Since the year 1950 Puerto Rico has been changing from an   3
agricultural society to an industrial community. A great economic and urban development has been taking place. There
is a large number of factories all throughout the island. Popular metropolitan areas have displaced the traditional small
towns. In these metropolitan areas there are many luxurious
hotel with their gambling places running without control. On
the other hand Puerto Rico has received more than 75,000
Cuban and Dominican immigrants. More than 20% of the
working force of the island is unemployed. The addicts population has been estimated in more than 100,000 and in the
year 1985 about 2,717 persons were arrested for violation of
the controlled substances law of which 1,637 were smugglers. Also the island is geographically located in the mid-
way of South and North America. Everybody know what that
mean for the business of drug traffic.

All those facts gives specific and logical bases to under-   4
stand why Puertoricans feel the fear of crime. The reason
crime is perceived as worse is because it affects the behavior
and sometimes the environment of a society. They feel fright-
ened for their security and we can see this in the manner that
people protect their house with iron bars and alarm systems.
The personal safety is affected by the crime, the right to have
a safe and secure home is affect too. It's not good for the head
of a family to live under such pressure condition and because
his family is at risk of being attack for a robbery or for a bur-
glary. For that reason the crime affects the social, moral and
personal values of all persons, society and country and those
values are our framework within the society in which we live.
We can see this problem of social values in the problem of social disorganization and the only tools to stop the social disorganization is the social rules.

My society, the Puertorican society, need to raise its social   5
rules to start to fight against crime. For better or for worse
crime is a disease created by the urban development and Puerto Rico is a victim of them. In the case of Puerto Rico something must be done to win this battle against this high
criminal activity.

♦ DISCUSSION QUESTIONS

Keep in mind that this is still only a second draft. Note what has been improved, and think about what needs further work.

1. What changes have been made?

2. Do they justify his judgment better?

3. Which paragraphs should be developed more? In what way?

The following student example is actually a second draft. During a conference with the instructor, the student decided that the problem with the first draft was that he was trying to write about the United States, and the draft was broad and vague. He made a wise choice to start again on the same topic, the value of certain kinds of education, focusing this time on education for Saudi Arabians, since that was what he knew most about. It is always best to start with what you know best and then expand from there.

Draft 2

EDUCATION IN SAUDIA ARABIA

Before 60 years ago, the education in Saudi Arabia was   1
poor and not compatitive. The highest level of education was
the high school diploma. With the high school diploma at
that time, the Saudis would get a good job and a good position
in the society. The wealthy families, they were few, sent their
children to Egypt to get higher education in the Egyptian
University. The Saudis who went to Egypt for higher education, studied non science majors. Those who came back from
Egypt find good jobs offered for them and good positions in
the society.

The second generation took the first generation as an ex-   2
ample of successful people, so they picked the same majors
and studied it. The Saudis at that time were not concerned
with science majors, so they did not encouraged their children to study a science majors. The first and the second generation did not think in the future of the country from the
development side.

With the discovery of the oil, money were available. The   3
Saudis did not think of studying science majors, but they

went to business majors. They find good job and good incomes with the business majors. When the Saudis student in high school asked what major they want to study, they answer bussenes. The reason behind this answer is that the Saudis students saw that the students graduating from bussness schools have good income in fact they become wealthy after few years.

The Saudis did not recognize that the situation was not usual. The reason behind all this money was the oil. The country was improving and needed engineers and sciences to support the development. The government was not able to find Saudis in this fields, so it depended on the foreign experts. The world improved, many countries are inventing and exploring new things and the Saudis still study business. The Saudis had a narrow thinking of the future. They thought that the oil prises will stay high and there will not be shortege in the income of the country.   4

The Saudis recognized an important thing that the oil prises went down and all the foreign power which is working in the country need to be changed with Saudi power, but it is late. Most of businesses faced money problems and some of them closed. The successful businessman with billions of dollers is not a very popular example for the student. The students began to recognize that the science majors are important for the government and the student will not be a billionaire in few years. All the foreign workers cost the government billions of dollers. This money the Saudis could benefit from it if they thought in the future.   5

The students in Saudi Arabia are going to science majors and trying to improve many sides in the country. It was mistack done by most of the Saudis, leaving the science fields and going for the business fields, but now they are trying to correct the mistack. I pelam [blame] the Saudis in this problem because they did not think in the future and they went to the money.   6

Abdullah Almaimanee

◆ DISCUSSION QUESTIONS

1. Is this essay about the value of certain kinds of education?

2. What is the thesis? Is it clearly stated?

3. Does the writer mention any clear standards to support the judgment that studying the sciences is *better* for Saudi Arabians?

After thinking about the answers to these questions, Abdullah wrote another draft.

Draft 3

Before 60 years ago, the education in Saudi Arabia was   1
poor and not competitive. The highest level of education was
the high school diploma. With the high school diploma at
that time, the Saudis would get a good job and a good position
in the government. The wealthy families, they were few, sent
their children to Egypt to get higher education in the Egyptian University. The Saudis who went to Egypt for higher education, studied a non scientific majors as political science,
business, and economics. Those who came back from Egypt
found good jobs offered for them and good positions in the
government.

The second generation took the first generation as an ex-   2
ample of successful people, so they picked the same majors
and studied it. The Saudis at that time were not concerned
with scientific majors as engineering and natural science
and math. The first and the second generation did not think
in the future of the country from the development side.

With the discovery of the oil, money were available. The   3
Saudis did not think of studying science majors, but they
went to business majors. They find good job and good incomes with the business majors. When the Saudis student in
high school asked what major they want to study, they answer business. The reason behind this answer is that the
Saudis students saw that the students graduating from business schools have good income infact they become wealthy
after few years.

The Saudis did not recognize that the situation was not   4
usual. The reason behind all this money was the oil. The
country was improving and needed engineers and sciences to
support the development. The government was not able to
find Saudis in this fields, so it depended on the foreign experts. The world improved, many countries are inventing and
exploring new things and the Saudis still study business.
The Saudis had a narrow thinking of the future. They
thought that the oil prises will stay high and there will not be
shortage in income of the country.

The best solution for the Saudis to concentrate in the engi-   5
neering majors, scientific majors, and in math for at least the
twenty years coming. Saudi Arabia need as many as engineers and scientific majors. To develop independence the
country must have people to support it. The foreign experts
cost the country billion of dollers each year. This money
could build more factories or to improve the services if there
are Saudis experts. Freedom is a very important issue. When
the country has her own experts and recherchers, will feel
more comfortable because if anything happened between
Saudi Arabia and other countries, the other countries will
take it is [its] experts and Saudi Arabia will be in a problem.

Prestige between the countries is important. The country   6
will be proud of her people when they discover new inventions between the countries. Winning one of the prestige
prizes will get the Saudis some confidence in their ability to
create and discover. The world is developed, the countries begin working with the nuclear power and discovering the
space. Building a car or even a factory became not complicated for the developed countries. With all this improvement
in science and in the inventions, Saudi Arabia does not have
the ability to build a car. It is a shame on the Saudis. The
Saudis could build a car and even a plane, but not without
more Saudi engineers.

The people are trying to involve in the scientific field and   7
compete with other international students. Saudi Arabia will
have to depend on the foreign experts for long period of time
until the Saudis can support their own development.

♦ DISCUSSION QUESTIONS

Keeping in mind that this draft, like José's second draft, is still "in process" consider the following points:

1. What are the changes he has made?

2. Do the changes express some criteria to support his judgment that Saudis should study the sciences now and not business?

3. What are those criteria?

♦ WRITING ASSIGNMENT

Take the first draft you completed before reading the preceding section and exchange it with a partner. Use peer review sheet 6 and write out the answers to each question, paying particular attention to the following ones:

What is/are the key value term(s) in the thesis?

What are the standards for the judgment?

Do you think the judgment is well supported?

Gathering More Information   Once you have completed peer review sheet 6, you may still have questions about what the key value terms are and what the appropriate criteria are for supporting your judgment. It is important to think about how an evaluation differs from other purposes mentioned earlier in this text.

You have already practiced writing to describe, to explain, and to analyze. You could write about almost any topic with a variety of purposes in mind, including writing to make a judgment. Consider the following examples of different thesis statements on the same topic, in this case VCRs:

Descriptive thesis   "A VCR is a simple, inexpensive machine that allows the average homeowner to show video recordings on his or her television set." A technician would write a far more detailed, technical description.

Explanatory thesis   "Buying a VCR is a process of using comparison shopping to come up with the best deal."

Analytical thesis   "The sudden popularity of VCR's for home use caused new problems of interpreting copyright laws."

Judgmental or evaluative thesis   "The Panasonic VCR is the best machine for your use."

The key value term in the last example is "best." How do you prove that it is the best? You must come up with appropriate criteria. Which of the following sets of criteria would be better to defend that statement?

[A]

how friendly the salesman was

how desperately Panasonic needs your business

what color it is on the outside

[B]

initial cost

its repair record

cost of repairs

number and quality of features

suitability for your uses (home, school, professional)

Coming up with a list of suitable criteria to make the judgment on your topic will help you to move forward with draft 2, especially if you or your partner had trouble completing peer review sheet 6.

Once you are more confident that you have a good list of criteria, then you can begin to search for more material to describe and support those points. Each point might be a separate paragraph or section in your essay, and you would probably do well to discuss them in order of importance, from least to most important.

Gathering more information may involve a number of different procedures. Just clarifying the criteria may make all sorts of new ideas come into your mind. If not, try one of the following:

◇ Brainstorm on any memories related to the topic.

◇ Brainstorm or freewrite on a projection of the future: "what should be."

◇ Do a map putting each criterion in the middle of the page.

◇ Do some research—go to the library and try to find an article in a good newspaper or newsmagazine on the topic.

◊ Interview someone—find someone who knows something about the topic and ask a few questions. Interviewing a nonexpert may help also if you ask what the person thinks of your ideas and what he or she would want to read about in your essay.

♦ WRITING ASSIGNMENT

If the peer reviewer helped you as much as needed, you are ready to write your second draft. You may want to schedule an appointment with a tutor in the writing center or you may have the opportunity to take the first draft to your instructor for a reading or conference. If you need more information, follow one of the suggestions listed above. In doing your second draft, work hard to support your judgment fully. After you finish working on the revisions to make the criteria clear and to support them with adequate detail, examples, and facts, you should try to do some editing.

Recopy this draft and turn it in to your instructor for comment.

Editing

Word Choice   One of the most important aspects of editing your work is to try, as much as possible, to use precise, accurate words. Choosing your words carefully is important first for clarity of meaning and second for the connotations they carry. You must know that the denotation (dictionary meaning or strict sense) of the word is correct for your meaning, and you must take into account the word's connotation (extended or implied meaning), so that you don't suggest some meaning that is inappropriate for the context or audience.

Think about how different your word choice is in addressing children versus a group of college students. Or think about how you change your wording depending on whether an instructor can hear you or whether you are just talking to a friend. For instance, saying someone is "fat" is not as kind as saying he or she is "overweight." Although the words mean the same thing, the connotation of "fat" is very negative. Words that have the same meaning often differ in their appropriateness for either speech or writing, their level of sophistication, their degree of intensity, and their degree of politeness, among other things. Compare the following examples:

◊ "The food in our cafeteria is *the pits*" (current student slang—spoken) vs. "The food in our cafeteria is *terrible*" (general audience—could be written).

◊ "Those people are *fools* not to study philosophy" (strong and potentially offensive) vs. "Those people are *shortsighted* not to study philosophy" (more polite).

◊ "He suffers from *arteriosclerosis*" (technical term—educated audience) vs. "He suffers from *hardening of the arteries*" (more general audience).

♦ WORD CHOICE EXERCISE

In the following sentences, find synonyms that can be used for the underlined words. Discuss with your instructor how the synonym differs in connotation. Some of the underlined words are from vocabulary exercises in this chapter, and some other vocabulary words could be used as the synonyms for the underlined words.

1. Her whole body was *swathed* in furs.

2. That boy *hassles* everyone around him.

3. The basement of her house is a *damp* place.

4. My childhood was a very *happy* time.

5. Those kids *look down on* the poor kids next door.

6. My directions *stipulate* very clearly that no one is to leave.

7. She has a very *open* nature.

8. There were *little raised bumps* all over the roots of that tree.

9. Professors shouldn't *harangue* their students.

When you are editing for word choice in your own work, you will probably need the help of a native speaker of English—another student or your instructor who can point out differences in connotation. You can do much to correct your own word choice, however, by thinking about the appropriateness of the words for the topic and the audience.

♦ EDITING EXERCISE

1. Look back at José's second draft and Abdullah's third draft and edit them, paying particular attention to word choice.

2. In the following draft, edit according to the instructor's marks (see Appendix B for a key to the abbreviations). Note that the instructor has helped by supplying some corrections for idioms and suggestions at certain points.

Draft 2

EDUCATION ABROAD AND ITS EFFECT
ON SOCIAL STANDING

It is obvious that Thai students are   1
going abroad to study in the countries_   *pn*
such as the United States, Australia,
Canada, or European countries. About
70 years ago ~~that~~ there was no university in Thailand, so a few people who
were wealthy or in the royal families
and had scholarship from the king   *number*
could go to study in European countries. All of the people who had high
education graduated from universities abroad. So the social classes
started being classified by education.
People were believing that education   *tense*
gained abroad made persons more intelligent, successful, and respectable.
The first university in Thailand,
Chulalongkorn University, was established by King Vachiralongkorn. Thai
people who wanted higher education
could attend the university without
going abroad. However, the belief, that *pn*
the foreign degree was better, was   *pn*
maintained. Now, there are at least 50
institutions which offer college education all over the country, and several
of them offer graduate school and doctorates. Many people have had master *tense*
degrees and doctorates from Thai uni-

versities. A lot of people, on the other
hand, keep going abroad with the idea

one that ^foreign degree is better than ^Thai   *art./art*

to create ⎰^for many good reasons such as to get   *pn*
a "parallel" ⎱
structure, new experience, better <u>educational</u>   *word choice*
use a verb
in each <u>knowledge</u> and to improve their social   *number*
part <u>standings</u>.

   In Thailand now the number of uni-   2
versities is not balanced and does not
relate to the number of high school
students. The public universities can
accept only 20%–25% of ^graduating   *art*
students each year. So the rest of the
students have to study at private universities and colleges and open universities with ^unlimited number of the   *art*
students. The students who do not
want to study in private universities
or open universities, and who have   *pn*
parents who can afford it, will go to   *pn*
study outside the country.

   Since Thailand is now trading and   3
has diplomatic relationship <u>with</u>   *number*
many countries, ~~so~~ the companies or
the government often <u>qualifies</u> the de-   *word choice*
gree from specific countries for job ap-
                              In the
plicants. ^Thai International Airline

cap company which has the best compensation, for example, ~~whose job,~~ *the*
                                      s
qualification ^for many positions <u>re</u>-

word choice quires applicants who know English
<u>well</u> or have ^foreign degree in order ~~to~~   *art*

word choice ~~be capable~~ <u>to deal</u> with internationals.

The officers of the Ministry of Foreign
Affirs ~~whose positions~~ *who* are diplomats,
for instance, must know foreign languages and understand many cul-
tures, and this is the reason why they   *wordiness*
need people who graduate from the
other countries.

    The reason ~~of~~ *for* going abroad is not   4
only to know the other language but
also to experience the other countries   *poss*
culture and new things. The reward of   *word choice*
studying abroad is not only ∧ degree   *art*
and pride but the great experience ~~is~~ ∧ *which*
~~being~~ *stays* with them forever. People who
involve international business are   *word choice*
needed to know ∧ culture different in   *number*
order to deal business effectively. The   *word choice*
consumer behavior is based on their   *poss*
culture, life style, and household pattern. To learn their behavior is not
to create | just reading books but being with
parallelism | them and learn *ing* them with six sences.   *sp*
    Knowing   ∧   *having*   *number*
~~To know the~~ other language and ∧ ex-   5
perience are not enough to get jobs
done successfully. But also educa-   *word*
tional knowledge is applied ~~to use~~ to   *choice*
get the jobs done. Most of the Thai ed-
ucational patterns have been improved | *improved over*
over   ?? | *copied from*
from the western models especially
    at
curricula. Now Thai curricula are ~~in~~
the same level and some of them are
better than the westerns models. But ∧   *adj./word missing*
some fields the westerns are still bet-   *word choice*

ter such as aircraft engineering,ₐmedi- *word missing*
cal science. Thai people still believe
the westerns educational pattern are *adj./number*
better. So people who get degree *number*
abroad are more accepted and com-
pensated by many companies and government organizations.

The most important reason is so- 6
cially based. This idea derives from
the perception of Thai people in the
past that only wealthy people and
royal families could go abroad to
study. It has been a pride of the family
if one goes abroad to study and comes
back with a degree. Especially in royal
families, one person at least, has to go
to study abroad, otherwise it will be
shameful. It became a tradition of the
royal family. The common people also
sent their children abroad in order to
improve their standing in the society,
even if they do not have enough
money. They probably have to loan *word choice*
money and have to suffer in order to
repay. But when their children come *it*
back with a degree, they will be happy
and will be able to tell that their son or *word choice*
daughter has graduated from France, *have they graduated from the country?*
England, American, or wherever.
Some people are still thinking that 7
persons who go out to study are coming under the influence of western
people. They think there are enough

universities in Thailand and the educational quality is better than in western countries. They are too patriotic___ *r.s.*
and they cannot see the truth. Whatever the reasons for people to go to
study abroad ~~are~~, it is a fact that if
they <u>return back</u> home and use the *rep.*
knowledge they have gained abroad, it
will help to develop the country. Thailand, now, is <u>still needing</u> educated *tense*
people with different creative ideas
and experiences from other more de-
velopped countries. *sp*

◆ WRITING ASSIGNMENT

Up to this point you should have done prewriting, a first draft, peer review, some exercises to clarify your thesis and criteria, and written a second draft. When you have received the second draft from your instructor or had a conference, you will be ready to make final revisions by adding more information and editing as carefully as you can for all elements of grammar, usage, and spelling. Pay particular attention to your word choice.

If, by chance, you do not want to continue with the topic you started with earlier in this chapter, then begin with some prewriting on another topic. Just to review, here are the steps you should follow:

◇ Prewrite to generate ideas on the topic.

◇ Think carefully about the purpose of this assignment.

◇ Draft a tentative thesis that expresses a judgment.

◇ Think about criteria or standards to support that judgment.

◇ Draft a first or discovery draft.

◇ Exchange it with a peer and use peer review sheet 6.

◇ Show it to your instructor or tutor in the writing center.

◇ Work on a second draft to clarify the criteria and support.

◇ Gather more information if needed.

◊ Give draft 2 to your instructor.

◊ Work on any further revisions needed and do careful editing based on the instructor's comments.

◊ Write draft 3.

◊ Proofread and prepare final draft.

Sample Student Essay for Writing to Form a Judgment

This final student writing sample is again one that you can read and comment on from a very rough discovery draft through revision, editing, and proofreading of the final draft.

Discovery Draft
THE VALUE OF EDUCATION

Education is very important to many people. It is the key   1
to success and it can also adapt sudden [certain] goal in life.
Education can teach us many things and it will bring us
more knowledge. The value of education are career, make
money, earned a degree, and gain knowledge.

Many people took education very seriously because they   2
want to have a career. They want to have skill and knowledge
on their job. They want to be proud and happy on what their
career is.

Earned a lot of money is one of the value of education. Peo-   3
ple want to live in a comfortable life and also in their own
style. They want to have everything houses, cars, and other
expensive items. Maybe sudden [certain] person want to have
a family. If they don't have enough money, how can they support themself?

Degree is very valuable. It show that one had finish its ma-   4
jor. If one went and apply for job between a person with a degree and a person without a degree who would have more
chance of getting a job? Of course the person with the degree.

Knowledge is the best value of education. Without knowl-   5
edge a person can be so enarance [ignorant]. Where did people get all those knowledge, is it from television and radio?

Maybe a little bit, but most of it is from reading books and learn things in school.

Phuong Mai

Peer Review 6
Writing to Form a Judgment

Writer: *Phuong Mai*
Peer Reviewer: *John Vornavarn*

1. What did you like best about this essay?

   I liked the idea that education come from book not just T.V. or radio.

2. What is the purpose?

   to show what value of education is — to make a judgment about education

3. What is the thesis?

   "The value of education are career, make money, earned a degree, and gain knowledge.

4. What are the key value terms in the thesis?

   value   ? ?

5. What are the standards for the judgment?

   have a career
   earn money
   degree is valuable
   knowledge

6. Do you think the judgment is well supported?

   not very well developed or explained

7. Do you have any suggestions for revision?

   say more about each part — need some examples every paragraph very short. I'm not sure about her standards

♦ DISCUSSION QUESTIONS

1. What do you think of this draft?

2. Do you agree with the peer reviewer?

3. What would you add to the peer reviewer's comments?

After writing this discovery draft, the student was asked what she had trouble with in starting this assignment. She said, "The problem that I had doing this essay are I can't find an idea that I can really go into more detail. I don't know if my paragraph support my thesis." After discussing the peer review sheet and doing an exercise similar to the one on p. 203, she wrote a second draft, trying to clarify the criteria used to support her belief that higher education is valuable.

In draft 2, the instructor commented on the left on needed revisions and on the right on editing, so that if the student wanted to use the same sentence she would not repeat those errors. But only two types of errors were addressed; word choice and fragments. Revision, not editing, is still the most important task at this point, but sometimes it is worth paying attention to a small number of problems even in an early draft.

Draft 2

Education is very important to   1
many people. It is the key to success
and it can also achieve sudden [cer-
tain] goal in life. Education is a <u>mass</u>   *wd*
<u>of knowledge</u>, no matter how long
better   ones study, the field will never end.
intro   Now the world is so modern and with
many new technique. It will make education even more valuable. New tech- ⎫
nique come out all the time, if one did ⎬ *frag*
not have an education and take more   ⎭
class. They will not know how to oper-
ate <u>things</u>. The value of education can   *wd*
prepare students for the real world,
make money, and get a degree.

Education can really prepare stu-   2
dents for the real world. For example,

the professor will give students tough assignments and expect them to do it right. Students must spend time observing and find the solution for it. On the outside world, when the boss give an employee a hard case. He must find a solution just like he did in college.

frag

good example here

Another example is many professors will put students under pressure. Students have three tests and an essay due on the same day. Students must not panic, but find time to organize oneself to study. Students must struggle through and be the best, get high grade. Many business man is under the same pressure, but in a different situation. He properly [probably] have three meeting to go to and a stack of paper work must be done at the same time. He must struggle through like he did in college, if he want to be the top business man.

what is a "good" major?

Many people want to have a good major for many reasons, but one of the reason most people want is make a lot of money. If one want to live in a comfortable life and also in their own style, one must have a high payment in their major. These major are mostly engineering, accounting, and many others require an education degree.

3

do you mean "major" or "career"?

wd

wd unclear

finished one's education

Degree is very valuable. It show that ones had finish its major. For example, if there are two people went and

frag

4

could you { apply for job. If one had a degree and
develop one don't have a degree. Who would
this # have more chance of getting a job? Of
and #3
more? course, a person with a degree. They

think that the person had a degree is

higher level than a person without a

what happened degree. Person with a degree will <u>ob-</u> *wd*
to the value
of knowledge? <u>served</u> things more quickly.

Some people had took education for 5

granted in America. They had all the

qualification to have an education and

be success people. Instead, people

turn it down and not take advantage of

it. They thought that they had known

everything about it, but not <u>really</u>. Ed- *wd*

ucation is not something one learn in

one life time, but it's study forever.

◆ DISCUSSION QUESTIONS

1. Has the thesis been changed?

2. Is it an improvement?

3. Is there better support in this draft?

4. Are the criteria for making the judgment clear?

5. Are all of the instructor's comments clear? Which, if any, are not?

6. What do you think needs to be worked on the most?

Now read the third draft.

Draft 3

could you be
more ────→ Education is very important to 1
specific
many people. It is the key to success___ *pn*

can "education" and it can also achieve certain goal in
achieve a
goal? life. Education is not <u>finish</u> after col- *vb*

lege, but it still continues. Now, people

have to keep up with ~~the~~ new tech- *s,*
nique on machine and computer or *s,* *s,*
new ideas to be on top of society. Education will give people knowledge.
Without knowledge a person can be <u>so</u> *wd*
ignorant. Where did people get all
are verb these knowledge, is it from television *agr/cs*
tenses
consistent? and radio? <u>Maybe</u> a little bit, but most *wd*
of it is from <u>reading books and learn</u> *par*
<u>things</u> in schools. The value of educa-
tion is to prepare students for the real
world, to allow them to make money,
and to get university degree. *art*

Education can <u>really</u> prepare stu- *wd*   2
dents for the real world. For example,
the professor will give students tough
assignments and expect the student to
do the assignment right. Students
must spend time <u>to observed</u> and to *vb*
find the solution for the assignment.
In the outside world, when the boss
gave an employee a hard case, he must
find a solution just like he did in college. Another example is many professors will put students under
pressure. Students have three tests
and an essay due on the same day. Students must not panic, but find time to
organize themselves to study. Stu-
dents must struggle <u>though</u> and be the *sp*
best, also get high <u>grade.</u> Many busi- *pl*
ness men are under the same pres-
sure, but in a different situation. <u>He</u> *ref*
might have three meetings to go to and

a stack of paper work must be done at
the same time. He must struggle
through like he did in college, if he
wants to be a successful business
man.

Many people want to have a good career for many reasons, but one of the
reasons most people want is to chose a
career that could make money. If people want to live a comfortable life and
also in their own style, they must try
don't you mean more than this? to obtain <u>a salary</u> in their career.
<u>These</u> career required an education *agr*
like <u>E</u>ngineering, pre-med, or ac- *l.c.*
counting.

ᴧUniversity degree is very valuable. *art*
It shows that people have finish <u>one's</u> *ref*
education. For example, if there are
two people apply for an office job, one *frag*
has a <u>college degree</u> and <u>another one</u>
doesn't have a degree. Who <u>wuld</u> have *sp*
more chance of getting a job? Of
course, a person with a degree. They
think that the personᴧhas a degree is *wd missing*
higher level than a person without a
degree and will learn things more
quickly.

Some people have taken education
for granted in America. They have all
the qualification to have an education
and be <u>a</u> successful <u>people</u>. Instead, *agr) tr*
people take it very lightly. Many peo-
ple took education very seriously because they want to have a career. They

3

4

5

want to have skill and knowledge ~~on~~ *in*
their job. They also want to be proud
and happy in their career. Education
is not something people learn in one
life time, but (it's study) forever. *can be pursued*

Notice the improvements that she has made in the third draft. Has her judgment about the value of an education become clearer and better supported? Notice also the amount of editing that still needs to be done. Phuong wrote a fourth draft, concentrating on editing and trying in a few places to continue her effort to be precise and clear.

Read the fourth draft and then see if you can find any places that she missed in her final editing and proofreading.

Draft 4

THE VALUE OF AN EDUCATION

Higher education is very important to many people. It is the key to success and it can also lead to certain goals in life. Education continues after people finish college. Now, people have to keep up with the new techniques, machines, computers, and ideas to be on top of society. For example, after the medical students had graduated and practiced with their license, they have to keep up with the medicines and learn how to use them. Education will give people knowledge. Without knowledge a person can be very ignorant. Where do people get all this knowledge? Is it from television and radio? Perhaps a little bit, but most of it is from reading books and learning things in school. The value of education is to prepare students for the real world, to allow them to make money, and to get a university degree.

Education can prepare students for the real world. For example, a professor will give students tough assignments and expect them to do the assignment right. Students must spend time to observe and to find the solution for the assignment. In the outside world, when the boss give an employee a hard case, he must find a solution just like he did in college. Another example is many professor will put students under pressure. Students have three tests and an essay due on the same day. Students must not panic, but find time to organize themselves to study. Students must struggle through and be the best, also get high grades. Many business men are under the same pressure, but in a different situation. They might have three meetings to go to and a stack of paper work must be done by a certain time. They must struggle through like they did in college, if they want to be a successful business man.

Many people want to have a good career for many reasons, but one of the reasons is to chose a lucrative career that could make money. If people want to live a comfortable life and also in their own style, they must try to earned a high salary in their career. These careers require an education like engineer, doctor, or accounting.

A university degree is very valuable. It shows that people have finished certain education. For example, if there are two people applying for an office job, one has a college degree and the other one doesn't have a degree, who would have more chance of getting the job? A person with a degree. The employer thinks that the person who has a degree is higher status than a person don't have a degree and will learn things more quickly.

Some people have taken education for granted in America. They have all the qualifications to have an education and be successful people. Instead, people take it very lightly. For example, students who had drop out of school because they think that education is not important to them or could not do them any good in life. On the other hand, many people take education very seriously because they want to have a career. They want to have skill and knowledge in their job. They also want to be proud and happy in their career. Education is not something people learn in one life time, but can be pursued forever.

Chapter Six

CONTEMPORARY SOCIAL ISSUES

Writing to Persuade

Convince yourself that you are working in clay not marble, on paper not eternal bronze: let that first sentence be as stupid as it wishes. No one will rush out and print it as it stands.

—*Jacques Barzun*

Geoffrey Nunberg (1945–)

Geoffrey Nunberg was born in New York City and received his PhD in Linguistics from the CUNY Graduate Center. He has taught at University of California in Los Angeles and at Stanford University. He has written articles for Atlantic Monthly *and numerous pieces for* The New York Times. *He currently lives in San Francisco and has a language commentary radio show on PBS entitled "Fresh Air" in addition to working with the Center for Study of Language and Information at Stanford University and the Xerox Palo Alto Research Center.*

In this editorial from The New York Times, *(October 1, 1986) Nunberg lays out the discussion surrounding proposed legislation to make English an official language in the state of California. The United States does not have, at the federal level, any legislation about language use, although some cities have declared themselves officially bilingual.*

Before reading, write in your journal for 10 minutes on why you think anyone in the United States would be worried about making English an official language.

An "Official Language" for California?

PALO ALTO, CALIF.—Strange as it may seem, the people of California—the creators of Marinspeak and Valley Girl Talk[1]—will vote this fall [1986] on a measure[2] intended to protect the English language from baneful foreign influences. Proposition 63 would amend the state constitution to make English California's "official language" to prevent state business from being transacted in other tongues.   1

The vote is the most important test to date for former Senator S. I. Hayakawa, whose organization, U.S. English, seeks ultimately to attach a similar amendment to the United States Constitution. Official language laws have already been passed recently by two state legislatures,   2

---

[1]The language of teenage girls (and others) who live in Marin County, Northern California, and in the valley south of the Los Angeles area.

[2]Here, an action designed to accomplish a purpose. Proposition 63 was an official measure placed on the ballot in the fall of 1986, and accepted by a strong majority of voters.

but the measure in California is the first to be put to a popular vote and to receive wide national attention.

The measure doesn't simply recognize English as the official state language in the way "California, Here I Come" might be recognized as the official state song. It specifically enjoins the legislature from taking any action that "diminishes or ignores" the role of English as the state language.

No one is sure how the courts or the legislature would interpret this, but attorneys on both sides suggest it could be used to end bilingual education programs and to prohibit the use of other languages in everything from employment compensation hearings[3] to government publications and public-service announcements.

The argument most frequently offered in defense of the amendment is that immigrants will not take the trouble to learn English if the government makes services available in other languages. In a short time, proponents say, we will have large, permanent non-English-speaking communities in our midst, with the prospect of separatist movements and ensuing "language wars."

What frightens them most is the large Hispanic communities, which they see as threatening not only because of their size and concentration but because they are perceived as being subject to the contagion by foreign political interests.[4] But Hispanic groups are adapting exactly as did earlier immigrants. A Rand Corporation survey in 1985 found that more than 95 percent of first-generation Mexican-Americans born in the United States are proficient in English and that more than half the second generation speaks no Spanish at all.

There are important questions about how to ease the acculturation of new immigrants, such as: Does it make sense to allow immigrant children to take math and social studies in their native language until they have learned enough English to enter the English-only course? But this is hardly a constitutional issue.

It's important not to lose sight of English's enormous appeal throughout the nation and the world. The notion of protecting it must seem bizarre to the French who fruitlessly write laws to keep its influence at bay. To them, English needs protecting about as much as crabgrass.[5]

What is most distressing about the prospect of a language amendment is that it demeans our own linguistic traditions. Men like Samuel

---

[3]Official sessions where citizens are aided with problems related to jobs or wages.

[4]This should probably read "subject to the influence of foreign political interests."

[5]A broad-leaf grass considered a weed.

Johnson[6] and Noah Webster[7] held that the language should not be subject to state control or interference. Our Founding Fathers also debated and wisely rejected proposals to make English an official language.

If the referendum passes, its main effect would be the opposite of its   10
ostensible goal. It would make it harder for immigrants who have not yet mastered English to enter the social and economic mainstream. The amendment won't do anything to help new immigrants learn the language, but it will deny them help in their own language when they go to a state employment agency or try to find out how to enroll their children in school. If some advocates have their way, it will even be impossible for them to get a driver's license.

The English-first proponents like to point out that earlier generations   11
of immigrants were faced with worse hardships and managed to acculturate themselves nonetheless. But there was nothing ennobling about the experience, nor did anyone learn English faster as a result. It is only through a very long and misted glass that someone can look back with nostalgia at the reception that our ancestors underwent at Ellis Island[8] and conclude that we owe the same treatment to recent arrivals.

◆ COMPREHENSION/DISCUSSION QUESTIONS

1. What is the issue involved in Proposition 63?

2. What is the difference between a state adopting an official song or flower and a state passing a measure such as Proposition 63?

3. What do people think the result will be if Proposition 63 passes?

4. What are the arguments in favor of it?

5. What is Nunberg's position on the issue?

6. How does he use the linguistic traditions of the United States as support for his position?

7. Why do you suppose the "Founding Fathers" rejected proposals to make English the official language?

8. What does Nunberg think will happen if the referendum passes?

---

[6]British lexicographer, critic, and author (1709–1784).

[7]American lexicographer (1758–1843)

[8]An island in upper New York Bay serving as the main U.S. Immigration center from 1892 to 1943. Site of the processing of thousands of immigrants. Now part of the Statue of Liberty National Monument.

9. Does he think that new immigrants should be treated as older ones were? Why or why not?

10. Is there a connection to be made between this essay and the Simon piece in Chapter 4?

11. Do you think that the government should support bilingual education?

12. How would you defend your own position on the issue of an official language?

♦ VOCABULARY

Write a definition of the following words and indicate their specific meaning in context. Write a sentence of your own using each one. Then try to write a paragraph using at least five of the words.

baneful [1]	mainstream [10]
contagion [6]	nostalgia [11]
demean [9]	ostensible [10]
enjoin [3]	referendum [10]
ennoble [11]	separatist (5)
fruitlessly [8]	

♦ IDIOMS AND FIGURES OF SPEECH

Study the following expressions and try to explain the comparisons being made.

1. "To keep its influence *at bay*" [8]—keep it away.

2. "English needs protecting about as much as crabgrass" [8].

3. "It is only through a very long and misted glass . . ." [11].

♦ JOURNAL ENTRY

Write for 20 minutes in your journal on your reactions to this essay. You might think of answering one or more of the following questions:

Did it surprise you that Americans would be worried about protecting English?

Do you think the government is obligated to help all citizens and immigrants by offering services in other languages?

Do you think immigrants will learn English faster if the government conducts all business in English?

♦ SMALL GROUP WORK

Divide into groups of 3–4 students and work in the library on finding out about public reaction to Proposition 63 as expressed in newspapers. Each group might take a different aspect, for example:

opinions pro and con prior to the vote

reactions after it passed on November 4, 1986

any subsequent results in California

any subsequent action taken in other states

Each member of the group should take a major U.S. newspaper,—the *New York Times*, the *Washington Post*, and at least two from California—and search indexes to find stories on the issue. A reference librarian or your classroom instructor can offer help in learning how to use electronic and other bibliographic resources.

The groups should report on their findings in a following class session. Students may want to use this exercise as a starting point for an essay.

Alvin Toffler   *(1928–   )*

Alvin Toffler began his career as a newspaper reporter and served as an Associate Editor of Fortune *magazine. He has been a freelance writer since 1961 and is best known for his works,* The Culture Consumers *(1964),* Future Shock *(1970), and* The Third Wave *(1980). His book* Future Shock *provided our language with a new term to designate the impact of rapid cultural and technological changes. The following selection, which is taken from that work, reflects Toffler's projections about what the family will be like in the future. Much of what he says reflects faith in new birth technology and a belief in the need for different patterns of parenting and marriage.*

Before you read, write in your journal for 10 minutes on what you think the differences are between your grandparents' generation and your own in regard to raising children and getting married.

The Family Fractured

The flood of novelty about to crash down upon us will spread from universities and research centers to factories and offices, from the marketplace and mass media into our social relationships, from the community into the home. Penetrating deep into our private lives, it will place absolutely unprecedented strains on the family itself.

The family has been called the "giant shock absorber"[1] of society— the place to which the bruised and battered individual returns after doing battle with the world, the one stable point in an increasingly flux-filled[2] environment. As the super–industrial revolution unfolds, this "shock absorber" will come in for some shocks of its own.

Social critics have a field day speculating about the family. The family is "near the point of complete extinction," says Ferdinand Lundberg, author of *The Coming World Transformation*. "The family is dead except for the first year or two of child raising," according to psychoanalyst William Wolf. "This will be its only function." Pessimists tell us the family is racing toward oblivion—but seldom tell us what will take its place.

[1]Mechanism on a vehicle that keeps the wheels from transfering the impact of bumps to the frame.

[2]In continuous change or movement.

Family optimists, in contrast, contend that the family, having existed   4
all this time, will continue to exist. Some go so far as to argue that the
family is in for a Golden Age[3] As leisure spreads, they theorize, families
will spend more time together and will derive great satisfaction from
joint activity. "The family that plays together, stays together," etc.

A more sophisticated view holds that the very turbulence of tomor-   5
row will drive people deeper into their families. "People will marry for
stable structure," says Dr. Irwin M. Greenberg, Professor of Psychiatry
at the Albert Einstein College of Medicine. According to this view, the
family serves as one's "portable roots," anchoring one against the storm
of change. In short, the more transient and novel the environment, the
more important the family will become.

It may be that both sides in this debate are wrong. For the future is   6
more open than it might appear. The family may neither vanish *nor*
enter upon a new Golden Age. It may—and this is far more likely—break
up, shatter, only to come together again in weird and novel ways.

THE MYSTIQUE OF MOTHERHOOD

The most obviously upsetting force likely to strike the family in the   7
decades immediately ahead will be the impact of the new birth technology. The ability to pre-set the sex of one's baby, or even to "program"
its IQ, looks and personality traits, must now be regarded as a real
possibility. Embryo implants, babies grown *in vitro*,[4] the ability to
swallow a pill and guarantee oneself twins or triplets or, even more, the
ability to walk into a "babytorium"[5] and actually purchase embryos—
all this reaches so far beyond any previous human experience that one
needs to look at the future through the eyes of the poet or painter, rather
than those of the sociologist or conventional philosopher.

It is regarded as somehow unscholarly, even frivolous, to discuss   8
these matters. Yet advances in science and technology, or in reproduc-
tive biology alone, could, within a short time, smash all orthodox ideas
about the family and its responsibilities. When babies can be grown in a
laboratory jar what happens to the very notion of maternity? And what
happens to the self-image of the female in societies which, since the very
beginnings of man, have taught her that her primary mission is the
propagation of and nurture of the race?

Few social scientists have begun as yet to concern themselves with   9
such questions. One who has is psychiatrist Hyman G. Weitzen, director
of Neuropsychiatric Service at Polyclinic Hospital in New York. The

---

[3] An idyllic time usually thought of as a re-creation of "the good old days."

[4] Latin for "in glass," such as a test tube or Petri dish.

[5] Toffler's word, after "emporium;" a fancy store.

cycle of birth, Dr. Weitzen suggests, "fulfills for most women a major creative need . . . Most women are proud of their ability to bear children. . . . The special aura that glorifies the pregnant woman has figured largely in the art and literature of both East and West."

What happens to the cult of motherhood, Weitzen asks, if "her offspring might literally not be hers, but that of a genetically 'superior' ovum, implanted in her womb from another woman, or even grown in a Petri dish?" If women are to be important at all, he suggests, it will no longer be because they alone can bear children. If nothing else, we are about to kill off the mystique of motherhood.
10

Not merely motherhood, but the concept of parenthood itself may be in for radical revision. Indeed, the day may soon dawn when it is possible for a child to have more than two biological parents. Dr. Beatrice Mintz, a developmental biologist at the Institute for Cancer Research in Philadelphia, has grown what are coming to be known as "multi-mice"—baby mice each of which has more than the usual number of parents. Embryos are taken from each of two pregnant mice. These embryos are placed in a laboratory dish and nurtured until they form a single growing mass. This is then implanted in the womb of a third female mouse. A baby is born that clearly shares the genetic characteristics of both sets of donors. Thus a typical multi-mouse, born of two pairs of parents, has white fur and whiskers on one side of its face, dark fur and whiskers on the other, with alternating bands of white and dark hair covering the rest of the body. Some 700 multi-mice bred in this fashion have already produced more than 35,000 offspring themselves. If multi-mouse is here, can "multi-man" be far behind?
11

Under such circumstances, what or who is a parent? When a woman bears in her uterus an embryo conceived in another woman's womb, who is the mother? And just exactly who is the father?
12

If a couple can actually purchase an embryo, then parenthood becomes a legal, not a biological matter. Unless such transactions are tightly controlled, one can imagine such grotesqueries[6] as a couple buying an embryo, raising it *in vitro*, then buying another in the name of the first, as though for a trust fund.[7] In that case, they might be regarded as legal "grandparents" before their first child is out of its infancy. We shall need a whole new vocabulary to describe kinship ties.
13

Furthermore, if embryos are for sale, can a corporation buy one? Can it buy ten thousand? Can it resell them? And if not a corporation, how about a noncommercial research laboratory? If we buy and sell living embryos, are we back to a new form of slavery? Such are the night-
14

[6]Grotesque or awful things.

[7]Money set aside until a child reaches maturity.

marish questions soon to be debated by us. To continue to think of the family, therefore, in purely conventional terms is to defy all reason.

Faced by rapid social change and the staggering implications of the   15
scientific revolution, super-industrial man may be forced to experiment with novel family forms. Innovative minorities can be expected to try out a colorful variety of family arrangements. They will begin by tinkering with existing forms.

THE STREAMLINED FAMILY

One simple thing they will do is streamline the family. The typical   16
pre-industrial family not only had a good many children, but numerous other dependents as well—grandparents, uncles, aunts, and cousins. Such "extended" families were well suited for survival in slow-paced agricultural societies. But such families are hard to transport or transplant. They are immobile.

Industrialism demanded masses of workers ready and able to move   17
off the land in pursuit of jobs, and to move again whenever necessary. Thus the extended family gradually shed its excess weight and the so-called "nuclear" family emerged—a stripped-down, portable family unit consisting only of parents and a small set of children. This new style family, far more mobile than the traditional extended family, became the standard model in all the industrial countries.

Super-industrialism, however, the next stage of ecotechnological de-   18
velopment, requires even higher mobility. Thus we may expect many among the people of the future to carry the streamlining process a step further by remaining childless, cutting the family down to its most elemental components, a man and a woman. Two people, perhaps with matched careers, will prove more efficient at navigating through education and social shoals, through job changes and geographic relocations, than the ordinary child-cluttered family. Indeed, anthropologist Margaret Mead has pointed out that we may already be moving toward a system under which, as she puts it, "parenthood would be limited to a smaller number of families whose principal functions would be child-drearing," leaving the rest of the population "free to function—for the first time in history—as individuals."

A compromise may be the postponement of children, rather than   19
childlessness. Men and women today are often torn in conflict between a commitment to career and a commitment to children. In the future, many couples will sidestep this problem by deferring the entire task of raising children until after retirement.

This may strike people of the present as odd. Yet once childbearing is   20
broken away from its biological base, nothing more than tradition suggests having children at an early age. Why not wait, and buy your

embryos later, after your work career is over? Thus childlessness is likely to spread among young and middle-aged couples; sexagenarians[8] who raise infants may be far more common. The post-retirement family could become a recognized social institution.

BIO-PARENTS AND PRO-PARENTS

If a smaller number of families raise children, however, why do the   21
children have to be their own? Why not a system under which "professional parents" take on the childbearing function for others?

Raising children, after all, requires skills that are by no means univer-   22
sal. We don't let "just anyone" perform brain surgery or, for that matter, sell stocks and bonds. Even the lowest ranking civil servant is required to pass tests proving competence. Yet we allow virtually anyone, almost without regard for mental or moral qualification, to try his or her hand at raising young human beings, so long as these humans are biological offspring. Despite the increasing complexity of the task, parenthood remains the greatest single preserve of the amateur.

As the present system cracks and the super-industrial revolution rolls   23
over us, as the armies of juvenile delinquents swell, as hundreds of thousands of youngsters flee their homes, and students rampage at universities[9] in all the techno-societies[10] we can expect vociferous demands for an end to parental dilettantism.

There are far better ways to cope with the problems of youth, but   24
professional parenthood is certain to be proposed, if only because it fits so perfectly with the society's overall push toward specialization. Moreover, there is a powerful, pent-up demand for this social innovation. Even now millions of parents, given the opportunity, would happily relinquish their parental responsibilities—and not necessarily through irresponsibility or lack of love. Harried, frenzied, up against the wall, they have come to see themselves as inadequate to the tasks. Given affluence and the existence of specially-equipped and licensed professional parents, many of today's biological parents would not only gladly surrender their children to them, but would look upon it as an act of love, rather than rejection.

Parental professionals would not be therapists, but actual family units   25
assigned to, and well paid for, rearing children. Such families might be multi-generational by design, offering children in them an opportunity to observe and learn from a variety of adult models, as was the case in

---

[8]Sixty-year-olds.

[9]A reference to demonstrations against the war in Vietnam.

[10]Highly developed nations.

the old farm homestead.[11] With the adults paid to be professional parents, they would be freed of the occupational necessity to relocate repeatedly. Such families would take in new children as old ones "graduate" so that age-segregation[12] would be minimized.

Thus newspapers of the future might well carry advertisements addressed to young married couples: "Why let parenthood tie you down? Let us raise your infant into a responsible, successful adult. Class A Profamily offers: father age 39, mother, 36, grandmother, 67. Uncle and aunt, age 30, live in, hold part-time local employment. Four-child-unit has opening for one, age 6–8. Regulated diet exceeds government standards. All adults certified in child development and management. Bioparents permitted frequent visits. Telephone contact allowed. Child may spend summer vacation with bio-parents. Religion, art, music encouraged by special arrangement. Five year contract, minimum. Write for further details." 26

The "real" or "bio-parents" could, as the ad suggests, fill the role presently played by interested godparents,[13] namely that of friendly and helpful outsiders. In such a way, the society could continue to breed a wide diversity of genetic types, yet turn the care of children over to mother-father groups who are equipped, both intellectually and emotionally, for the task of caring for kids. . . . 27

THE ODDS AGAINST LOVE

Minorities experiment; majorities cling to the forms of the past. It is safe to say that large numbers of people will refuse to jettison the conventional idea of marriage or the familiar family forms. They will, no doubt, continue searching for happiness within the orthodox format. Yet, even they will be forced to innovate in the end, for the odds against success may prove overwhelming. 28

The orthodox format presupposes that two young people will "find" one another and marry. It presupposes that the two will fulfill certain psychological needs in one another, and that the two personalities will develop over the years, more or less in tandem, so that they continue to fulfill each other's needs. It further presupposes that this process will last "until death do us part."[14] 29

These expectations are built deeply into our culture. It is no longer respectable, as it once was, to marry for anything but love. Love has 30

---

[11]A home and the land around it.

[12]Grouping people by age.

[13]Adults selected by the parents to be special protectors of a child, usually done at the time of baptism.

[14]Part of the traditional marriage vows.

changed from a peripheral concern of the family into its primary justification. Indeed, the pursuit of love through family life has become, for
many, the very purpose of life itself.

Love, however, is defined in terms of this notion of shared growth. It   31
is seen as a beautiful mesh of complementary needs, flowing into and
out of one another, fulfilling the loved ones, and producing feelings of
warmth, tenderness and devotion. Unhappy husbands often complain
that they have "left their wives behind" in terms of social, educational
or intellectual growth. Partners in successful marriages are said to
"grow together."

This "parallel development" theory of love carries endorsement   32
from marriage counsellors, psychologists and sociologists. Thus, says
sociologist Nelson Foote, a specialist on the family, the quality of the
relationship between husband and wife is dependent upon "the degree
of matching in their phases of distinct but comparable development."

If love is a product of shared growth, however, and we are to measure   33
success in marriage by the degree to which matched development actually occurs, it becomes possible to make a strong and ominous predic-
tion about the future.

It is possible to demonstrate that, even in a relatively stagnant society, 34
the mathematical odds are heavily stacked against any couple achieving
this ideal of parallel growth. The odds for success positively plummet,
however, when the rate of change in society accelerates, as it now is
doing. In a fast-moving society, in which many things change, not once,
but repeatedly, in which the husband moves up and down a variety of
economic and social scales, in which the family is again and again torn
loose from home and community, in which individuals move further
from their parents, further from the religion of origin, and further from
traditional values, it is almost miraculous if two people develop at anything like comparable rates.

If, at the same time, average life expectancy rises from, say, fifty to   35
seventy years, thereby lengthening the term during which this acrobatic
feat of matched development is supposed to be maintained, the odds
against success become absolutely astronomical. Thus, Nelson Foote
writes with wry understatement: "To expect a marriage to last indefinitely under modern conditions is to expect a lot." To ask love to last
indefinitely is to expect even more. Transience and novelty are both in
league against it.

♦ COMPREHENSION/DISCUSSION QUESTIONS

1. Toffler wrote *Future Shock* in 1970, so we are in a position today
   to discuss whether he accurately predicted some trends for the
   future. To what extent was he correct?

2. In what way is the family a "giant shock absorber?"

3. What is the new birth technology Toffler refers to?

4. Why does he suggest that we need to look at the future through the eyes of a painter or a poet?

5. Explain the last sentence in paragraph 10.

6. What are some of the legal and ethical implications of the new birth technology?

7. What is the difference between extended and nuclear families? Which is more common in the United States?

8. Why will super-industrialism reduce the size of families?

9. Why would pro-parents be better at raising children than the natural parents?

10. Explain his statement in paragraph 30: "It is no longer respectable, as it once was, to marry for anything but love."

11. How has the idea of "shared growth" changed our understanding of what marriage should be?

12. After you finished reading this selection, what did you think about?

13. Do you think the new birth technology is beneficial?

14. Do you think using pro-parents is a likely or desirable development in child-rearing practices?

15. Discuss some issues in the news that relate to the changes in family structure and birth technology that Toffler predicted.

16. Do you want the "old-fashioned" marriage for yourself, or would you like to follow some of Toffler's ideas?

♦ VOCABULARY

Define the following words, paying particular attention to their meaning in context. Then write two paragraphs (they don't have to be connected) using at least 20 words in all.

accelerate [34]	cope [24]
acrobatic [35]	cult [10]
affluence [24]	deliquents [23]
complementary [31]	dilettantism [23]

embryo [7]

endorsement [32]

frivolous [8]

innovation [24]

jettison [28]

mesh [31]

mystique [10]

nurture [8]

oblivion [3]

ominous [33]

peripheral [30]

pessimist [3]

plummet [34]

presuppose [29]

propagation [8]

rampage [23]

relinquish [24]

shoals [18]

stagnant [34]

streamline [16]

tandem [29]

therapist [25]

tinkering [15]

transient [5]

turbulence [5]

vociferous [23]

womb [11]

♦ IDIOMS

Study the use of the following idioms in their context; then try writing a sentence of your own using them.

1. "Doing battle with" [2]—struggling with.

2. "Come in for" [2]—receive.

3. "Have a field day" [3]—have a great time.

4. "To try his [or her, one's] hand at"[15]—experiment, try out.

5. "Up against the wall" [24]—having nowhere to go.

6. "Odds are stacked against" [34]—it is unlikely.

♦ JOURNAL ENTRY

Write in your journal for 20 minutes on what you think your own life will be like ten years from now. Will you marry? Will you have children? Will you be living near your parents?

♦ SMALL GROUP WORK

Exercise 1   Divide into small groups of 3–4 students. Brainstorm a list of circumstances or conditions that you think all children need in order to become healthy, happy, and successful as adults (5 minutes). One condition might be good nutrition, for example. Once the group has listed these conditions, then put them in order of importance from 1 (highest importance) to 10 (lowest) or whatever number. When the groups reassemble, the recorders or another student should put the results on the board. The class as a whole should compare the lists and discuss whether the biological parents are necessarily the only ones who can provide for those needs.

Follow-up Writing   Write several paragraphs describing the three most important things children need and who can best provide them.

Exercise 2   Divide into small groups of 3–4 students and discuss solutions to the following problem: let us say that the population of the world is increasing at such a rate that food supplies, even in developed countries, will be in short supply by the year 2020. Given this situation, what should the "techno-societies," as Toffler called them, do with the birth technology they have? Should the government of the United States or any other country restrict the number of children per family? After a general discussion, list the factors for and against a government policy on birth control (10 minutes). Each small group should then share its list of pro and con factors with the class as a whole. The class should try to come to some agreement about which list, the pros or the cons, has the greatest weight or value (10 minutes).

Follow-up Writing   Write a few paragraphs explaining your feelings on this issue.

Martin Luther King, Jr. *(1929–1968)*

Martin Luther King, Jr. received a Ph.D. and a D.D. (Doctor of Divinity) from Boston University and another D.D. from Chicago Theological Seminary. He was an ordained Baptist minister and served as pastor of Ebenezer Baptist Church in Atlanta, Georgia, where his father had also been a minister. He founded the Southern Christian Leadership Conference (SCLC), which was a highly influential group leading demonstrations in favor of civil rights for blacks during the 1960's. He was also a prolific writer. "I Have a Dream" was originally delivered on August 28, 1963 as a speech from the steps of the Lincoln Memorial in Washington, D.C. The speech was the culminating event of the March on Washington during which 200,000 black people went to the capital to celebrate the 100th anniversary of the signing of the Emancipation Proclamation freeing all slaves (1863).

Since this was delivered as a speech, the text is full of the dramatic illustrations, parallel structures, repetitions, and pauses that characterize good oral language. King draws on the history of the black people in America and tries to alert the nation to the need to respond quickly to their legitimate demands for the full privileges of citizenship. He urged black people to remain calm while he urged the white power structure to realize that the basic tenets of our government and our moral heritage were being violated every time a black person was denied his or her rights.

Before reading this eloquent speech, write in your journal for 10 minutes on what you know about Martin Luther King, Jr., or what the term "civil disobedience" means to you.

I Have a Dream

Five score[1] years ago, a great American, in whose symbolic shadow we stand, signed the Emancipation Proclamation.[2] This momentous decree came as a great beacon light of hope to millions of Negro slaves who had been seared in the flames of withering injustice. It came as a joyous daybreak to end the long night of captivity. 1

But one hundred years later, we must face the tragic fact that the Negro is still not free. One hundred years later, the life of the Negro is 2

[1]A score is twenty years.

[2]The address given by Abraham Lincoln on January 1, 1863 which led to the end of the Civil War.

still sadly crippled by the manacles of segregation and the chains of discrimination. One hundred years later, the Negro lives on a lonely island of poverty in the midst of a vast ocean of material prosperity. One hundred years later, the Negro is still languishing in the corners of American society and finds himself an exile in his own land. So we have come here today to dramatize an appalling condition.

In a sense we have come to our nation's capitol to cash a check. When the architects of our republic wrote the magnificent words of the Constitution and the Declaration of Independence, they were signing a promissory note to which every American was to fall heir. This note was a promise that all men would be guaranteed the unalienable rights of life, liberty, and the pursuit of happiness.

It is obvious today that America has defaulted on this promissory note insofar as her citizens of color are concerned. Instead of honoring this sacred obligation, America has given the Negro people a bad check; a check which has come back marked "insufficient funds." But we refuse to believe that the bank of justice is bankrupt. We refuse to believe that there are insufficient funds in the great vaults of opportunity of this nation. So we have come to cash this check—a check that will give us upon demand the riches of freedom and the security of justice. We have also come to this hallowed spot to remind America of the fierce urgency of *now*. This is no time to engage in the luxury of cooling off or to take the tranquilizing drug of gradualism.[3] *Now* is the time to make real the promises of Democracy. *Now* is the time to rise from the dark and desolate valley of segregation to the sunlit path of racial justice. *Now* is the time to open the doors of opportunity to all of God's children. *Now* is the time to lift our nation from the quicksands of racial injustice to the solid rock of brotherhood.

It would be fatal for the nation to overlook the urgency of the moment and to underestimate the determination of the Negro. This sweltering summer of the Negro's legitimate discontent will not pass until there is an invigorating autumn of freedom and equality.[4] 1963 is not an end, but a beginning. Those who hope that the Negro needed to blow off steam and will now be content will have a rude awakening if the nation returns to business as usual. There will be neither rest nor tranquility in America until the Negro is granted his citizenship rights. The whirlwinds of revolt will continue to shake the foundations of our nation until the bright day of justice emerges.

But there is something I must say to my people who stand on the warm threshold which leads into the palace of justice. In the process of gaining our rightful place we must not be guilty of wrongful deeds. Let

[3]The theory that civil rights would come eventually if blacks just didn't make trouble.

[4]Play on the wording of the title of John Steinbeck's novel *Winter of Our Discontent* (1961).

us not seek to satisfy our thirst for freedom by drinking from the cup of bitterness and hatred. We must forever conduct our struggle on the high plane of dignity and discipline. We must not allow our creative protest to degenerate into physical violence. Again and again we must rise to the majestic heights of meeting physical force with soul force. The marvelous new militancy which has engulfed the Negro community must not lead us to a distrust of all white people, for many of our white brothers, as evidenced by their presence here today, have come to realize that their destiny is tied up with our destiny and their freedom is inextricably bound to our freedom. We cannot walk alone.

And as we walk, we must make the pledge that we shall march ahead. We cannot turn back. There are those who are asking the devotees of civil rights, "When will you be satisfied?" We can never be satisfied as long as the Negro is the victim of the unspeakable horrors of police brutality. We can never be satisfied as long as our bodies, heavy with the fatigue of travel, cannot gain lodging in the motels of the highways and the hotels of the cities. We cannot be satisfied as long as the Negro's basic mobility is from a smaller ghetto to a larger one. We can never be satisfied as long as a Negro in Mississippi cannot vote and a Negro in New York believes he has nothing for which to vote. No, no, we are not satisfied, and we will not be satisfied until justice rolls down like waters and righteousness like a mighty stream. 7

I am not unmindful that some of you have come here out of great trials and tribulations. Some of you have come fresh from narrow jail cells. Some of you have come from areas where your quest for freedom left you battered by the storms of persecution and staggered by the winds of police brutality. You have been the veterans of creative suffering. Continue to work with the faith that unearned suffering is redemptive. 8

Go back to Mississippi, go back to Alabama, go back to South Carolina, go back to Georgia, go back to Louisiana, go back to the slums and ghettoes of our northern cities, knowing that somehow this situation can and will be changed. Let us not wallow in the valley of despair. 9

I say to you today, my friends, that in spite of the difficulties and frustrations of the moment I still have a dream. It is a dream deeply rooted in the American dream. 10

I have a dream that one day this nation will rise up and live out the true meaning of its creed: "We hold these truths to be self-evident; that all men are created equal."[5] 11

I have a dream that one day on the red hills of Georgia the sons of former slaves and the sons of former slave owners will be able to sit down together at the table of brotherhood. 12

---

[5]Words in the Declaration of Independence.

I have a dream that the state of Mississippi, a desert state sweltering   13
with the heat of injustice and oppression, will be transformed into an
oasis of freedom and justice.

I have a dream that my four little children will one day live in a   14
nation where they will not be judged by the color of their skin but by the
content of their character.

I have a dream today.   15

I have a dream that the state of Alabama, whose governor's lips are   16
presently dripping with the words of interposition and nullification,[6]
will be transformed into a situation where little black boys and black
girls will be able to join hands with little white boys and white girls and
walk together as sisters and brothers.

I have a dream today.   17

I have a dream that one day every valley shall be exalted, every hill   18
and mountain shall be made low, the rough places will be made plain,
and the crooked places will be made straight, and the glory of the Lord
shall be revealed, and all flesh shall see it together.[7]

This is our hope. This is the faith with which I return to the South.   19
With this faith we will be able to hew out of the mountain of despair a
stone of hope. With this faith we will be able to transform the jangling
discords of our nation into a beautiful symphony of brotherhood. With
this faith we will be able to work together, to pray together, to struggle
together, to go to jail together, to stand up for freedom together, knowing that we will be free one day.

This will be the day when all of God's children will be able to sing   20
with new meaning.

> My country, tis of thee
> Sweet land of liberty,
>   Of thee I sing:
> Land where my fathers died,
> Land of the pilgrims' pride,
> From every mountainside
> Let freedom ring.[8]

And if America is to be a great nation this must become true. So let   21
freedom ring from the prodigious hilltops of New Hampshire. Let freedom ring from the mighty mountains of New York. Let freedom ring
from the heightening Alleghenies[9] of Pennsylvania!

---

[6]The governor was George Wallace, who refused to admit blacks to all white public
schools. He opposed federal intervention in Alabama politics.

[7] A paraphrase of *Isaiah* 40:4.

[8]Lyrics to *My Country 'Tis of Thee.*

[9]Mountains in Western Pennsylvania.

Let freedom ring from the snowcapped Rockies of Colorado! 22

Let freedom ring from the curvaceous peaks of California! 23

But not only that, let freedom ring from Stone Mountain[10] of Georgia! 24

Let freedom ring from Lookout Mountain[11] of Tennessee! 25

Let freedom ring from every hill and molehill of Mississippi. From 26
every mountainside, let freedom ring.

When we let freedom ring when we let it ring from every village and 27
every hamlet[12] from every state and every city, we will be able to speed
up that day when all of God's children, black men and white men, Jews
and Gentiles, Protestants and Catholics, will be able to join hands and
sing in the words of the old Negro spiritual,[13] "Free at last! free at last!
thank God almighty, we are free at last!"

♦ COMPREHENSION/DISCUSSION QUESTIONS

1. What was the role of Martin Luther King during the civil rights movement of the 1960s?

2. Why does he begin with an old-fashioned expression "five score years ago?"

3. In what sense was the Negro still not free when King gave this speech?

4. Explain the figure of speech (an extended metaphor) in paragraphs 3 and 4.

5. Why is there the sense of urgency expressed in the repeated "*Now* is the time?"

6. How does he expect "his" people to act?

7. Does he offer any specific solutions to end racial discrimination?

8. In calling for freedom, to what American qualities and beliefs does he appeal?

9. Why do you suppose there is so much repetition in the second half of the speech?

10. What were your reactions while reading this?

11. Do you think Martin Luther King is an inspiring writer? If so, why?

---

[10]Granite mountain located outside Atlanta which has carved figures of Southern Civil War heroes.

[11]In the Smokey Mountains of Tennessee.

[12]Small village.

[13]Religious song.

12. What did you think of his choice of words? Do you recognize one of the sources for this language?

13. Who do you think his intended audience was? How do you know?

14. Do you believe that his message is still valid today?

♦ VOCABULARY

Write a definition of the following words and indicate their specific meaning in context. Write two paragraphs (not necessarily related to each other) using at least 20 of the words.

beacon [1]	militancy [6]
curvaceous [23]	momentous [1]
default [4]	oasis [13]
degenerate [6]	prodigious [21]
discrimination [2]	promissory note [3]
engulf [6]	quicksand [4]
ghetto [7]	righteousness [7]
hallowed [4]	sear [1]
hew [19]	segregation [2]
inextricably [6]	sweltering [5]
invigorating [5]	tribulation [8]
jangling [19]	unmindful [8]
languish [2]	wallow [9]
manacle [2]	whirlwind [5]

♦ FIGURES OF SPEECH

Figures of speech are more important and more prominent in this selection than in any other one in this book. Study them all carefully to understand the comparisons being made. Discuss the sources for King's metaphors, and then read them aloud to hear how powerful they sound. Why do you suppose he uses so many? Do you think they contribute to the effectiveness of his argument?

1. "This momentous decree came as a great beacon light of hope to millions of Negro slaves who had been seared in the flames of withering injustice. It came as a joyous daybreak to end the long night of captivity" [1].

2. ". . . the life of the Negro is still sadly crippled by the manacles of segregation and the chains of discrimination . . . the Negro lives on a lonely island of poverty in the midst of a vast ocean of material prosperity . . . the Negro is still languishing in the corners of American society and finds himself an exile in his own land" [2].

3. ". . . tranquilizing drug of gradualism" [4].

4. "Now is the time to rise from the dark and desolate valley of segregation to the sunlit path of racial justice. Now is the time to open the doors of opportunity to all of God's children. Now is the time to lift our nation from the quicksands of racial injustice to the solid rock of brotherhood" [4].

5. "This sweltering summer of the Negro's legitimate discontent will not pass until there is an invigorating autumn of freedom and equality" [5].

6. "The whirlwinds of revolt will continue to shake the foundations of our nation until the bright day of justice emerges" [5].

7. ". . . people who stand on the warm threshold which leads into the palace of justice" [6].

8. "Let us not seek to satisfy our thirst for freedom by drinking from the cup of bitterness and hatred" [6].

9. ". . . we will not be satisfied until justice rolls down like waters and righteousness like a mighty stream" [7].

10. ". . . your quest for freedom left you battered by the storms of persecution and staggered by the winds of police brutality" [8].

11. ". . . the state of Mississippi, a desert state sweltering with the heat of injustice and oppression, will be transformed into an oasis of freedom and justice" [13].

12. ". . . every valley shall be exhalted, every hill and mountain shall be made low, the rough places will be made plain, and the crooked places will be made straight, and the glory of the Lord shall be revealed, and all flesh shall see it together" [18].

13. ". . . we will be able to hew out of the mountain of despair a stone of hope . . . we will be able to transform the jangling discords of our nation into a beautiful symphony of brotherhood" [19].

14. In many cases, King uses parallel (similar) sentence structure and repetitions to emphasize points and increase the emotional im-

pact of what he is saying. Note this especially in paragraphs 2, 4, 6, 7, 9.

♦ JOURNAL ENTRY

Write for 20 minutes in your journal about any firsthand experience you have had with discrimination (either as a minority, a woman, a foreigner, a student, or a member of a particular religion); or write about your own observations about race relations in the United States.

♦ SMALL GROUP WORK

Divide into groups of 3–4 students and select a recorder. The problem to be discussed is the protection of minority rights in a democratic country. It is clear that in a democracy, the majority can pass laws that may hurt a minority of the people. The majority can also take most of the advantages in a given situation just because of its numbers. Choose *one* of three specific examples for your group to discuss.

1. Admission to graduate schools (medicine, law, etc.): should a certain number of places in the entering class be set aside for minorities (blacks, Hispanics, American Indians) and women?

2. Political representation (elections of representatives, council members, senators, etc.): should minorities be assured of proportional representation (a percentage of the total population)?

3. Minority rights to educate children according to religious principles (such as not sending them to school at all, or refusing to teach them scientific versions of the origin of the world, etc.): should they be protected?

Choose 1, 2, or 3 and brainstorm reasons for and against these specific measures designed to protect minorities. Then identify the five most important pros and cons before presenting them to the class as a whole.

The class should discuss for each example whether the pros outweigh the cons. If the consensus is that the reasons in favor of special measures (pros) are stronger, then the class should brainstorm ideas for overcoming the reasons against, so that implementation of the measures would go smoothly. If the reasons against (cons) are stronger, then the problem to discuss is how to protect minorities and overcome their discontent.

Follow-up Writing Write a few paragraphs on how you felt about this issue before and after the group discussions. Several students might be asked to read their paragraphs aloud and comment on whether they think they could use this material for an essay designed to persuade others of their point of view.

WRITING TO PERSUADE

The readings in this chapter have probably evoked some strong responses from you that are recorded in answers to discussion questions, journal entries, or follow-up writing from the small group exercises. You may have already begun to work on a counterstatement to Toffler's view of the future family. Each of the authors presented a position on an issue that is designed to provoke discussion. For example, Nunberg presents two sides of a political issue that is very controversial, and he clearly takes a stand. Martin Luther King, Jr. attacks one of the most difficult and painful social problems in America by appealing to our best instincts and awakening in us a sense of justice. Each author in his own way has written to persuade us or argue a point.

All essays are persuasive in some sense because they represent the opinion of the writer, who certainly wants the audience to accept his or her point of view. Any good essay must also be based on clear, logical thinking. When the primary purpose, however, is to influence the audience to accept a certain idea or argue a specific case, rather than just explaining or analyzing it, then the writer may use a variety of strategies you already know—definitions, comparisons, descriptions, analysis of causes, and judgments—all organized to present clear, critical thinking that will persuade the audience.

In this chapter, we will emphasize the elements of good argumentation and a few points that have special importance. Persuasive writing relies to some degree on an appeal to the emotions and on the character of the writer or speaker. In other words, if the writer has strong credibility, then the audience is likely to be persuaded by his or her position on the issue. But the persuasive essay as we know it best is based on logical thinking, supported by evidence and an appeal to authority. Certainly in writing within an academic setting, you will be expected to present support for your point of view, and you will be asked to draw logical conclusions from whatever evidence or support you have presented.

To prepare your audience to accept your argument, you need to let them know that you are aware of points of view other than your own. It is good psychology to try to acknowledge what the audience may think about the topic, or at least let them know you realize there is more than one way to see the issue. If you don't, someone might consider you to be uninformed or prejudiced. It will then be difficult to convince the reader of your point of view.

Even if you prepare the audience well to receive your ideas, they may be eager to "find a hole" in the argument. The writer therefore must be prepared to make all points clear, well documented, and coherent. Other key elements in persuasive writing are choice of words and tone. Think back to how impressive Martin Luther King's speech is because of his word choice and powerful figures of speech that are based on the Bible. Likewise, you will want to think carefully about your choice of words and tone. It is easy to sound overly emotional in writing a persuasive paper, and that tone will have a negative effect on your audience.

The first step, as always, is to do some "priming of the pump," i.e., work to get the ideas flowing.

Prewriting

Brainstorming   Try brainstorming for 5 minutes on one of the following ideas:

>   arguing against an "English only" country
>
>   arguing for an "English only" country
>
>   convincing someone to buy a baby from a "babytorium"
>
>   arguing against the extended family
>
>   defending surrogate parenting
>
>   arguing against discrimination in job opportunities

Freewriting   Write for 10 minutes nonstop on one of the following key terms from the reading selections:

>   official language
>
>   bilingual education
>
>   genetic engineering
>
>   racial discrimination
>
>   Martin Luther King's "dream"

Small Group Work   Divide into small groups of 3–4 students. Select a recorder and begin to brainstorm on a controversial topic related to making a big change in society (it might be related thematically to one of the readings, or it might be on a completely different subject). For instance, "Highly competitive intercollegiate sports should be eliminated from American universities." Once the group has decided on a controversial statement related to making a major social change, then the members should do a *force field* analysis. This means setting up a pro and con column on a sheet of paper and listing under the appropriate column the factors that are for or against your statement. For instance:

Highly competitive intercollegiate sports should be eliminated from American universities.

PRO	CON
[they] promote corruption	promote healthy, clean fun
distract from studying	help build school spirit
cost university too much	bring in money and fame
distort values	build character and
other countries don't have	competitiveness
the same system	

The lists can be as long as time permits, and the points do not have to be matched evenly as they are in this example. The results should be shared with the entire class.

In the second stage of the exercise, the group can brainstorm ideas for overcoming the ''cons,'' trying to write up a plan of action to implement the statement.

This exercise should give you some ideas on generating supporting points and potential opposition points for an essay on one side of an issue.

♦ WRITING ASSIGNMENT

Take one of the ideas from the prewriting and draft a tentative thesis for an essay that will persuade someone of your point of view. The thesis and the topic must clearly be something that someone could debate or argue on several different sides. Get together with a partner and discuss your ideas for this paper. Tell each other about the tentative thesis and help each other to determine if it is truly an arguable point; then discuss the points you think you might use to support your opinion.

Once you feel that you have a workable tentative thesis and some sense of how you will develop the essay, start on a first draft.

Drafting and Revising

As you are drafting and starting to think about revision, you will want to consider the following basic strategies—acknowledging the opposition, logic, evidence, appeal to authority, clarity, word choice, and tone. The examples will help you to see how other students have worked with this type of writing.

Acknowledging the Opposition Letting the audience know you are aware that there is more than one side to an issue may be accomplished by mentioning one or more opposing arguments as you begin your essay. By stating other arguments, you will show maturity of thought, even if the arguments are just hypothetical. If you know specifically what your audience has said or written on an issue, it is good to use a technique popularized by the psychologist Carl Rogers for improving interpersonal communications. Rogers suggests that we restate what someone else has said before we present our own side of the argument. The value in doing this is to let the other person know we have heard and understood his or her position. If people see that we are intelligent and fair enough to truly listen and accurately restate their opinions, then they are more likely to listen to ours. It is best, however, to acknowledge your opposition at the beginning of your essay, and, if possible, find some common ground between their position and yours to begin the development of your own position.

In his editorial on Proposition 63, Geoffrey Nunberg starts with some of the points which support the proposition, although he is writing against it. Whether you start by acknowledging other points of view or merely with the opposite side of an argument, it is always wise to present your point second and build your case so that you leave your reader with your ideas at the end.

Sample Student Writing

As you read the following student essay, watch for how the student has tried to acknowledge potential opposition from a Western audience on the controversial topic of women's liberation.

THE FREEDOM OF SAUDI WOMEN

People in this world behave and act depending on the culture and the society in which they have been brought up. Each person looks to other societies and points out the good and the bad sides, but trying to study some of the facts and analyzing them might be helpful in some cases. Both men and women have their problems in this world, but women in Western societies have more pressure on them than Saudi women.

Women in Saudi Arabia enjoy a better life style than Western women. It might surprise Western women when they realize that the Saudi women have the same freedom that the

Western women have. The simple meaning of the word freedom is to do what you want to do. In this sense both Western women and Saudi women have it. Western women think of Saudi women as unimportant things in the society who do whatever the men tell them to do. However the Saudi men respect the women and bestow to them all their rights.

It is true that Saudi women must wear a long black cloth, called an abayah when they go outside their homes. However they can wear whatever they like in the privacy of their homes. In public they must wear an abayah and a tarhas to cover their hair so none of their beauty can be seen. Western women see this behavior as a restriction of the Saudi women's freedom. In Saudi Arabia the abayah and the tarbah are thought of as a protection against rape and other crimes. The percentage of rapes in Saudi Arabia is much lower than in the western world. Perhaps western women can learn from this Saudi example.

Women in Saudi Arabia do not have to worry about financial problems because earning money is the job of the man. So women are free for other things like continuing their education and raising their children. The women are not required to help their husbands financially and their husbands support them completely. Women have the opportunity to work, but they are not under pressure to earn a living. The Saudi women can concentrate on raising their children. On the other hand, Western wives face pressure to work and help their husbands earn the living. This problem may cause Western women to ignore or give less time to their children or have less opportunity to continue their education.

You may ask how do Saudi men respect the women when he marry up to four wives. I have been asked this question several times by many western people. They say this is not fair and Western women would not accept this. But the answer is very simple. In Western societies when there is a problem between two people they are quick to chose divorce as a solution. Divorced women will always face more problems than divorced men especially in raising the children and how to support them. Men in Saudi Arabia rarely choose divorce. Instead they try very hard to work out their problems. If they can not work out their problems, the husband will marry another woman, but will continue to care for his first wife and their children.

Western women might not recognize all the advantages that the Saudi women have. They might wear the abaya, but they do not live in the fear of rape. In order to better understand, Western women have to go to Saudi Arabia and experience living there.

Abdullah Almaimanee

♦ DISCUSSION QUESTIONS

1. Does his direct reference to Western attitudes make his essay stronger? Why or why not?

2. Even if members of another culture would not accept his point of view, does he help us understand Saudi men's attitude toward Saudi women? How does he achieve that?

Appealing to Emotion   Since the issue may be controversial or emotional for the audience, an appeal to the emotions has to be very carefully handled. A good speaker and persuasive writer draws his or her audience in and carries it along on the power of words to create emotional states. Martin Luther King, the eloquent moralist, is a master at this when he evokes his audience's suffering and frustration, then plays on the emotions of patriotism, faith, and hope for the future. Since King's speech is such an emotional one, we might wonder why people who pride themselves on being cool and logical don't criticize King for overemotionalism or sloppy sentimentality. It is probably because the emotions he plays with—indignation against injustice, patriotism, and hope—are admirable ones. He is using emotion for a "good" goal; he is not appealing to base emotions for personal or disrespectable goals.

Also, if we are honest, we must admit that we are all sensitive to an emotional appeal. Just think how advertising appeals to our emotions and persuades us every day to buy certain products. What distinguishes a "good" emotional appeal from a "bad" one may be subjective, but we can hope that if a negative emotion such as anger is aroused by the writing, it is in the service of a good cause, i.e., improvement of a social condition.

Sample Student Writing

Read the following student essay and underline or note places you think evoke emotion.

Why Drive When You're Drunk?

A drunk man comes stumbling out of a bar. He walks to his car, fumbles with his keys, jumps in and peels out in the street. A few blocks away, a little girl is slowly walking in the street with her dog, unaware of what is soon going to happen. The intoxicated man is weaving up the street. The girl crosses the street, and the man who is driving too fast and too close, does not hit the brakes soon enough. The man in this illustration represents a serious and big problem in modern society: drunk driving. Alcohol, the foundation of this problem, is a drug known to reduce our senses and abilities to act and react. This drug should be separate from the act of driving in order to protect all peoples safety. People tend to think that driving drunk is wrong but there are still people doing it.

A lot of accidents that occur in the streets are caused by people with alcohol in their blood driving vehicles. The alcohol affects the driver's comprehension about himself. The man in the early illustration believes that he is able to handle the situation perfectly well, but in fact he is not. His judgment ability was very reduced. He couldn't understand that he was driving too fast, and maybe his sight was so deteriorated that he could not even see the girl.

The girl was hit by the car. If the driver of the car hadn't been drunk, the odds that the girl would have been able to cross the street without getting hurt, would have been much higher than they really were in this situation. The girl obviously got injured in some way; she might even have died. In drunk driving accidents people end up with one or two limbs missing or they can become brain dead for the rest of their lives. We treat that as being something better than a death, but in the case of the family and the suffering they go through, sometimes it is not.

The man might have got off without a single scratch, as 4
they usually do, but he would surely have deep cuts in his
conscience when he sobered up and realized what he really
had done. Some people that are involved in drunk driving accidents, get lasting feelings of guilt and fear of driving cars,
which can make them cease driving all together. Maybe not
until an accident occur people will understand that they have
made a mistake and will consider never to drive a car again,
when they are drunk. But then it is too late.

It is a horrible fact that most people do not realize the mis- 5
take of drunk driving until they are confronted with a painful situation like a accident. If we go to a fatal accident, look
at it, and there is a drunk involved, we get so aggravated because the drunken driver usually comes out alive and the innocent person is dead. This situation, this mistake, is not
just a mistake made by individuals, but a mistake made by
the whole society. Happy-hours and even liquor stores with
drive-in windows indicates that our society approves that you
can drink and drive an automobile.

It is time we all woke up and told ourselves that what is 6
happening is wrong and that we have to do something about
it. We all have to start showing respect, both to ourselves as
much as to other people. It seems like roadblocks with police
officers and laws are not doing enough to stop the problem of
drunk driving, because people are actually getting killed in
the street everyday due to people that have been driving
drunk.

Annika Svensson

♦ DISCUSSION QUESTIONS

1. What emotions are evoked by the first paragraph?

2. Does the writer appeal to other emotions throughout the essay?

3. Are the emotions used effectively to make some points?

4. Does the essay seem predominantly reasonable or predominantly emotional?

Logic   Logic is the science of sound reasoning or valid argumentation. It is the basis of much of Western thought, especially scientific thinking. In the American culture, it has a very high value because of the dominance of science and technology over other aspects of our culture. For instance, people are not as convinced by an argument based on aesthetic value (something is good because it is beautiful) or affective value (something is good because it evokes emotion) as they are by a logical argument (something is good because it makes sense). Writing done for an academic or business setting is almost always expected to be logical because that mode of thinking dominates our culture.

Facts and evidence are the building blocks of a logical argument, but we know that facts can be used to draw conclusions that we or someone else might not accept. A good argument needs examples and facts to support its points, but the test of the argument will be whether the evidence is put together in a manner that supports good or valid conclusions. The assumptions must be reasonable, and the conclusions drawn from the evidence presented must be valid. Rather than trying to learn what logical fallacies (incorrect arguments) are by their Latin names, it is more important at this point for you to develop your ability to ask critical questions (see p. 254) about a piece of writing in order to challenge the logic of its arguments. If you learn to ask such questions about your own writing, you will make a great deal of progress toward improving its logic and clarity. If you are curious about the logical fallacies and want more instruction on logical arguments, consult a traditional English rhetoric or a logic textbook.

Evidence   You have practiced many times throughout this text the use of detail, examples, and illustrations to support your points. Evidence for an argument is all these: detailed descriptions of a situation, historical examples, scientific facts, statistical data, and case studies. Even hypothetical cases and personal examples can be used effectively in an argument so long as not too much emphasis is put on individual or unique experiences that would not be valid in a broader context.

Appealing to Authority   If you were to write that county schools should be integrated because the Supreme Court of the United States has ruled that racial segregation violates an individual's civil rights, you would be making an appeal to the authority of the law and the highest court in the country. When Martin Luther King, Jr. refers to Lincoln's Emancipation Proclamation and to the Constitution, he is appealing to two of the most important documents in the development of American law. When he paraphrases the Bible, he appeals to the sacred writings of the dominant religions in America, Judaism and

Christianity. Since law and religion are powerful sources of authority for many Americans (his audience), most people would accept at least one of these authorities as legitimate support for his arguments.

On the other hand, if the writer appeals to an authority that no one in the audience believes in, the argument might not be very convincing. Remember that in general an appeal to the authority of religion is dangerous unless the principles, morals, or attitudes referred to are broad interpretations that can be shared by many people. In other words, the writer must choose wisely an authority that his or her specific audience is likely to respect.

Authority comes from many sources, not just the law or major written documents. An authority can be an individual who is well known and well respected for a certain expertise in a given field, such as a Nobel Prize winner or someone who has published many well known books. The writer could quote this person or refer to his or her opinions to support a particular point in the argument.

♦ WRITING ASSIGNMENT

To help yourself with the development of a solid argument, take the draft you wrote after the prewriting section and exchange it with a partner. Have your partner answer the following questions (peer review sheet 7) about your draft and then work together on suggesting ways to revise. Once you have completed the peer review, study the drafts of student writing on the following pages and try to apply what you learn from them in revising your own draft.

Who is the audience for the argument?

What is the argument or claim it makes?

What are the assumptions on which the argument is based?

How is the argument supported?

Do the points made support the primary claim or another one?

Does the conclusion follow from the supporting evidence?

♦ DISCUSSION QUESTIONS

Look back at the essay on drunk driving (p. 251). Answer the following questions about that essay.

1. Who is the audience for this essay?

2. What is the main argument?

3. Are there any secondary arguments?

4. What assumptions does the writer make?

5. Does she acknowledge any opposition to her point of view? Is it necessary in this particular essay? Why or why not?

6. What is her evidence, or on what authority does she base her argument?

7. Does the conclusion follow well from the supporting statements?

8. Can you think of some revisions that would strengthen her argument?

Sample Student Writing

The following unedited drafts are illustrations of revising to build a more logical argument. The student was writing in response to the selection by Toffler, and he wrote a discovery draft for himself, then this one for a conference with the instructor.

Draft 2
COHABITATION LICENSES

Delivering a birth or marriage certificate might seem very normal if we are describing some of the tasks of a common city hall in a common French town. But who has heard of a city hall delivering cohabitation certificates for those people who wish one? To obtain one is not much of a hassle. The only thing an applicant has to do is to go with the chosen partner and two witnesses. Ten minutes later they are the fortunate possessors of a sealed, signed, and very legal paper that states that two individuals are married without really being so. 1

Funny? Perhaps, especially for those of us who come from a country where divorce is not even considered legal. Convenient? Certainly, one hundred percent! It helps save taxes because the tax collection agency considers them as a family of two or more members, thus the amount to be paid will be reduced. Otherwise each one would pay a higher amount of taxes because earnings would be considered individually. There are also the rent, food, and other expenses to be shared. 2

When the last drop overflows the glass, and one of the individuals is fed up with the other, it is time for farewells, and the search for a new partner begins. This process will be repeated as many times as the candidate wishes, or until the suitable partner for life arrives. 3

This situation can be viewed in two different ways. On one hand, it might show that people don't care and do not want to have the burden of marriage, raising a family, and all that it implies, thus discharging themselves of any responsibility. On the other hand, it can be a sign of maturity and caution, because couples want to wait until they find the best permanent partner. In any case, if cohabitation continues for a very long period of time due to indecision or a reluctance to change, the family ties will be based on tenuous and fragile bindings mainly caused by insecurity. 4

In the last decades the rate of divorces in developed countries rose alarmingly, and many children found themselves without a stable home where they could enjoy the presence of both parents. Those same children, now grownups and looking for a companion, are trying to avoid committing the same mistake their parents did. The ideal situation would be to cohabitate for a period of one to two years, which is a reasonable enough time to make a decision. 5

It is very difficult to know beforehand if the person we think we would like to marry is the right choice after dating him or her for some time. This problem is caused by the fact that two people dating each other are getting to know the other in a special atmosphere that does not correspond to the life they will have when they are married. Some people who get married after a short period of time of knowing each other, divorce when they encounter problems they cannot cope with in their daily lives. It also depends on the character of each individual to adjust and make concessions to the other for the sake of the couple. 6

It is a good idea to experiment in a real atmosphere of marriage so that each one can see if the couple they form is suitable to last for a rather long period of time, as long as there are no children in between. In such a case, if children are 7

born during cohabitation, it is an act of irresponsibility or ignorance of contraceptive measures.

Perhaps in the future, marriage will become the exception,   8
rather than the rule due primarily to the liberalization of
the laws and also the diminishing pressure of religious
thoughts. In many countries religious marriages are no
longer compulsory. In the French case, cohabitation has become a frequent and normal way of life that no longer needs
to be hidden.

Marcelo Riemer

♦ DISCUSSION QUESTIONS

1. He begins by making fun of cohabitation certificates. Is the essay
   itself making fun of the practice of cohabitation?

2. He acknowledges different points of view (paragraph 4) which set
   up the statement "In any case, if cohabitation continues for a
   long period of time due to indecision or a reluctance to change,
   the family ties will be based on tenuous and fragile bindings
   mainly caused by insecurity." Is this the main claim in his argument? If it is, does he actually develop this point? If this is not the
   claim, what is?

3. Does the major portion of the essay seem to support the benefits
   of cohabitation for a short time before marriage? If so, then why
   does the conclusion say that there may be no marriage in the
   future?

4. Can you tell how Marcelo feels about the ideas in his final paragraph? Does he regret or look forward to that future?

The answers to these questions show that there are some problems in
the essay that have not yet been resolved, perhaps because the writer
seems to have changed his mind during the drafting process. After
thinking about these questions, Marcelo rewrote to clarify his position.

Draft 3

COHABITATION LICENSES

Delivering a birth or marriage certificate might   1
seem very normal if we are describing some of the
tasks of a common city hall in a common French

town. But who has heard of a city hall delivering cohabitation certificates for those people who wish one? To obtain one is not much of a hassle. The only thing an applicant has to do is to go with the chosen partner and two witnesses. Ten minutes later they are the fortunate possessors of a sealed, signed, and very legal paper that states that two individuals are married without really being so.

Funny? Perhaps, especially for those of us who come from a country where divorce is not even considered legal. But after the first reaction of laughter, we might think about whether this scene could occur. After all, it would be convenient. Definitely, one hundred percent. Cohabitation helps save taxes because the tax collection agency considers the couple a family of two or more members, thus the amount to be paid will be reduced. Otherwise each one would pay a higher amount of taxes because earnings would be considered individually. There are also the rent, food, and other expenses to be shared. 2

Then, when the last drop overflows the glass, and one of the individuals is fed up with the other, it would be time for farewells, and the search for a new partner would begin. This could be repeated as many times as the candidate wishes, or until the suitable partner for life arrives. That's convenient too! 3

This situation can be viewed in two different ways. On one hand, it might show that people don't care and do not want to have the burden of marriage, raising a family, and all that it implies, so they discharge themselves of any responsibility. On the other hand, it could be a sign of maturity and caution, because couples want to wait until they find the best permanent partner. In either case, if cohabitation continued for a very 4

long period of time due to indecision or a reluctance to change, the family ties will be based on
tenuous and fragile bindings mainly caused by
insecurity. That does not mean, however, that it is

new idea a bad idea under any circumstances. The ideal sit-

&
material uation would be to cohabitate for a period of one

from old to two years, which is a reasonable enough time

¶ 5 to make a decision. Cohabitation in this case
would be desirable no just for convenience but for
the strength of the future family.

In the last decades, the rate of divorces in de-   5
veloped countries has risen alarmingly, and
many children have found themselves without a
stable home where they could enjoy the presence
of both parents. Those same children, now
grownups and looking for a companion, are trying to avoid making the same mistake their parents did. We might wonder why there are so many
divorces.

One reason is that it is very difficult to know be-   6
forehand if the person we think we would like to
marry is the right choice after dating him or her
for only a short time. This problem is caused by
the fact that two people dating each other are getting to know the other in a special atmosphere
that does not correspond to the life they will have
when they are married. Some people who get married after a short period of knowing each other,
divorce when they encounter problems they cannot cope with in their daily lives. A successful
marriage also depends on the character of each
individual to adjust and make concessions to the
other for the sake of the couple. Therefore, it is a

material good idea to experiment in a real atmosphere of

from old marriage so that each one can see if the couple

¶ 7 they form is suitable to last for a rather long
period of time.

Living together as an experiment does not   7

re-worded mean, however, that people should have every-thing exactly like a marriage. They should not have children, for instance. To have them when not married shows irresponsibility or an igno-rance of contraceptive measures.

re-worded In the future, due to the liberalization of the laws and also the diminishing pressure of re-ligious ideas, marriage will probably not be the only way couples can live together. Even now in many countries, religious marriages are no longer compulsory. In France, cohabitation has become a frequent and normal way of life that no longer needs to be hidden. It is not something to *new* laugh at or criticize as a simple convenience. Co-*concluding* habitation for a year or two may be the best way *sentence* to assure happier marriages and better home sit-uations for children, and that will benefit the whole society.

8

♦ DISCUSSION QUESTIONS

1. Notice all the underlined changes. What is their function?

2. Do they make the logic of his argument clearer?

Editing

Clarity   Clarity of thought results from a number of elements. The most obvious one is that ideas are organized and supported well enough to help the reader pay attention to the ideas instead of getting lost and wasting time trying to figure out where the writer is going. This is why we suggest that the introduction be a way of bringing the reader into the subject and that the thesis should be made clear early in the essay.

Another important element of clarity is unity. Each paragraph should be unified around a central idea, and all paragraphs should be related to the major thesis of the essay. If a sentence or two goes off on another topic, it should be developed as a separate paragraph, if the idea is important in the essay. If it is not particularly important, then it should be eliminated as irrelevant.

Clarity also results from coherence within paragraphs. It is not enough that all the sentences be related to a central idea; they must also be put together in a sequence that is coherent, i.e., logical. Each sen-tence must flow naturally from the preceding one and lead to the next sentence; the sentences should not seem strung together like beads on a string. Just putting the sentences next to each other does not create a connection between them. The relationship between sentences is indicated by frequent use of transitions. Remember that transitions are also important between paragraphs, and that whole sentences and even short paragraphs can play the role of creating a smooth transition from section to section in an essay.

Ultimately clarity is dependent upon careful word choice. As was mentioned in Chapter 5, word choice means deciding on the most accurate and specific words for the context as well as taking into account their connotations. If you do not have words that are accurate, precise, and appropriate, you will not be able to achieve clarity of thought.

Tone From careful word choice appropriate to the audience, topic, and purpose comes the tone of the essay. If your purpose is to persuade, then you want just enough spirit in your writing to arouse the audience but not so much emotion that they think you are ranting and raving. As was mentioned above, using emotion, which is conveyed through tone, is a bit risky. If you want to provoke, then you may need to adopt a very strong tone. You may choose instead to sound authoritative, understanding, or lighthearted, depending on your subject.

For example, the selection from *Future Shock* has an objective tone compared to King's speech. Toffler makes no appeals to great traditions or higher authority. His objective tone makes us think he is presenting facts when he is actually just speculating about the future. He may be manipulating our emotions in a much more subtle way by assuming a distant, matter-of-fact tone about emotional issues such as childbirth, marriage, and child rearing. If the subject is human rights and race relations, such a tone would be inappropriate. Certainly, you do not want a bitter, condescending, or threatening tone in your writing, or you will lose the audience. In trying to analyze the tone of your writing or a peer's writing, consider the level of the vocabulary (is it too elementary or too sophisticated for your audience?); the use of adverbs or any intensifiers ("this report is extremely poor" vs. "this report shows some weaknesses"); and the relative strength or weakness of the verbs ("John absolutely crushed his opponent" vs. "John soundly defeated him"). Try to establish a tone that will win over your audience, not make it angry or defensive.

Sample Student Writing

As you read the following student essay, underline specific words or phrases that you think create the tone, and check places you think are not clear or not unified.

Draft 1

THE CARE OF CHILDREN

Our society is going through many changes. One of the 1
most discussed changes today is women's liberation. It's not
obvious anymore that women are going to stay home and
bring up their children.

How is the question of raising of children going to be 2
solved in the future world? One opinion is that neither the
woman or the man are going to have time to raise their children anymore. They are going to leave them to some professional parents during childhood and then pick them up again
after ten years. Another opinion is that families will have
children after their productive life, after they have been retired and have done everything to develop their own life.
These two opinions can be read in "The Fractured Family"
by Toffler. Let us hope dear Mr. Toffler is wrong. The raising
of children will be done as it is now and always has been
done; the mother and father will raise the children during
their middle-age and develop together with them.

Our primary mission here on earth is to propagate and 3
raise our children. It's in each person's genes to raise and
teach their children, so that they can survive and develop the
human race. It has been so for hundreds of thousands of
years and to believe that a person should be able to change
that is almost absurd. A good example can be collected from
the animal kingdom. If you look at a female tiger during a
birth, you can see that she does some things determined by
genes. She knows the importance of getting the "baby" to
breathe by licking it and cutting the navel cord, and she gives
it quick food. During the growing up time she has to teach the
baby tiger to hunt, fight, and many other things to survive.
It's the same with human beings. During our development a
need arises to raise children; without that a person is not a
whole, satisfied person.

It's impossible to believe that a couple will bring a child to 4
life, without living and witnessing happy and sad times together. They won't do it to rescue the human race from exter-

mination. They will do it because they love children and want to see them grow up to be a good person, a person to be proud of.

In the future jobs will be boring. The jobs tend to be more and more mechanical, and therefore it will be harder and harder to fulfill yourself and enjoy your work. That means that your leisure time is going to be more and more important. A couple without children has to find other things to spend their time on which in a couple of months or years will be rather monotonous and boring. They will soon realize that a good and happy leisure time will include children.

Another point that is quite dangerous for the society is that all pro-parents will have the same judgments, because they have been educated with similar views. This will make the whole society's views rather similar, which will in the long run slow down development.

To have children after your productive life is not especially fair to the children. First of all, the average age of death will probably go down because of all the new diseases and stress factors, so the possibility of young people without parents will increase. Second, all rapid changes in the society will make the old parents' attitudes and norms out of date, which will make it hard for the children to fit in the new society.

Society today has real problems with children that have to live with some pro-parents, because their real parents for some reason couldn't keep them. The children get insecure about who their parents are, and why they couldn't be loved by their real parents. They can't find any place and they don't feel welcome into the society. Only a few of them can continue into a normal life, the rest of them become criminals, drug addicts or even worse, they commit suicide. There is just one question to ask, how will the future world be able to handle thousands more abandoned children, when we can't handle the few we have now?

A society with families without children is hard for me to see. If the world goes to that point, which it probably won't, the whole society will be very insensitive, hard, and filled with complacency. It's going to be filled with human beings, who are very mechanical and without any true happiness. There are going to be many criminals, bums, drug adicts, and maniacs who have no feelings and are dangerous, because of their background. Let's hope this future is not going to happen because if it does, I'm afraid it's going to be the end of mankind.

Thomas Hogstedt

♦ DISCUSSION QUESTIONS

1. How would you describe the overall tone of this essay?

2. Are there some specific places you think the language should be changed to achieve a different tone?

3. Are there any places where the essay seems unclear or not unified?

4. Now read the second (still unedited) draft and note all the underlined changes which were made to improve the organization, clarity and tone of the essay.

Draft 2

THE CARE OF CHILDREN

<u>Western</u> society is going through many <u>social</u> changes.   1
One of the most discussed changes today is womens' liberation. It's not <u>inevitable</u> any more that women are going to stay home and bring up their children.

How is the question of raising of children going to be   2
solved in the future world? One opinion is that neither the woman or the man are going to have time to raise their children anymore. They are going to leave them to some professional parents during childhood and then pick them up again after ten years. Another opinion is that parents will have children after their productive life, after they have been retired and have done everything to develop their own life. These two opinions can be read in ''The Fractured Family'' by Toffler, <u>but I hope</u>

Toffler is wrong. The raising of children will be done as it
has been throughout time; the mother and father will
raise the children during their middle-age and develop
together with them.

Parents will continue to raise their children because
our primary mission here on earth is to propogate ourselves. It's in each person's genes to produce and then
teach their children, so that they can survive and develop the human race. It has been so for hundreds of
thousands of years and to believe that a person should
be able to change that is almost unbelievable. A good example can be collected from the animal kingdom. If you
look at a female tiger during a birth, you can see that she
does some things determined by genes. She knows the
importance of getting the "baby" to breathe by licking it
and cutting the navel cord, and she gives it quick food.
During the growing up time she has to teach the baby tiger to hunt, fight, and many other things to survive.

It's the same with human beings. During our development a need arises to raise children, without that a person is not a whole, satisfied person. It's impossible to
believe that a couple will bring a child to life, without living and witnessing happy and sad times together. They
won't do it only to rescue the human race from exter-
mination. They will do it also because they love children
and want to see them grow up to be a good person they
can be proud of.

Finding satisfaction in life may also not come just
from working all the time. In the future jobs will be boring. They will tend to be more and more mechanical, and
therefore it will be harder and harder to fulfill yourself
and enjoy your work. That means that your leisure time
is going to be more and more important. A couple with-

3

4 paragraphs organized for unity

5

out children has to find other things to spend their time on which in a couple of months or years will be rather monotonous and boring. They will soon realize that a good and happy leisure time will include children.

It is natural to raise your own children, and giving them to pro-parents may create problems. One reason pro-parents would be quite dangerous for the society is that they will have the same judgments, because they have been educated with similar views. This will make the whole society's views rather similar, which will in the long run slow down development. Another reason is that society already has real problems with children that have to live with some pro-parents, because their real parents for some reason couldn't keep them. The children get insecure about who their parents are, and why they couldn't be loved by their real parents. They can't find any place and they don't feel welcome into the society. Some can continue into a normal life, but many of them become criminals, drug addicts or even worse, they commit suicide. One question to ask is how the future world will be able to handle thousands more abandoned children, when we don't handle them very well now?   6

Combining of 2 A's including old A-8

Toffler also mentioned having children after the productive years of work. Having children after your retirement is not especially fair to the children. First of all, the average life span will probably go down because of all the new diseases and stress factors, so the possibility of young people without parents will increase. Secondly, all rapid changes in the society will make the old parents' attitudes and norms out of date, which will make it hard for the children to fit in the new society.   7

A society of families with pro or retired parents or even without children is hard for me to see. If the world   8 goes to that point, which it probably won't, the whole society <u>might</u> be insensitive, hard, and filled with complacency. It <u>would be</u> filled with human beings, who are very mechanical and without any true happiness. There <u>would</u> be many criminals, bums, drug addicts, and maniacs who have no feelings and are dangerous, because of their background. Let's hope this future is not going to happen because if it does, I'm afraid it's going to be the end <u>of the good life as we live it now.</u>

♦ DISCUSSION QUESTIONS

1. How has the tone of the essay changed?

2. In what ways has the writer improved the essay's clarity?

♦ WRITING ASSIGNMENT

Turn the revised draft 2 that you completed in to the instructor for comment or take it to a conference. Once you have received reactions from your instructor, work on additional revisions and begin your editing.

This would be a good point for the class to take one or two students' drafts and duplicate them, or project them for the whole class to see, and to work on a group editing exercise.

In doing the editing of this draft, whether as a group or by yourself, pay attention to all the grammar or usage points you have had trouble with before, and make every effort to correct them. Then work hard to make your word choice accurate for the tone you want to achieve and for clarity. If you need or want to, take this draft to the writing center for further assistance.

Once you have done all the revising and editing you can, prepare a final draft and exchange it with a partner for one last proofreading session before you turn it in for evaluation.

Sample Student Essay for Writing to Persuade

As with each chapter, we end our last one with a student paper that you can follow from prewriting stage to the final draft. Do not be worried if you cannot read the handwritten brainstorming and notes. These have been included in their original form to demonstrate how messy the process of writing can be. As long as you can read your own

Brainstorming

The U. T. athletic fee
$35 each semester for full-time student
parking decal cost $15 per student a year

U. T. Student who need money for school are
complaining about the cost of a good education
Why do the every- full student have to pay for an
athletic fee every semester. I for example, a
art major who will probably never show up
at a game of soccer or baseball. But why
does they have to pay such a large amount

the sport department
why does ⟩ should full-time student have to
pay an athletic fee?
of $70 a year
Half of these students is probably never in
touch with the sport department they didn't
that if every department Take

handwritten material, it does not matter what it looks like. If you are
sharing it with a partner, of course, it must be readable. But keep in
mind that writing is not usually a neat, linear process.

Notice also that another peer review sheet is used (peer review sheet
8) which is slightly different from peer review sheet 7. Both are useful
for persuasive writing, and you may want to try one or both with your
own writing.

Draft 1

IS THE ATHLETIC FEE FAIR TO ALL STUDENTS?

As the hues of fall tinted away, the signs of spring are al-   1
ready present. Especially in the hallways of the University, it
is the time of year when students are busy studying for semester exams, organizing the spring semester classes and

making payments on their tuition fees. Some, the freshmen and independent students, will look at their pre-billing checklist again and again at the charge for athletic fee with disappointment.

Every semester, each fulltime student must pay an athletic   2
fee of thirty-five dollars. This mandatory funding fee is sponsored by the sport department which will covered the students' spectator ticket in sports such as soccer, baseball, swimming, etc. This fee may be alright for the student who involved with sports events, but what happen to the student who won't ever be with the program? Is the athletic fee fair to all students?

The student that will loose out the most are the one who   3
registered as fulltime student because this fee only effect the fulltime student. It is not true that some student don't like sports, but they can't find the time for them because of being a fulltime student. The athletic fee is almost senseless. It sounded good when a student walk into a game which said to be free to all student with an ID card. But actually the student didn't feel it was free at all when they said $35 a semester to a ticket that they probably use only once.

Still some student says that the athletic fee is like a bill   4
that charged a baby for a piece of steak when he or she could only eat baby food. To make this rational issue fair for all student, there shuld be certain regulation pertaining to this fee. For example, the fee should be lower to a more reasonable price and all studet should pay not just the fulltime student. Thirty five dollaras may not seem to be much, but for a financially tight student, it may means a whole semester worth of school materials.

Hoang Van Bui

♦ DISCUSSION QUESTIONS

1. What do you think of this draft?

2. Do you agree with the peer reviewer?

3. Is there anything you would add to the review?

4. Note how Van gathered more information by jotting down some additional notes for himself before he wrote the second draft.

Peer Review 8
Writing to Persuade II

Writer: *Van*
Peer Reviewer: *John Vornavarn*

1. What do you think is most interesting?

In ¶ 2 they pay the fee but they can't participate anything. It seems to waste the money.

2. What is the thesis?

$35 is not fair for full-time student who pay and not enjoy the programs.

3. Are there any points that seem unclear or illogical?

When the students use the ticket for free but don't think it is free

4. Are you persuaded by the argument?

yes, I agree with him that we've paid $35 but get nothing because we don't use that benefit because of our full-time student status

5. Restate in one short sentence the main idea of each paragraph.

This is about the
1) Students thinking about how much they have to pay
2) this explains the athletic fee and asks the question about fairness (thesis)
3) The student who suffers is one who doesn't go because he busy
4) The fee not fair — should be lower price

6. What is the tone?

You disagree but it is not so strong. You don't mind to pay this. You may or may not join the program.

7. What do you think needs the most revision?

In the end ¶ 2 and 3 needs more detail
No acknowledgement of opposition or conclusion.

NOTES

on the other hand This unpopular

<u>TIII</u> fee really is an important factor
for intermural sports. The athletic
fee also benefit

general budget
therefore For UT spot department as we
already know

The athletic fee has increased 27.8 percent
due to last year's dificit and this year's
like every university increases the financial
ration sports is almost the center obligation
attraction for students. therefore, it
cost money to run the department,
<u>renovate</u> <u>new</u> facilities and keep
<u>sponsoring</u> <u>activities</u> weekly.
the sports department also sponsor
intermural sports which mostly benefit
and enrich the student social
activities

is it purpose to

end   the foremost need of a change in the
athletic fee —— is a new policy
which that all student could a apply by
not every semester
It would be a nice if we could bring
change that not only could
help the financial needy students but
also to enrich the student social and
educational environment

In draft 2, the comments in the left margin point out revisions and the instructor's marks in the right margin are to help Van with word choice, logic, and verbs. (The draft has not been edited.)

Draft 2

It is only mid-November yet the   1
signs of spring are already present,
especially in the hallways of the University. It is the time of year when students are busy studying for semester
exams, organizing the spring semester classes, and making payments on
their fall tuition fees. Some, the freshmen and the independent students,
will look at their pre-billing checklist
again and again at the charge for the
athletic fee with disappointment.

At the University, every fulltime   2
student must pay an athletic fee of
thirty-five dollars each semester. This
mandatory fee is <u>sponsored by</u> the   *wd*
<u>sport</u> department which will <u>covered</u>   *wd/vb*
the student's spectator tickets ~~in~~ *for*
sports, such as soccer, baseball, and
swimming. This fee may be alright for
those who <u>involved</u> with sport events,   *tense*
but what happen to the student who
won't ever <u>be with</u> the program? Is the   *cl?*
athletic fee fair to all students? The
part ⌈students that will loose out the most
of old │ are the one who registered as fulltime
#3 │ students because its only effects the
└ fulltime students. It is not true that

part of old ¶3

some students don't like sports, <u>but</u>   *log*
they can't find the time for them on
account of the <u>busy</u> homework that a   *wd*
fulltime student has.

The athletic fee is almost senseless.   3
It sounded good when a student <u>walk</u>   *tense*
into a game which <u>said to</u> be "free" to   *wd*
all students with an ID card. But actu-
ally they didn't feel it was free at all
when they paid thirty-five dollars a semester for a ticket that they probably
got the chance to use only once.

acknowledging the opposition   On the other hand, this unpopular   4
fee is really an important factor for
the general budget. The athletic fee
has increased 27.8 percent due to last
year's deficit and this year's financial
obligations. Plus, there is a 13.5 increase in student activities fee. Like
other universities across the nation,
sports is the center of attraction for
the students <u>therefore</u> it cost money   *log?*
to run the department, purchase new
equipment, and sponsoring student
activities such as intramural sports.
As a whole, the athletic fee serves a
purpose to benefit and to enrich the
students social activities.

Still, some students say the athletic   5
fee is like a <u>bill that charged</u> a baby for   *cl?*

old ¶4

a piece of steak when he or she could
only eat babyfood. To make this <u>ra-</u>   *wd*
<u>tional</u> issue fair for all students, there

should be certain regulation pertaining to this fee. For example, the fee should be <u>lower</u> to a more reasonable   *vb*
price and all student should pay not just the fulltime students. Thirty-five dollars may not seem to be much, but for a financially <u>tight</u> student, it may   *wd*
mean a whole semester worth of school materials.

new conclusion   The foremost need of a change in the athletic fee policy is a solution that all student could <u>live</u> ^{*with*} <u>by</u>. Maybe we   *id*   6
should take Louis Thomas's philosophy in his essay, "To Err is Human." He wrote, "We can assume as a working hypothesis that all the right ways of doing this are unworkable. What we need, then for moving ahead, is a set of wrong alternatives." It would be nice that we could bring a change that not only help the financially needy students but also <u>endow</u> the student so-   *wd*
cial and educational environment.

♦ DISCUSSION QUESTIONS

1. In what ways has this draft been improved?
2. Do you think paragraphs 2 and 3 are well organized?
3. How is paragraph 4 connected to paragraph 5?
4. Is the conclusion a good one? If so, why?
5. Note the marks on the right. Are there any other places where you think the writer should revise for clarity or tone?

♦ EDITING EXERCISE

Read draft 3 and then edit it to correct any remaining errors.

Draft 3

It is only mid-November yet the signs of spring are already   1
present everywhere. Especially in the hallways of the University, it is the time of year when students are busy studying
for semester exams, organizing the spring semester classes,
and making payments on their tuition fee for the fall. Some,
the freshmen and independent students, will look at their
pre-billing checklist again and again with disappointment at
the charge for the Athletic Fee.

At the University every full-time student must pay an ath-   2
letic fee of thirty-five dollars each semester. This mandatory
fee is required by the athletic department to cover the student's tickets for sports, such as soccer, baseball, and swimming. This fee may be logical for those who are involved with
sports events, but what happen to the student who won't ever
attend a game? Is the Athletic Fee fair to all students? The
students that will lose out the most are those who registered
as full-time students because the fee only effects the full-time
students. It is not true that some students don't like sports;
they can't find the time for them on account of the heavy load
of homework that a full-time student has.

The Athletic Fee is almost senseless. It sounded good to   3
think that a student could walk into a game which is "free"
to all students with an ID card, but it actually wasn't free at
all when they paid thirty-five dollars a semester for a ticket
that they probably got the chance to use only once.

On the other hand, this unpopular fee is really an impor-   4
tant factor for the University's general budget. The Athletic
Fee has increased 27.8 percent due to last year's deficit and
this year's financial obligations. Plus, there is a 13.5 percent
increase in student activities fee. Like other universities
across the nation, sports are the center attraction for the students. The University's sports center, for example, is a big in-
vestment. Every year the budget increases due to annual
spending such as purchasing new equipment and machin-
ery, sponsoring student and city activities, and even just to
keep the auditorium open for the student's personal enjoy-

ment. As a whole, the Athletic Fee serves to benefit and to enrich the students' social life.

Still, some students say that the Athletic Fee is like charging a baby for a piece of steak when he or she could only eat baby food. To make this policy fair for all students, there should be certain regulation pertaining to this fee. For example, the fee should be lower to a more reasonable price and all students should pay, not just the full-time students. Thirty-five dollars may not seem to be much, but for a financially strapped student, it may mean a whole semester worth of school materials. 5

The foremost need is to make a change in the Athletic Fee policy that all student could live with. Maybe, we should take Louis Thomas's philosophy in his essay, "To Err is Human." He wrote, "We can assume as a working hypothesis that all the right ways of doing this are unworkable. What we need, then for moving ahead, is a set of wrong alternatives." It would be nice that we could bring a change that not only help the financially needy students but also enhance the student social and educational environment. 6

A Few Thoughts on Concluding
Or, How I Will Revise the Next Draft

I have now completed a textbook that has gone through many drafts and been revised many times with the help of my students, readers, and editors. I have always had difficulty concluding a piece of writing because I keep thinking of things I want to change at the beginning and in the middle. Next time, I would explain even more ways to do prewriting, include student examples of complete false starts that had to be thrown away before the student found a clear direction, and include many more hints on editing. But every piece of writing must be brought to conclusion at some point. We exist in a world of deadlines and the need to move on to new projects. So I have stopped, if not concluded, this piece of writing.

Students too must conclude, write the final essay, take a final exam, and move on to another course. I hope that in moving on, you will carry with you some helpful advice from this text. You have completed many reading and writing assignments that I hope have stimulated your thinking and led you to express yourself in writing in new and better ways. If you have gained more confidence in your ability to write mature essays that will prepare you for academic or job-related writing assignments, then the book will have served its purpose. If you have also learned that prewriting, drafting, revising, and editing are manageable tasks that lead to better writing no matter how lost you may feel at first, then you have learned one of the true "tricks of the trade." As William Stafford wrote in the selection at the very beginning of the text, "A writer is not so much someone who has something to say as he is someone who has found a process that will bring about new things he would not have thought of if he had not started to say them."

You too are a writer. Go on into your other courses or your job, and enjoy the process of taking half-formed feelings and ideas and molding them into concrete language. You may surprise yourself with the quality of the product.

THE PEER REVIEW SHEETS

Peer Review 1 **Writer:**
Personal Writing **Peer Reviewer:**

What is most interesting?

Where would you like to have more detail?

Peer Review 2   **Writer:**
Narrative/Descriptive   **Peer Reviewer:**

1. What did you like the most about this composition?

2. What is the purpose? Is each paragraph related to that purpose?

3. Is the writing appropriate for the audience?

4. Is there any place that is unclear?

5. Are there any places where the writer should add more detail or eliminate any repetitions?

Peer Review 3   **Writer:**
Summary   **Peer Reviewer:**

1. Does the first sentence identify the original?

2. Is the major thesis restated at the beginning? What is it?

3. Are all the major points included?

4. Is there anything missing or anything that doesn't belong in the summary?

5. Are the ideas presented in the same order as in the original?

6. Are there any places where the wording is too close to the original?

Peer Review 4   **Writer:**
Writing to Inform   **Peer Reviewer:**

1. What did you think was most interesting?

2. What is the purpose?

3. What is the thesis?

4. Are there any places where you want more information?

5. Are there any places that are not related to the thesis?

Peer Review 5   **Writer:**
Writing to Analyze   **Peer Reviewer:**

1. What do you think is most interesting?

2. What is the purpose?

3. What is the thesis?

4. How is the essay organized? Make a brief outline of major points.

5. Does it have a good introduction and conclusion?

6. Does the organization need any revision?

Peer Review 6   **Writer:**
Writing to Form a Judgment   Peer Reviewer:

1.   **What did you like best about this essay?**

2.   **What is the purpose?**

3.   **What is the thesis?**

4.   **What is/are the key value term(s) in the thesis?**

5.   **What are the standards for the judgment?**

6.   **Do you think the judgment is well supported?**

7.   **Do you have any suggestions for revision?**

Peer Review 7   **Writer:**
Writing to Persuade I   **Peer Reviewer:**

1. Who is the audience for the argument?

2. What is the argument or claim it makes?

3. What are the assumptions on which the argument is based?

4. How is the argument supported?

5. Do the points made support the primary claim or another one?

6. Does the conclusion follow from the supporting evidence?

Peer Review 8   **Writer:**
Writing to Persuade II   **Peer Reviewer:**

1. What do you think is most interesting?

2. What is the thesis?

3. Are there any points that seem unclear or illogical?

4. Are you persuaded by the argument?

5. Restate in one short sentence the main idea of each paragraph.

6. What is the tone?

7. What do you think needs the most revision?

Appendix B

KEY TO INSTRUCTOR'S MARKS

ab	faulty abbreviation
adj	misuse of adjective
adv	misuse of adverb
agr	agreement
art	article
cap	capital
case	error in case
cl	clarity
coh	coherence
coord	faulty coordination
cs	comma splice
dev	development
frag	sentence fragment
id	idiom
lc	lower case (no caps)
log	logic
no ¶	no paragraph
par	parallelism
¶	paragraph
pl	plural
poss	possessive
pn	punctuation
ref	reference
rep	repetition
rs	run-on sentence
sp	spelling
sub	faulty subordination
tnse	faulty verb tense
tr	transition
vb	faulty verb form
wd	word choice
ww	wrong word

Index